Christmas '08

To dear Alex,
Hoping this will
rekindle some happy
memories!
With lots of love,
from
Susan + Mike

AF378291

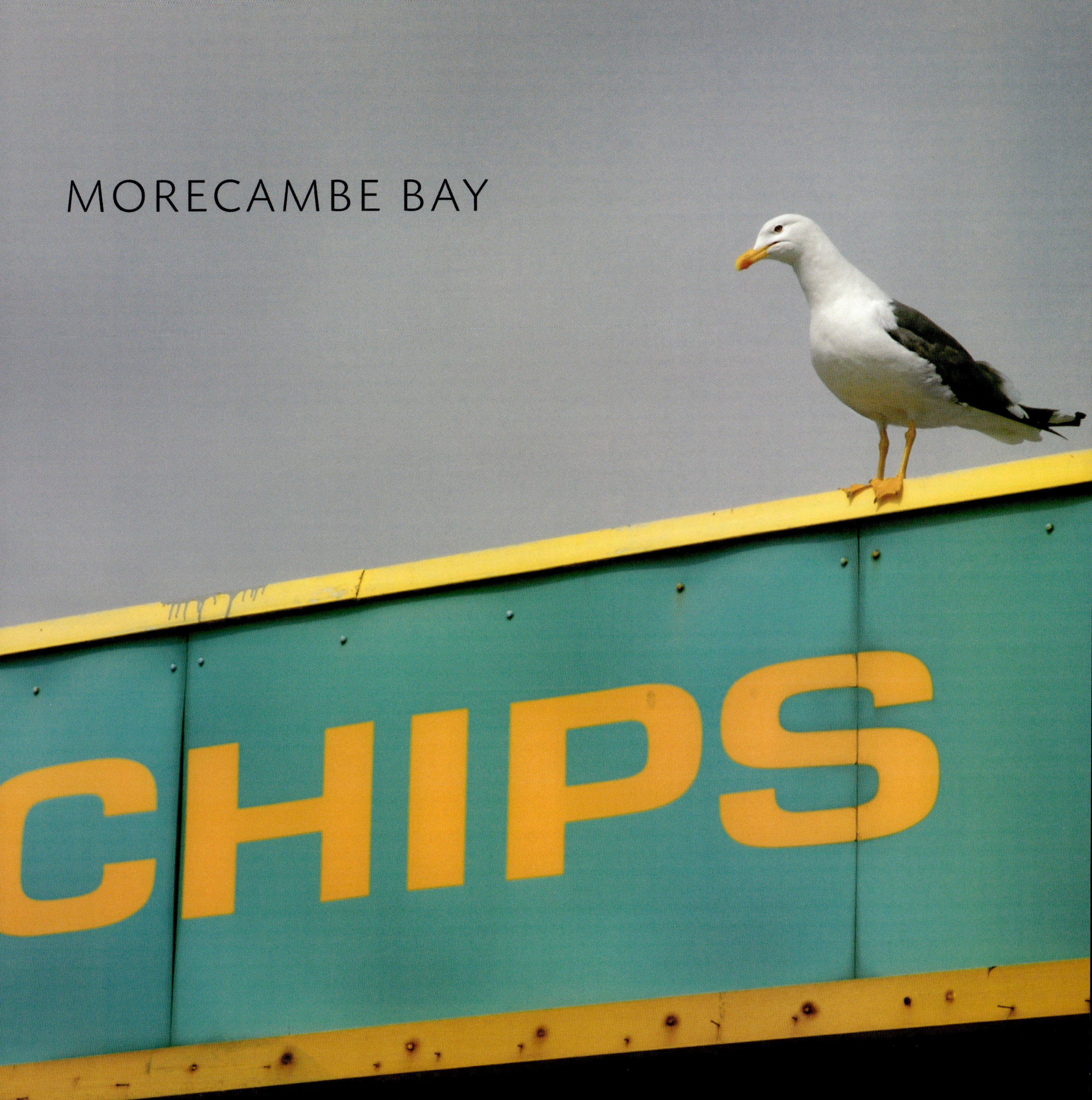
MORECAMBE BAY
CHIPS

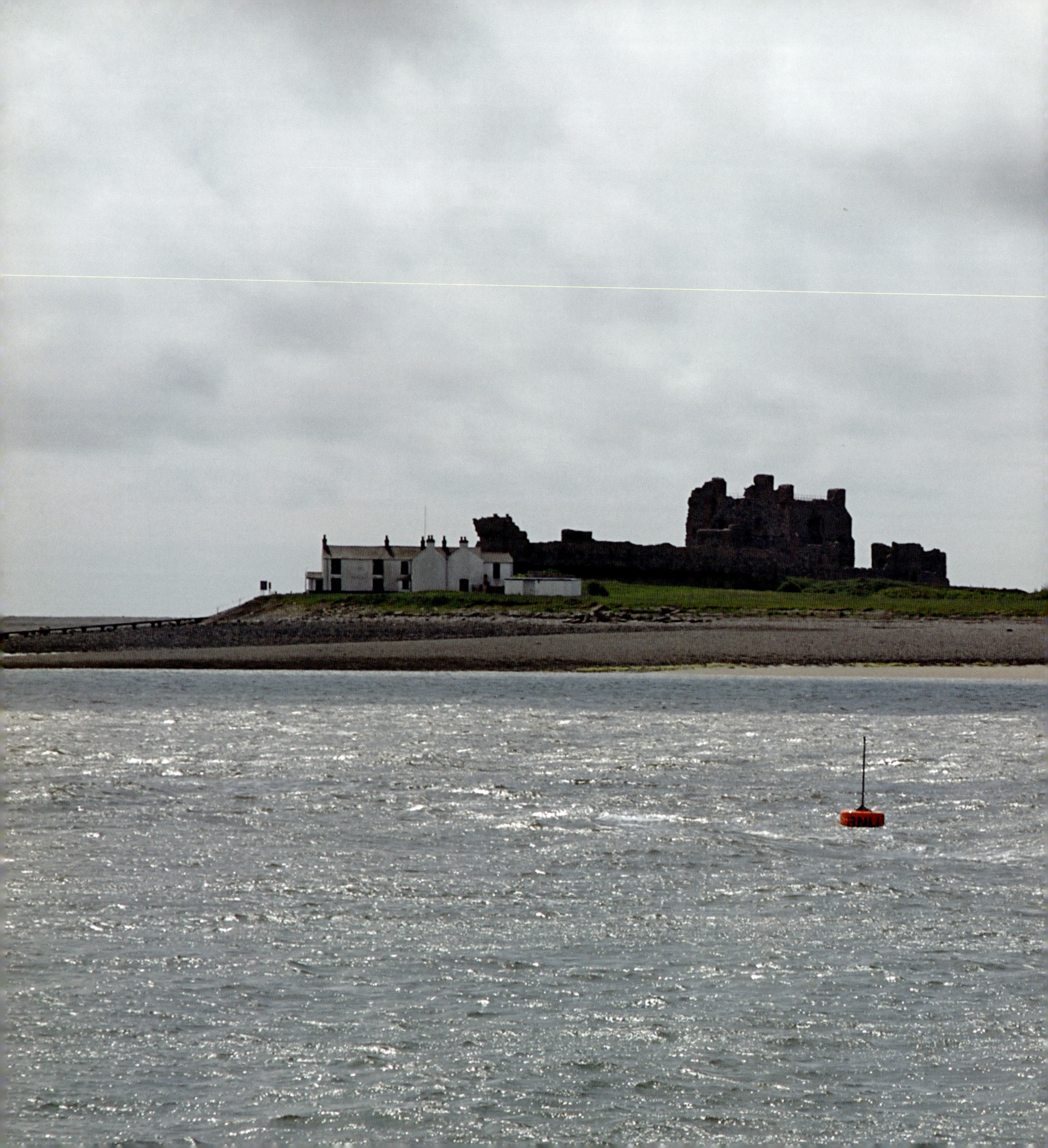

# MORECAMBE BAY

## John Morrison

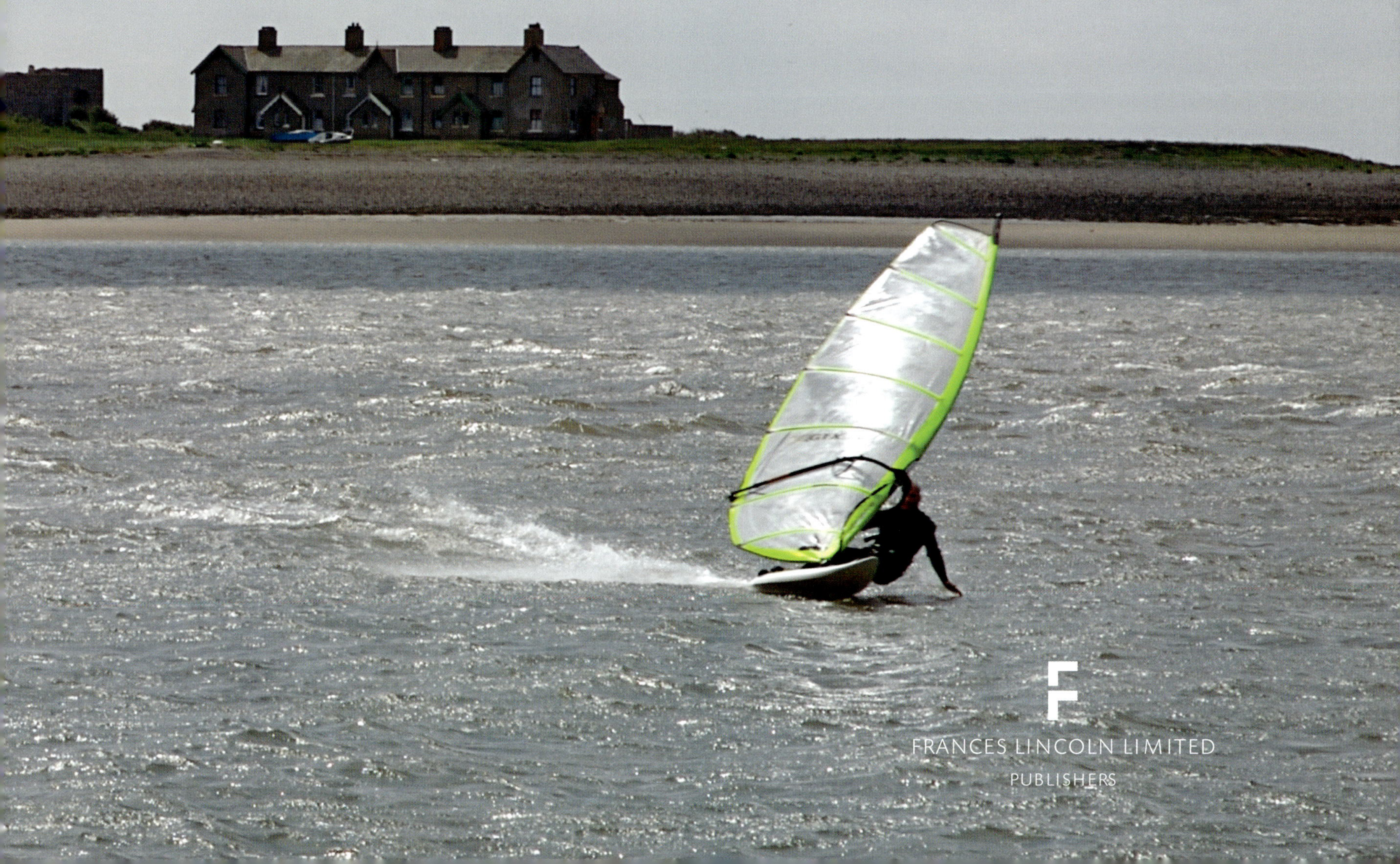

Frances Lincoln Limited
PUBLISHERS

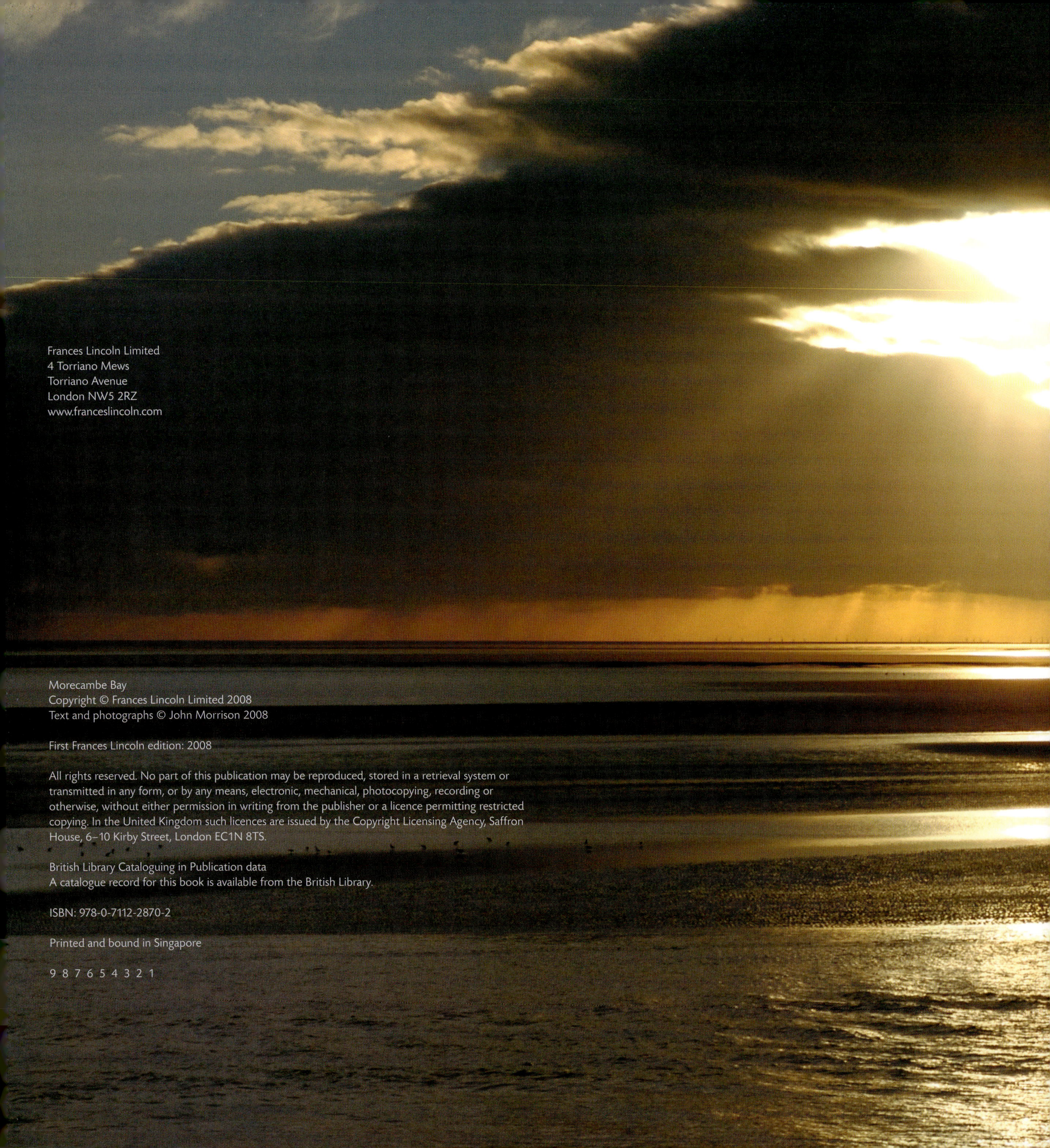

Frances Lincoln Limited
4 Torriano Mews
Torriano Avenue
London NW5 2RZ
www.franceslincoln.com

Morecambe Bay
Copyright © Frances Lincoln Limited 2008
Text and photographs © John Morrison 2008

First Frances Lincoln edition: 2008



British Library Cataloguing in Publication data
A catalogue record for this book is available from the British Library.

ISBN: 978-0-7112-2870-2

Printed and bound in Singapore

9 8 7 6 5 4 3 2 1

# CONTENTS

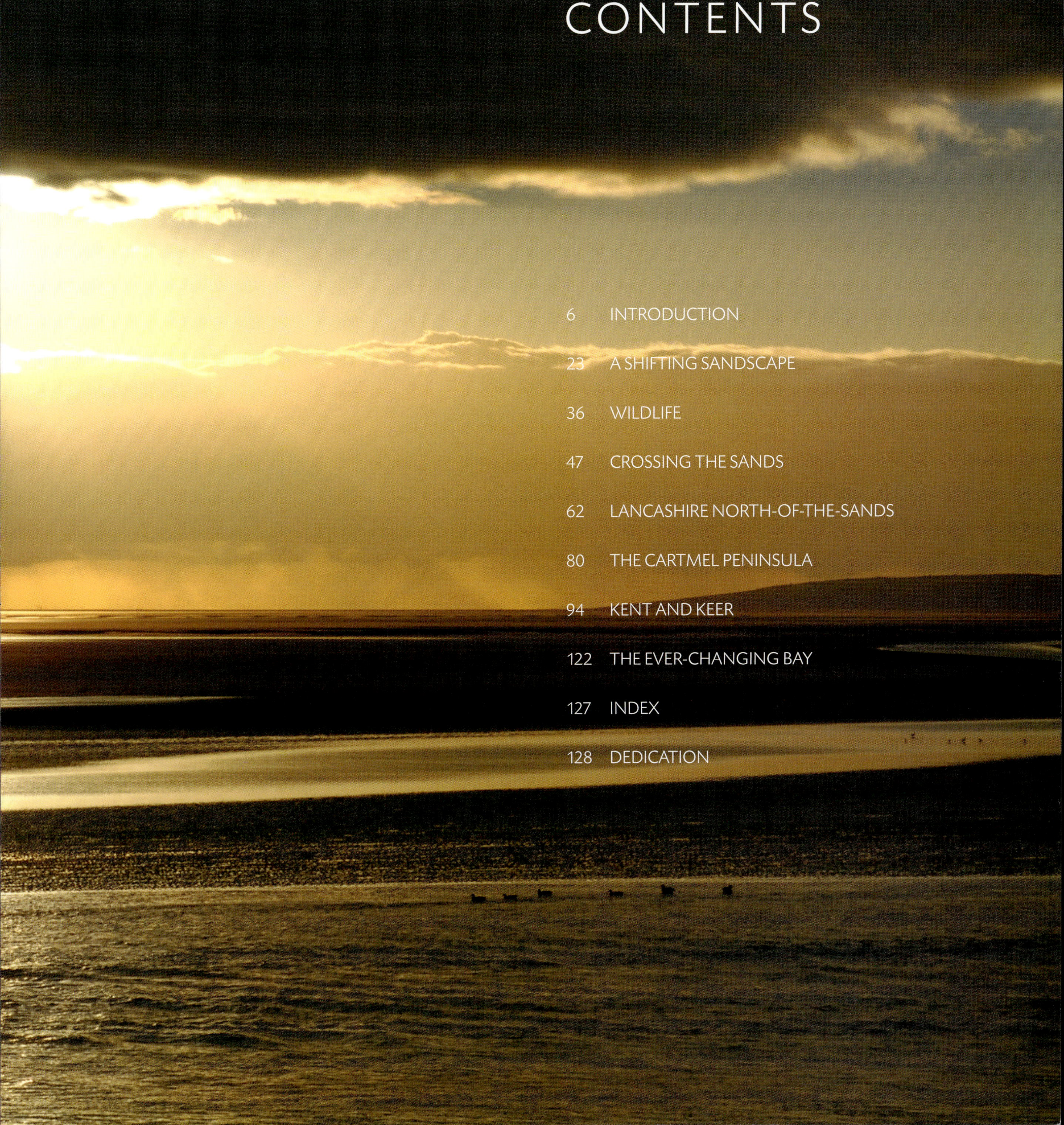

# INTRODUCTION

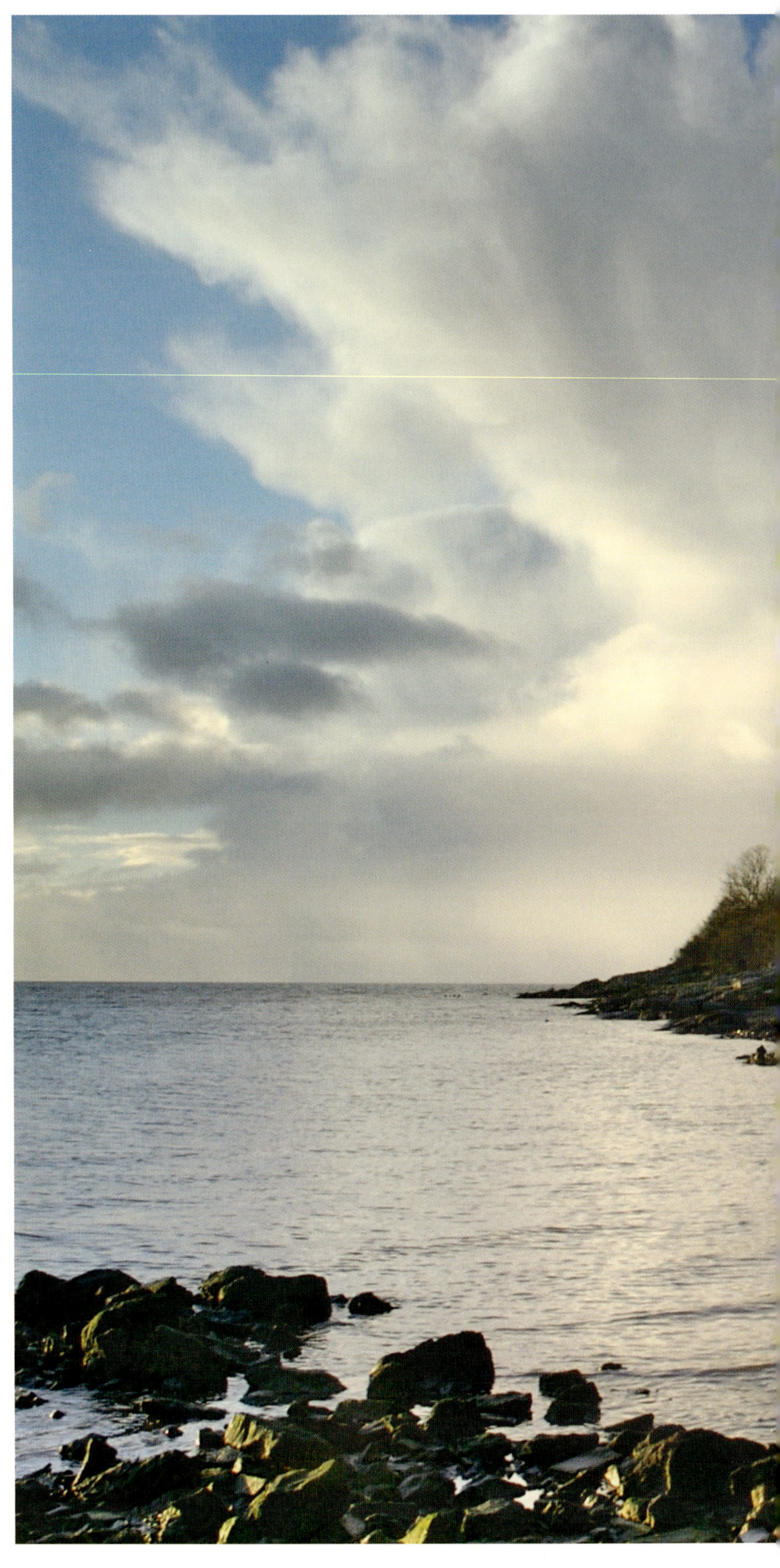

Morecambe Bay means different things to different people. It depends how you look at it; it depends who you ask. To birdwatchers the bay is one of the most important habitats in the country for waders and wildfowl. To the holidaymakers who come to the faded resort of Morecambe, it's a windswept promenade and a 'Kiss Me Quick' hat. To those with a taste for adventure sports, it's a place for adrenalin-fuelled recreation. To those who love wild places, it means fresh air and freedom.

For a landscape photographer like me, Morecambe Bay is a constantly changing seascape of big skies and shimmering sands, backed up by a frieze of Lakeland hills. While the trawlermen of Fleetwood – a dwindling number – drop their nets into deeper waters, the bay has traditionally been 'farmed' for shrimps, mussels, flukes and cockles. Tragically, to a gang of Chinese cockle-pickers, stranded by rising tides in 2004, the bay proved to be a graveyard.

The name of the bay is a recent coinage; to early map-makers Morecambe Bay was, simply, 'The Sands'. Unlike a national park, the bay has no definitive boundary, so I had to decide for myself how far it extends. 'My' Morecambe Bay starts at the northern tip of Walney Island – which shelters Barrow-in-Furness from the ravages of the sea – and ends at the Lancashire port of Fleetwood. I haven't ventured far inland for pictures, concentrating mostly on places associated with the sea, plus the major river estuaries which add so much interest and variety to the topography of the bay.

Photographers and painters have long been inspired by this remarkable land and sea-scape, and Morecambe Bay is rightly

Jenny Brown's Point, near Silverdale, framed by clouds.

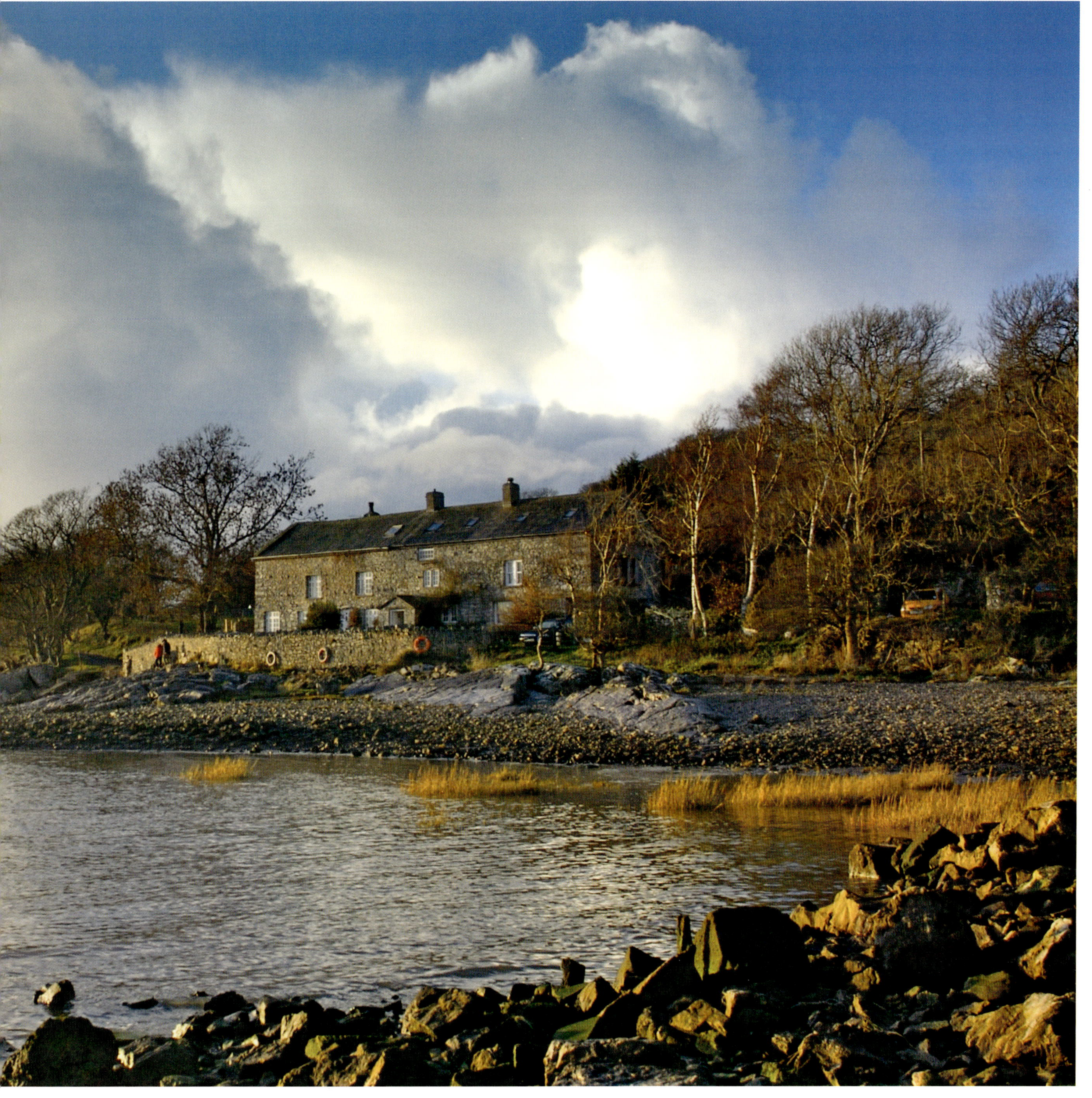

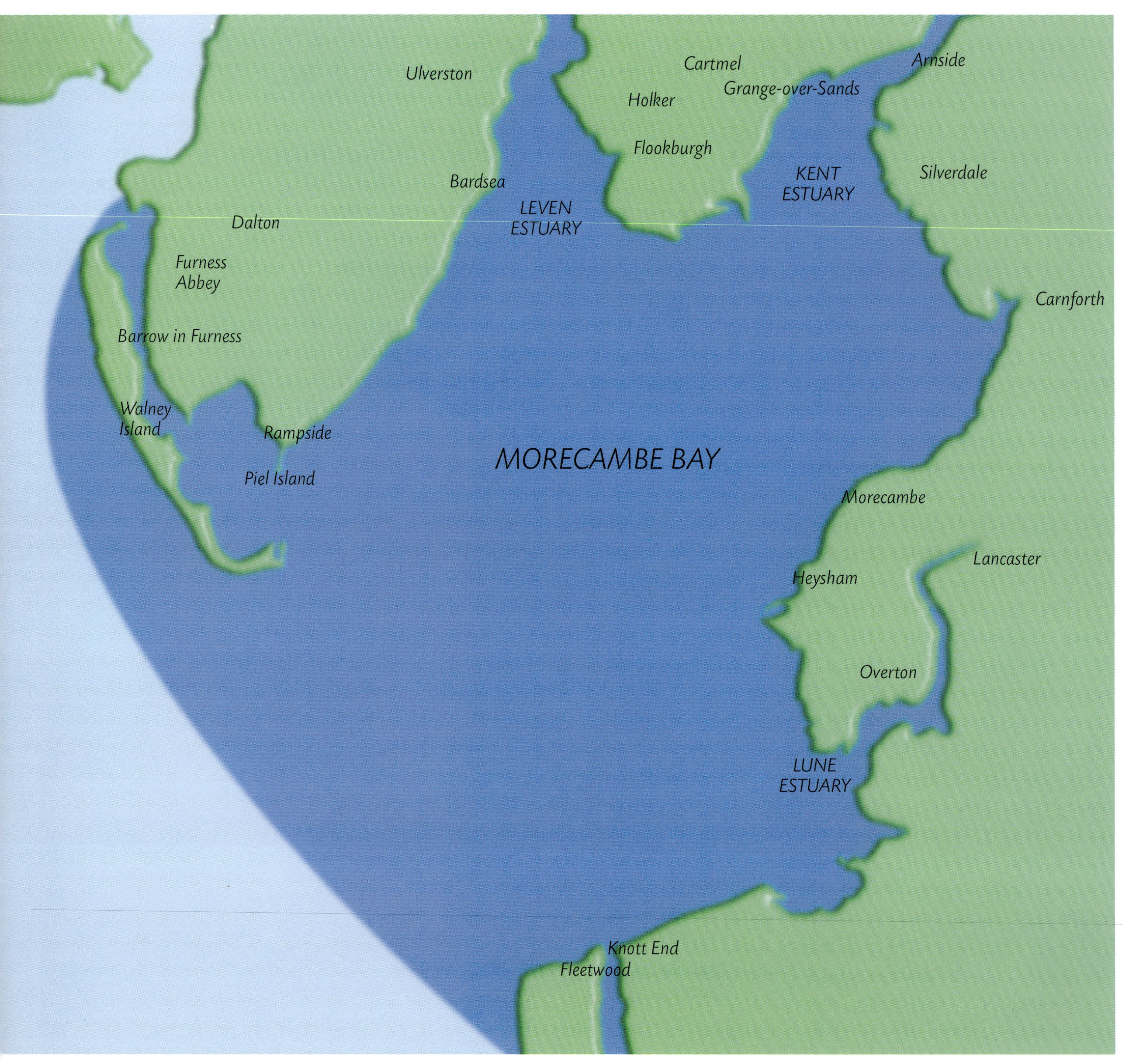

Ulverston
Cartmel
Arnside
Holker
Grange-over-Sands
Flookburgh
KENT ESTUARY
Silverdale
Bardsea
LEVEN ESTUARY
Dalton
Carnforth
Furness Abbey
Barrow in Furness
Walney Island
Rampside
MORECAMBE BAY
Piel Island
Morecambe
Lancaster
Heysham
Overton
LUNE ESTUARY
Knott End
Fleetwood

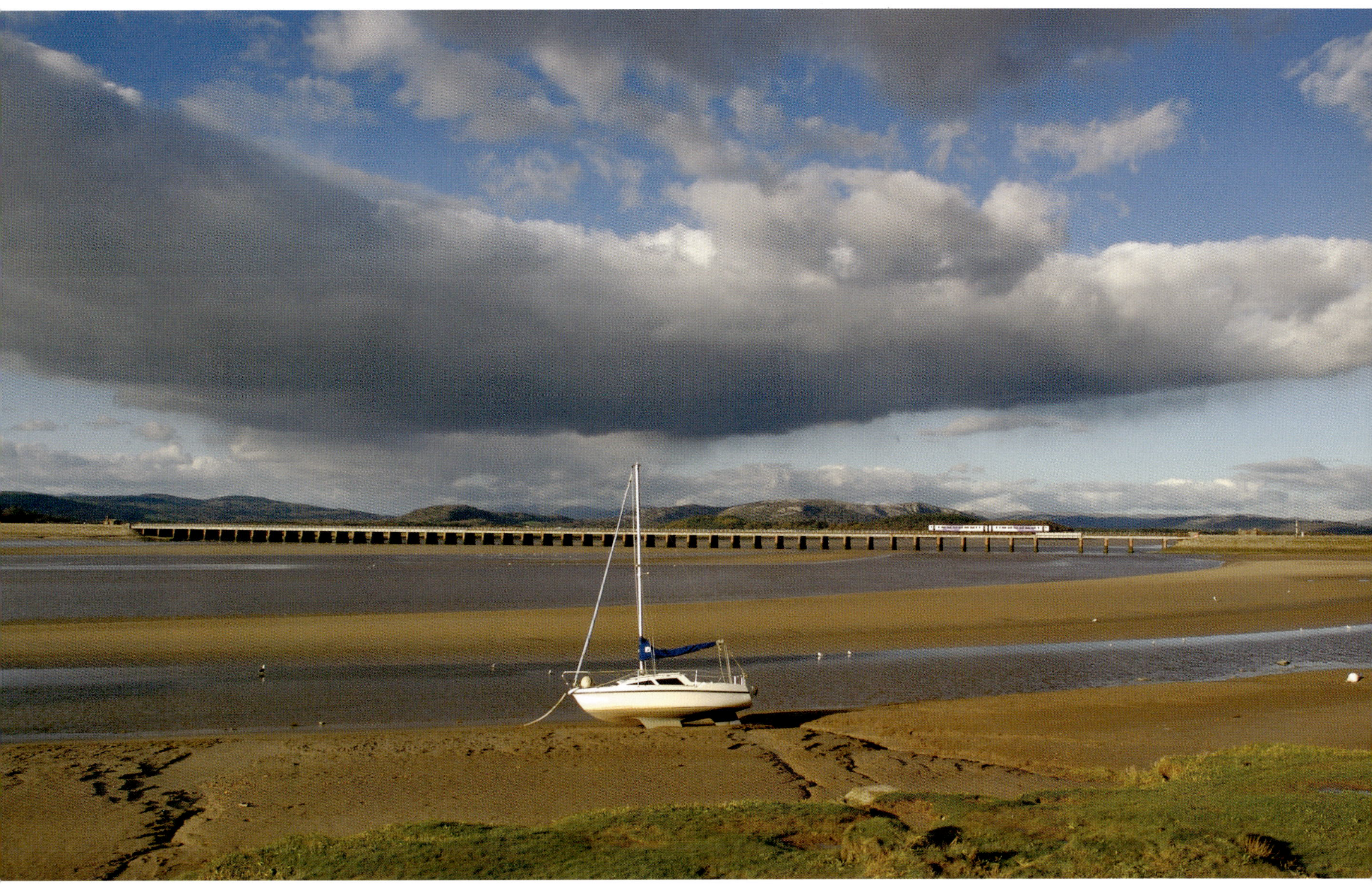

A train crosses the estuary of the River Kent at Arnside.

famous for its dramatic sunsets. When the blood-red ball of a sun is sinking towards the horizon after a long, hot summer's day, the bay can seem peaceful and benign. But appearances can be deceptive, and the sands of Morecambe Bay are no place for the inexperienced and unwary.

It's an emotional landscape. So I have tried, with my photographs, to show not just what Morecambe Bay looks like, but what it feels like, with light chasing shadows across the sands and the mood changing from minute to minute. If, like me, you enjoy getting off the beaten track and avoiding the tourist honeypots, then take the time to visit this fascinating, volatile and mildly eccentric corner of England.

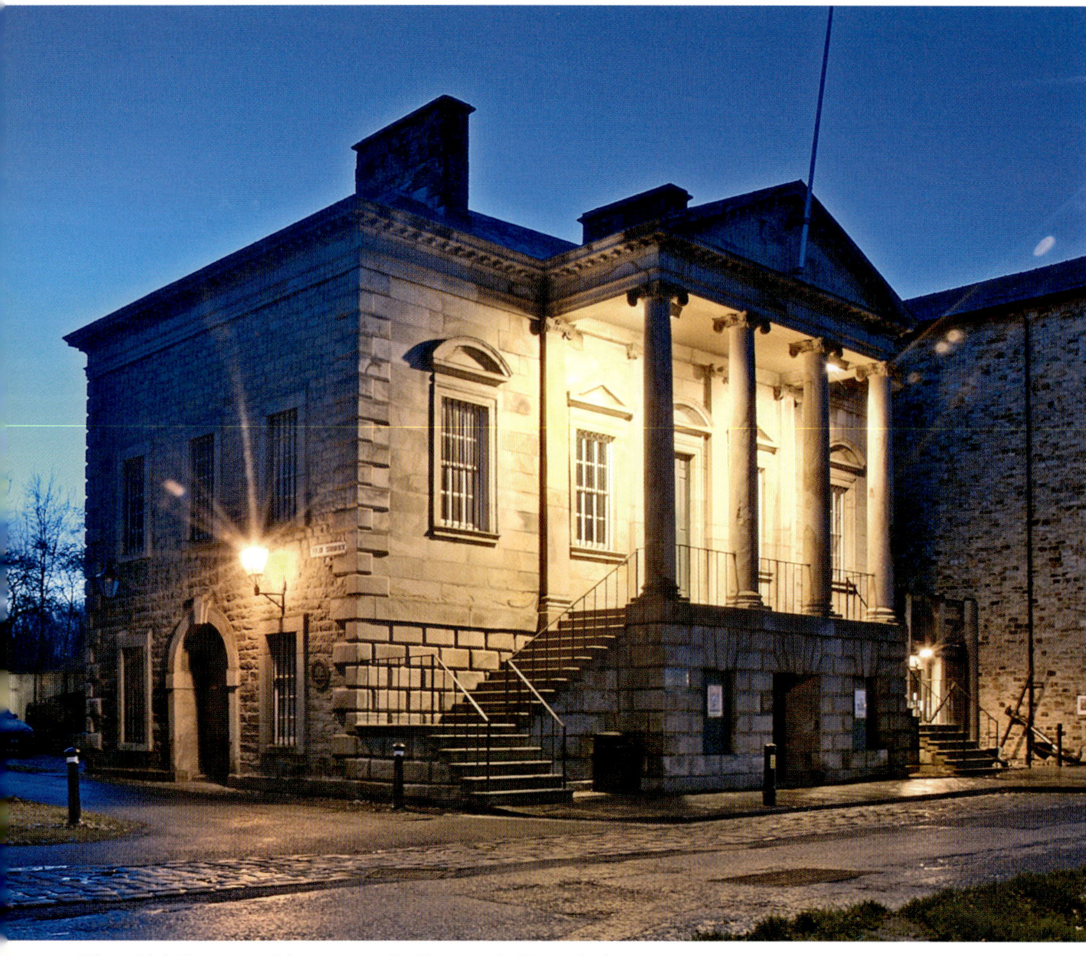

The Old Customs House, on St George's Quay in Lancaster,
has a new lease of life as a maritime museum.

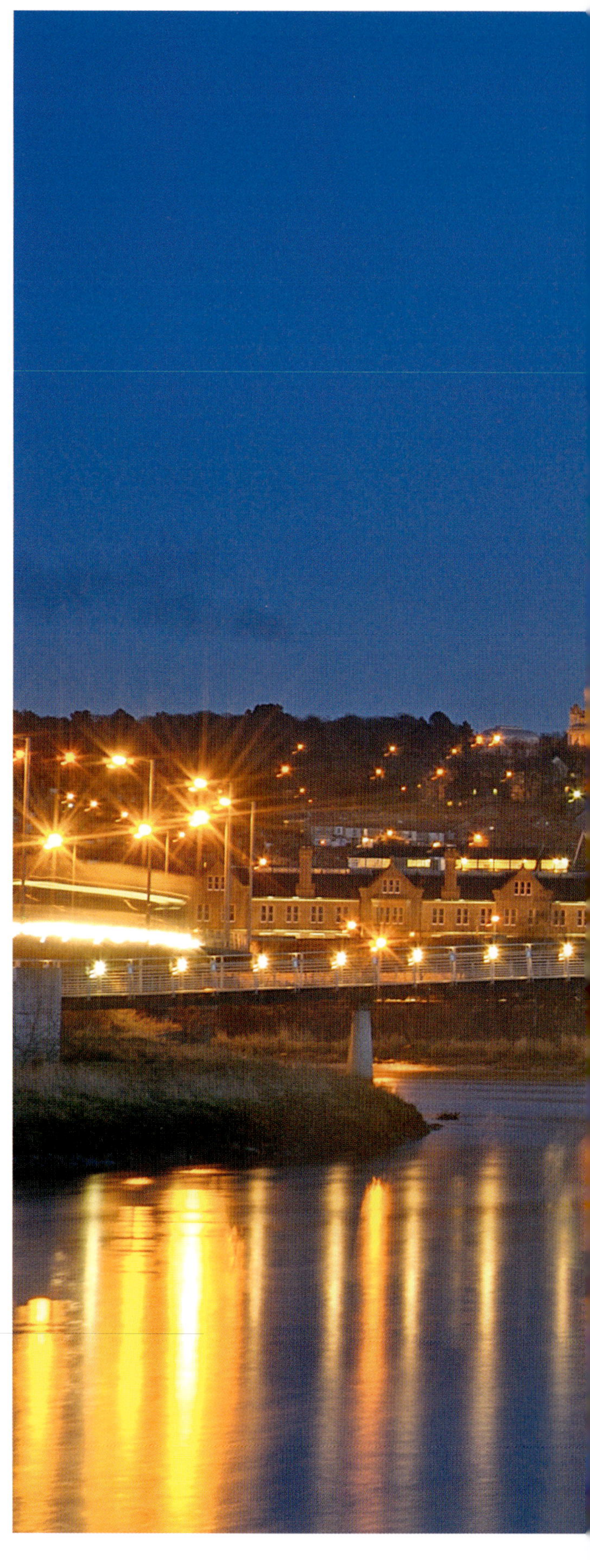



RIGHT
The River Lune at Lancaster, spanned by the Millennium
Footbridge.

FOLLOWING PAGES
Farmland near Milnthorpe, with the rounded contours of the
Howgill Hills as a backdrop.

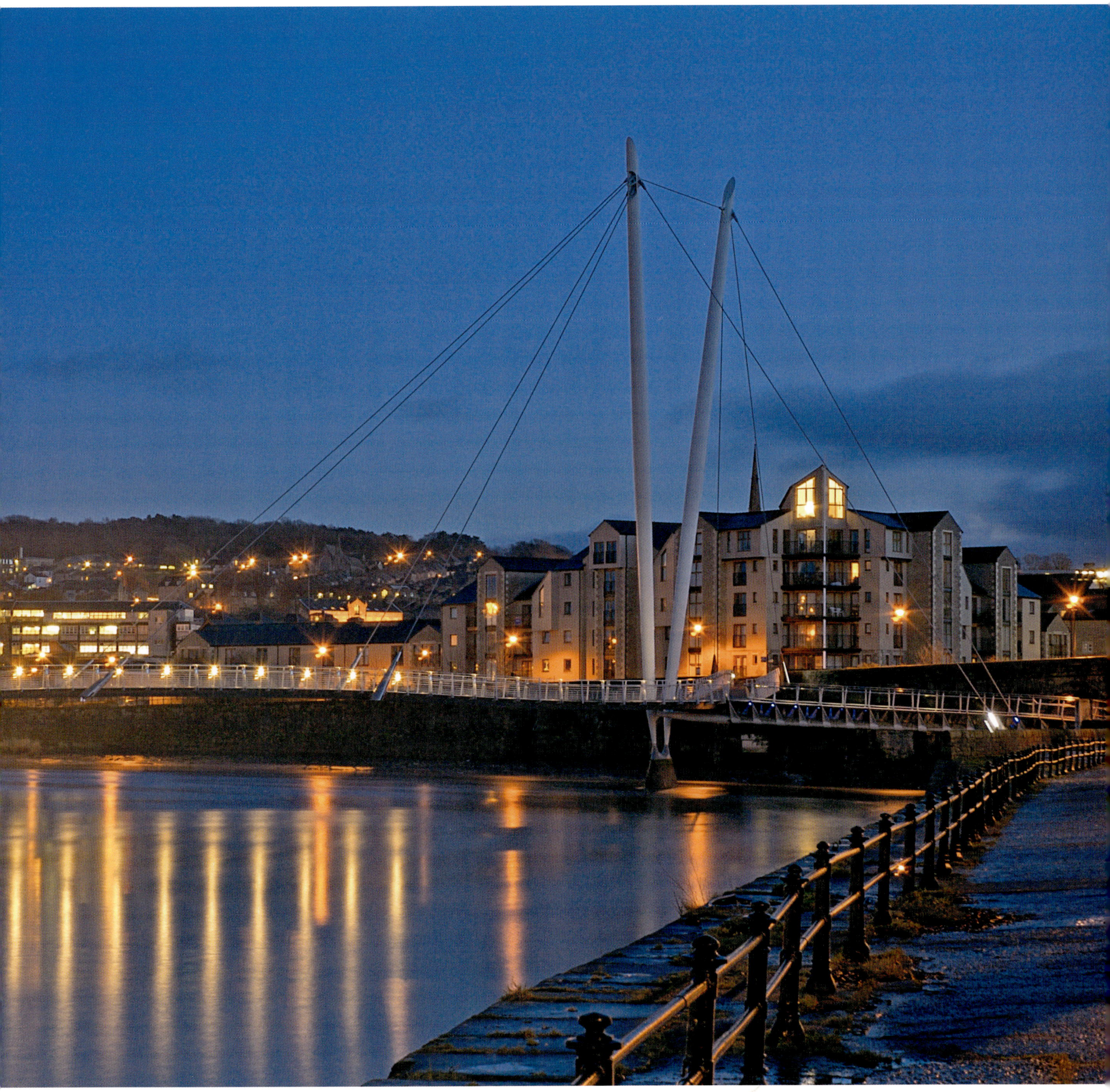

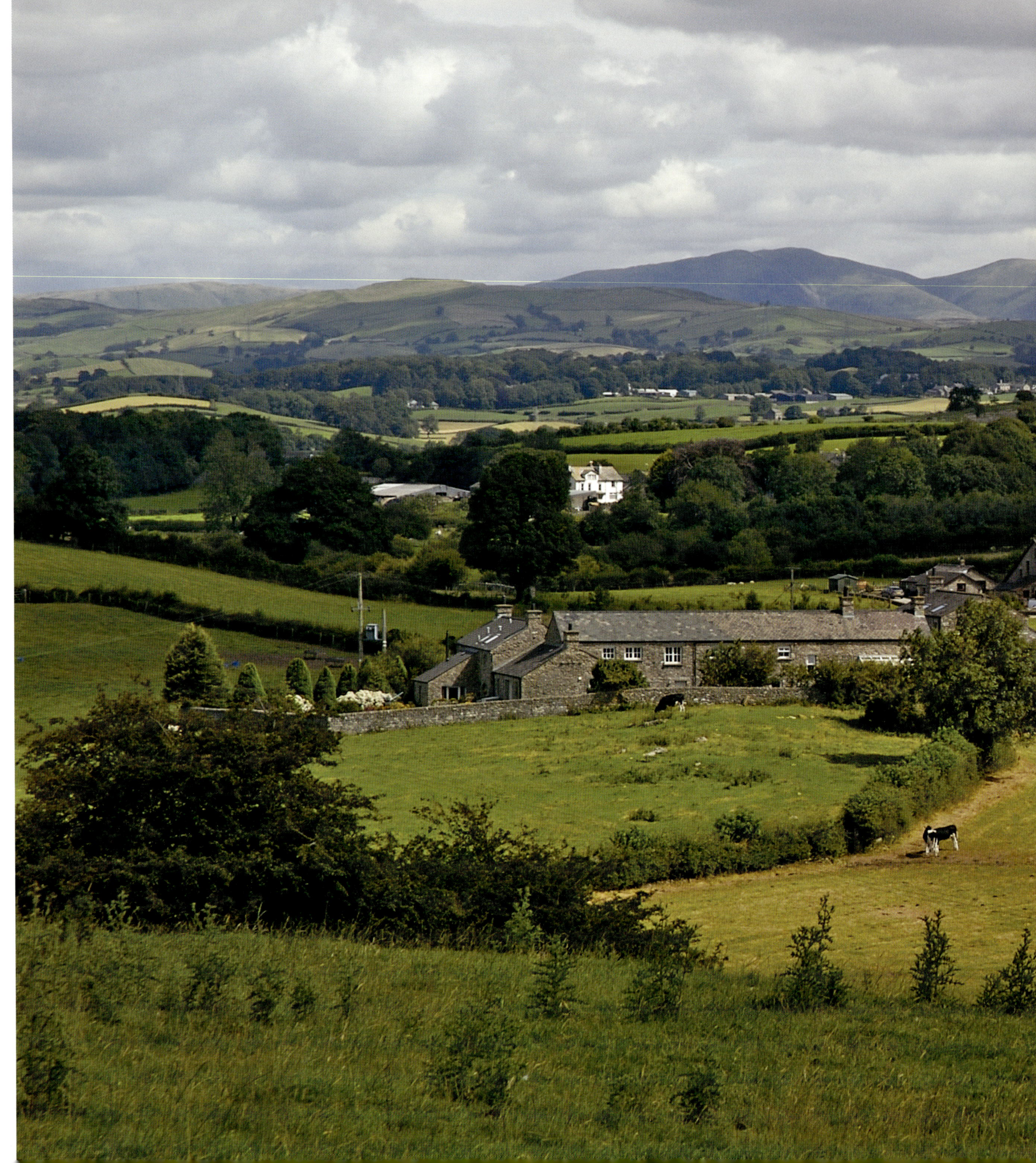

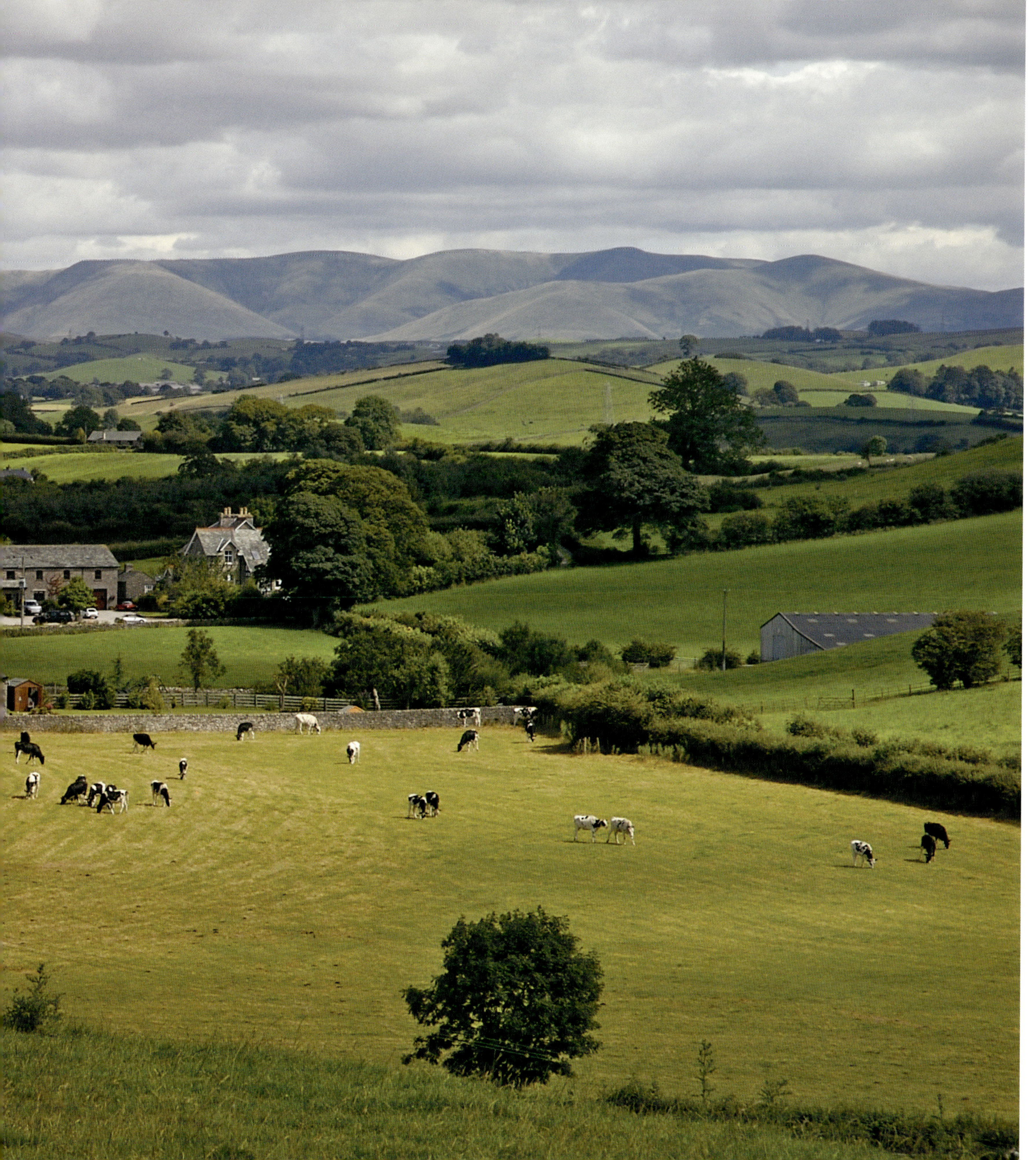

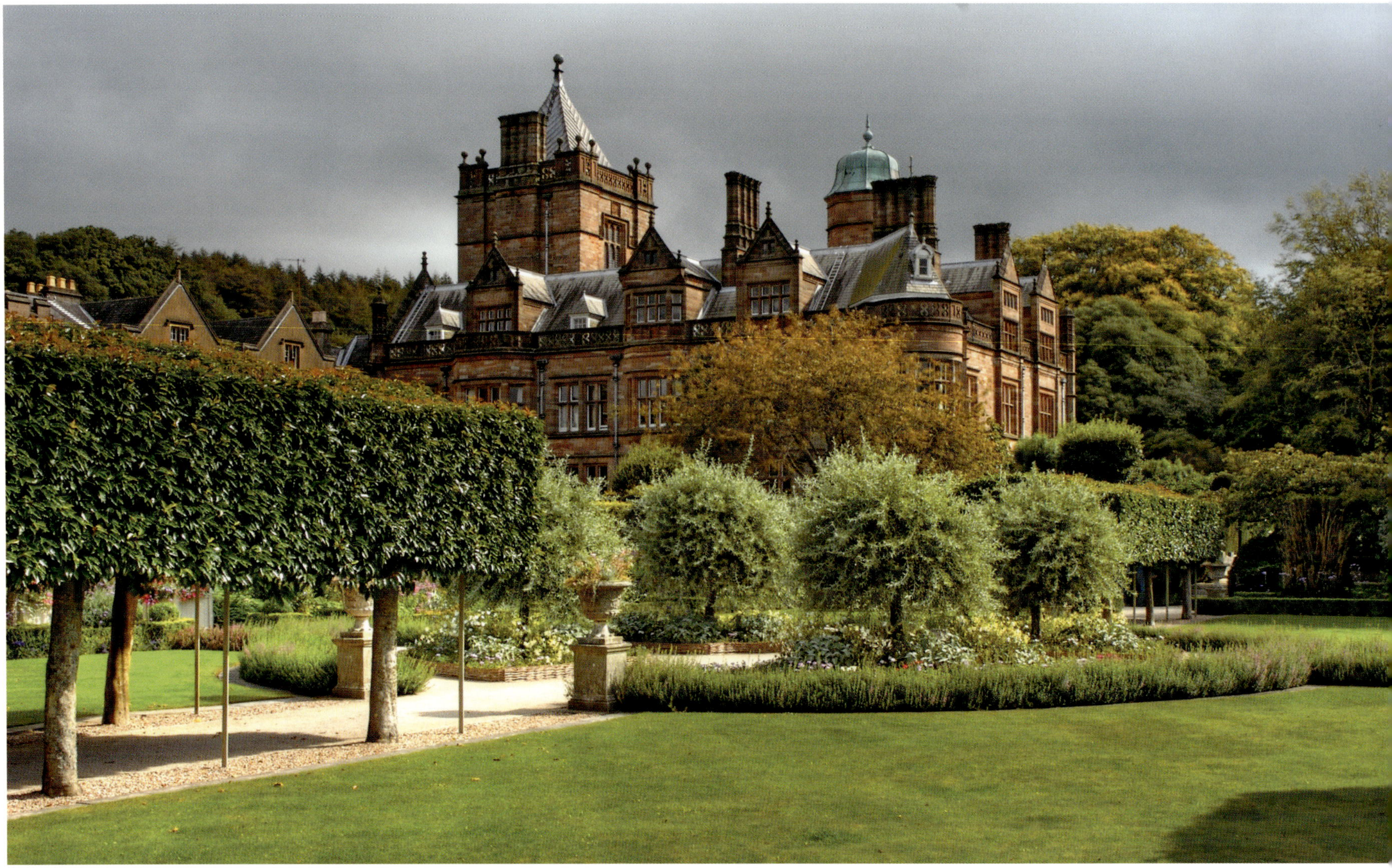

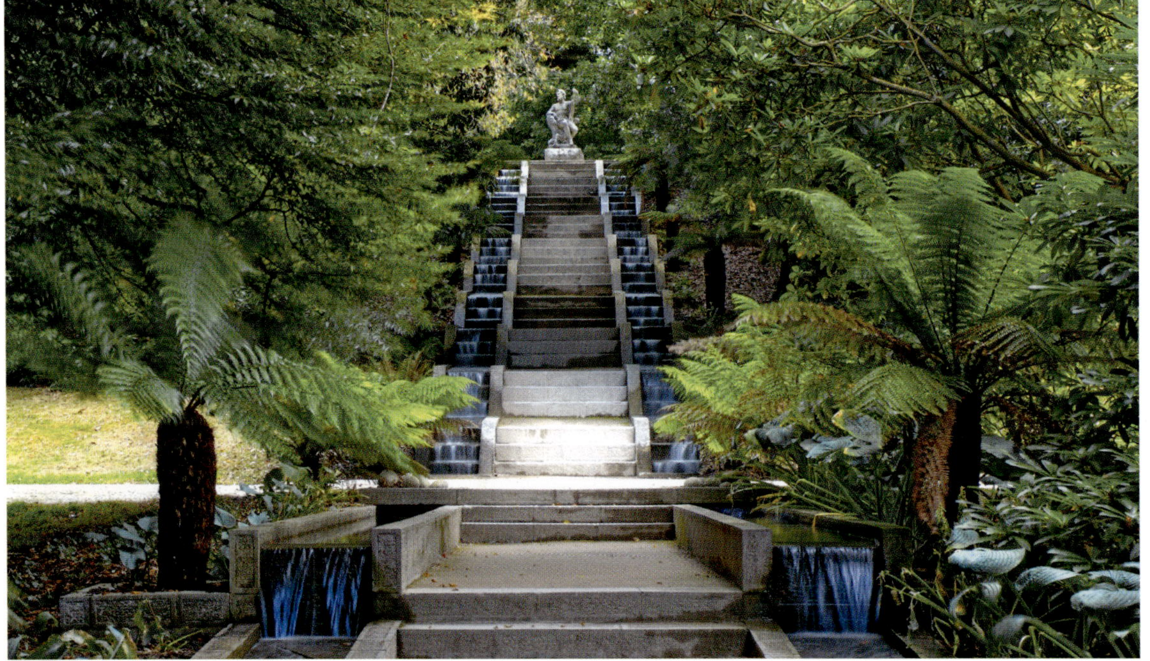



ABOVE
Holker Hall, a Victorian rebuild in red sandstone of an
earlier house on the Cartmel peninsula.

LEFT
The cascade, one of the water features in the
celebrated gardens of Holker Hall.

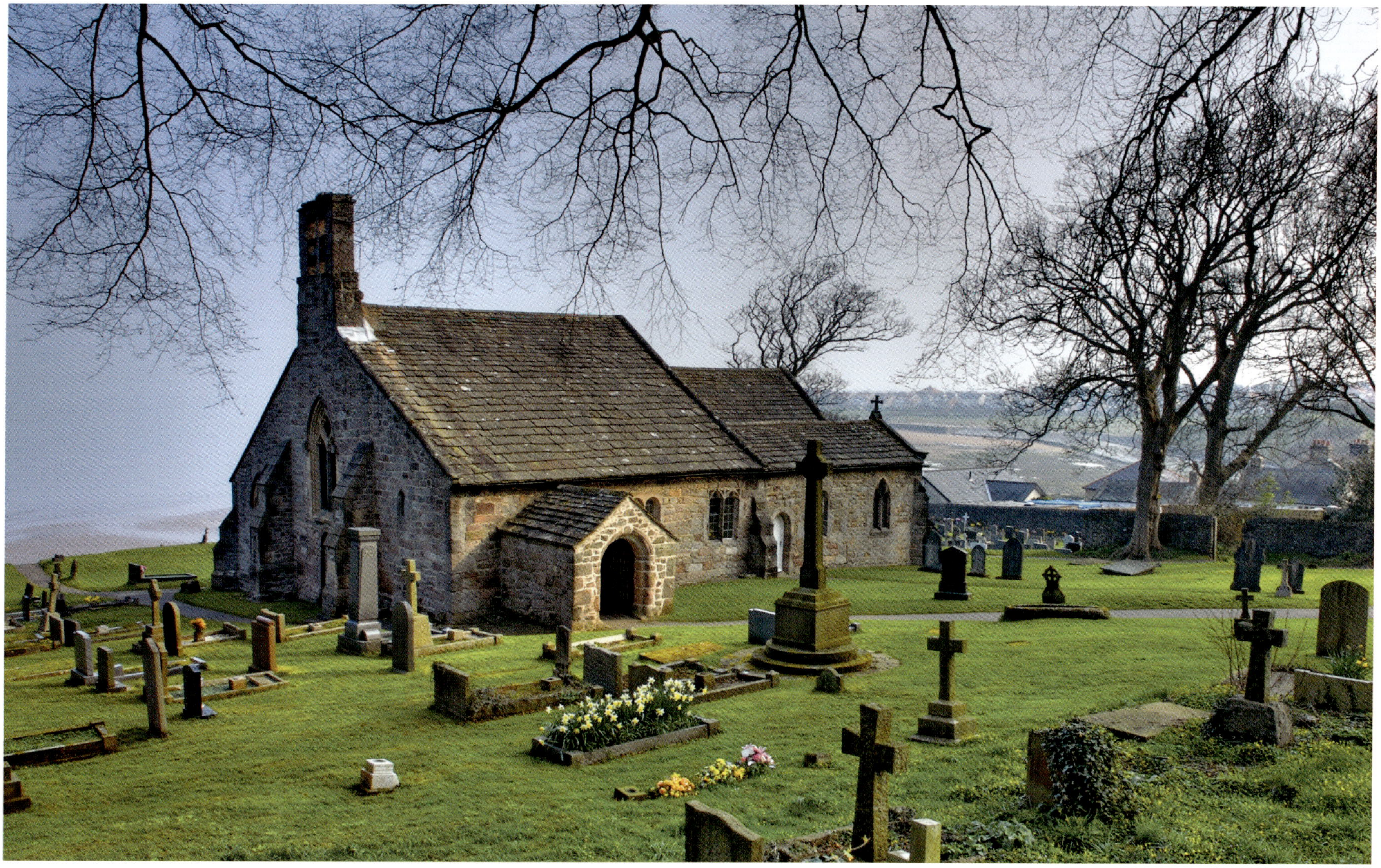

St Peter's Church, an ancient site of worship on Heysham Head.


The graveyard of St Peter's Church, just yards from the sea, with Morecambe beyond.

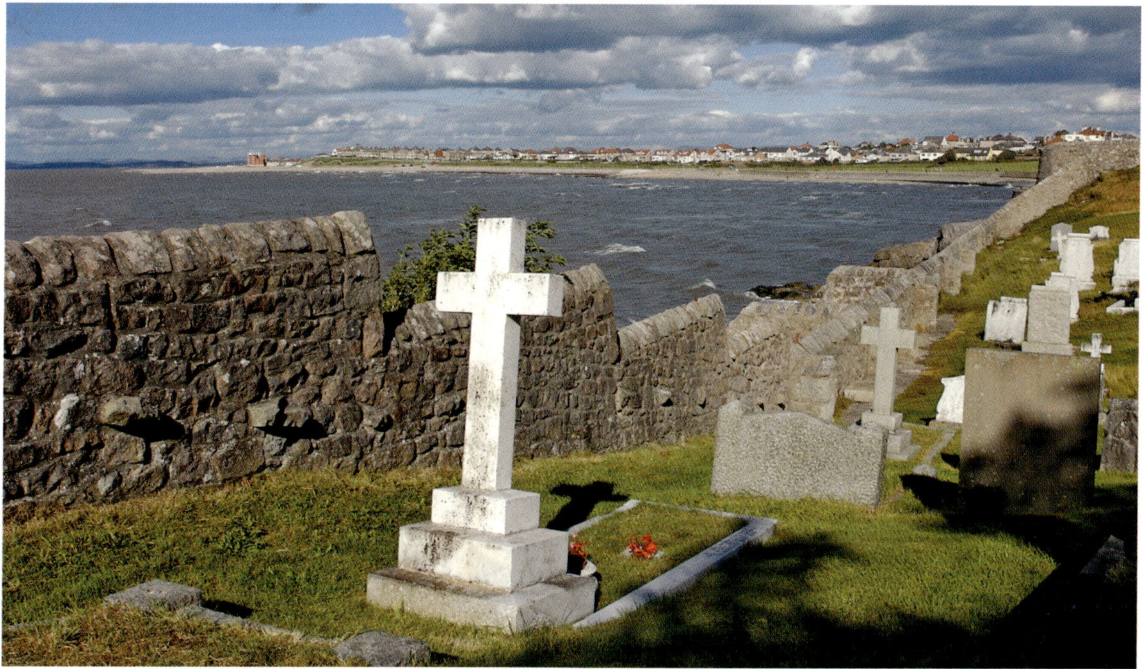

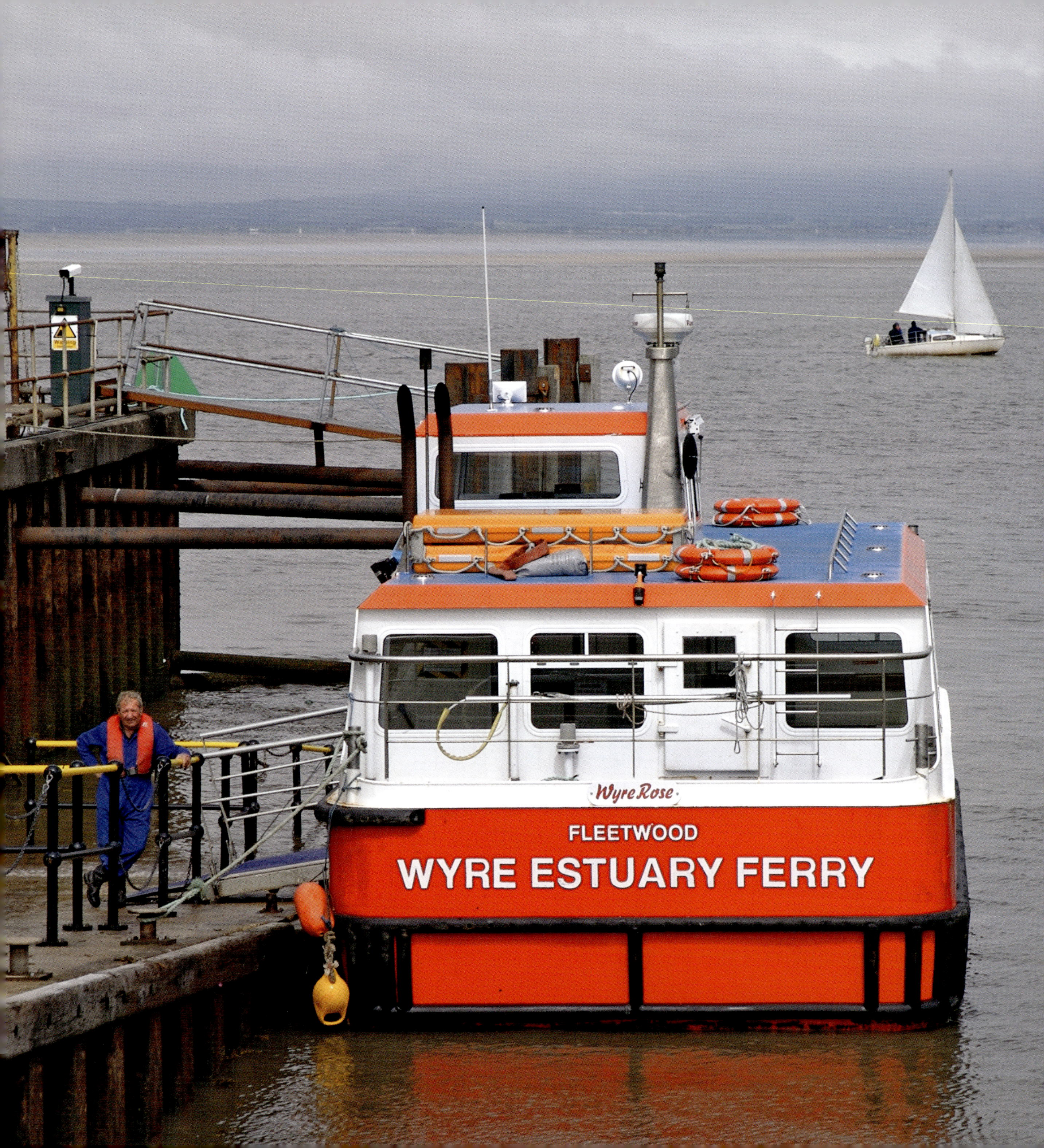

Wyre Rose
FLEETWOOD
WYRE ESTUARY FERRY

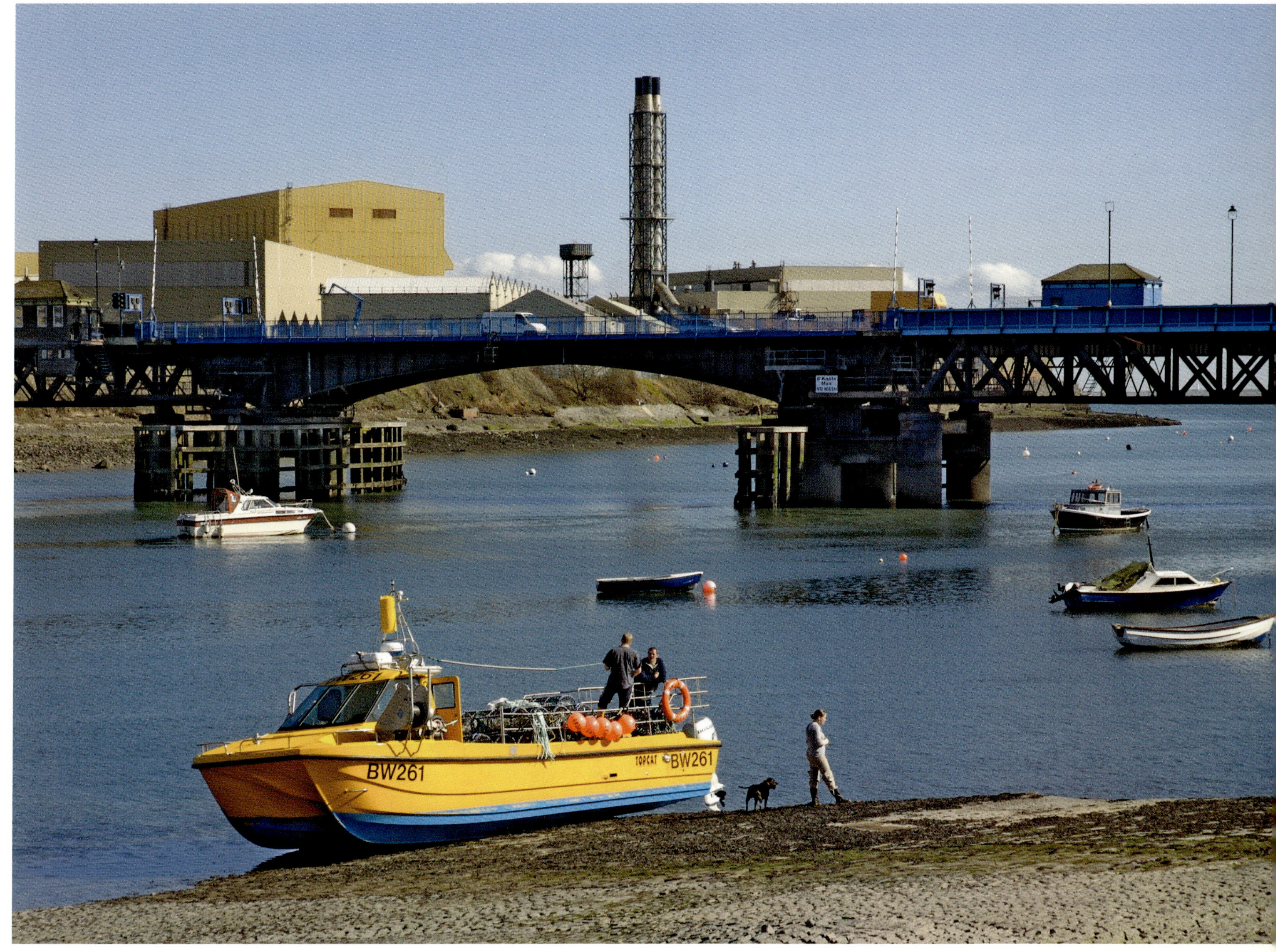

The Jubilee Bridge, built exactly a hundred years ago to link
Barrow-in-Furness and the island of Walney.



LEFT
The ferry waits to take passengers across the River Wyre,
from Fleetwood to Knott End and back.

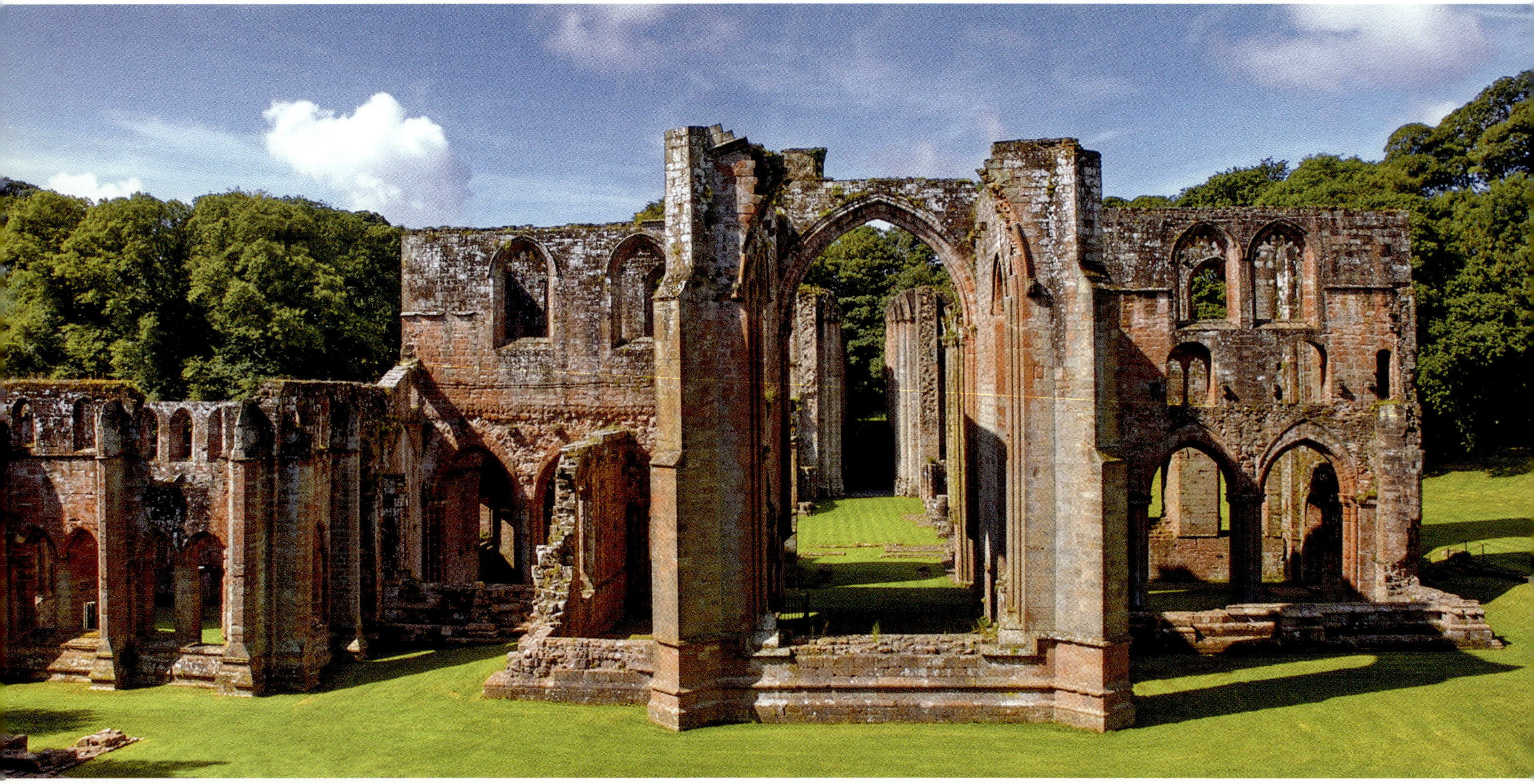

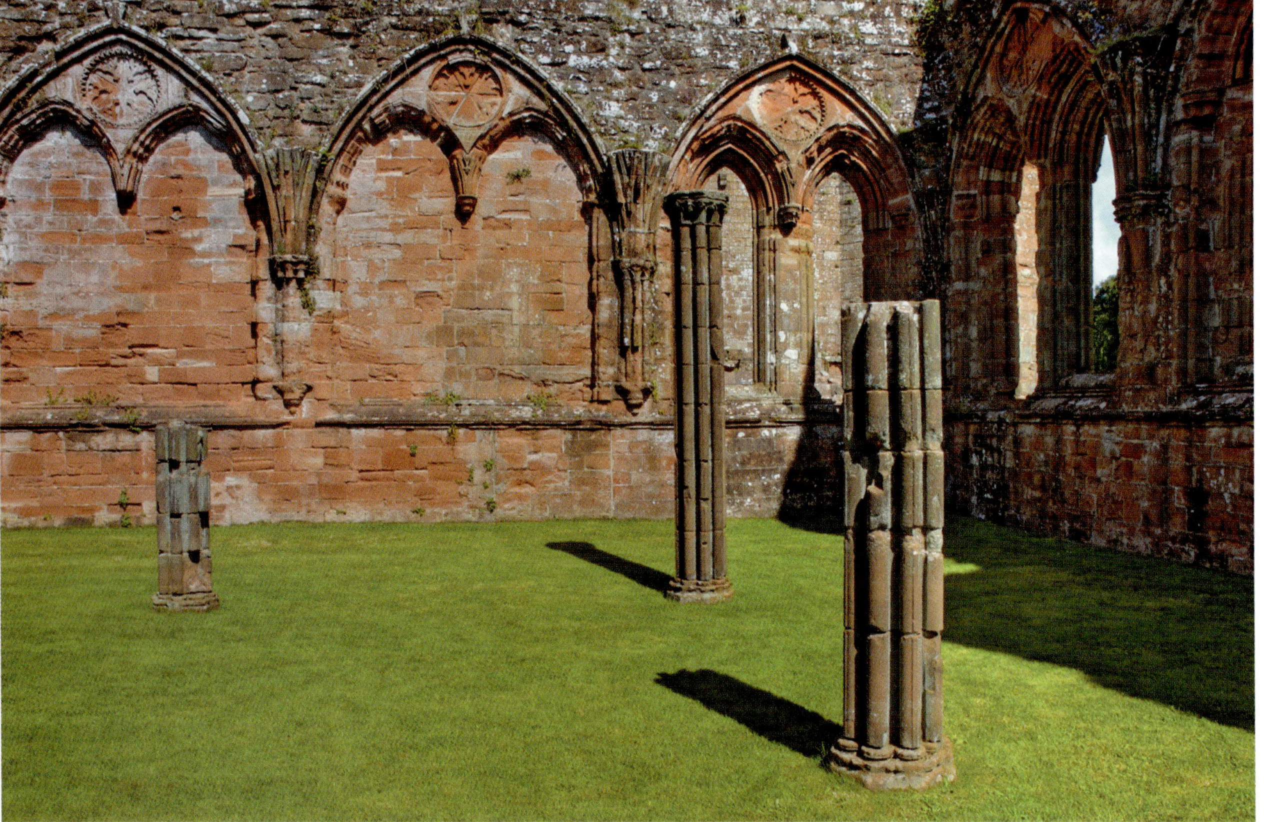

ABOVE
The red sandstone nave of Furness Abbey, one of the wealthiest Cistercian abbeys in England.

LEFT
Pillars and arches in the chapter house, where the daily business of Furness Abbey was carried out.

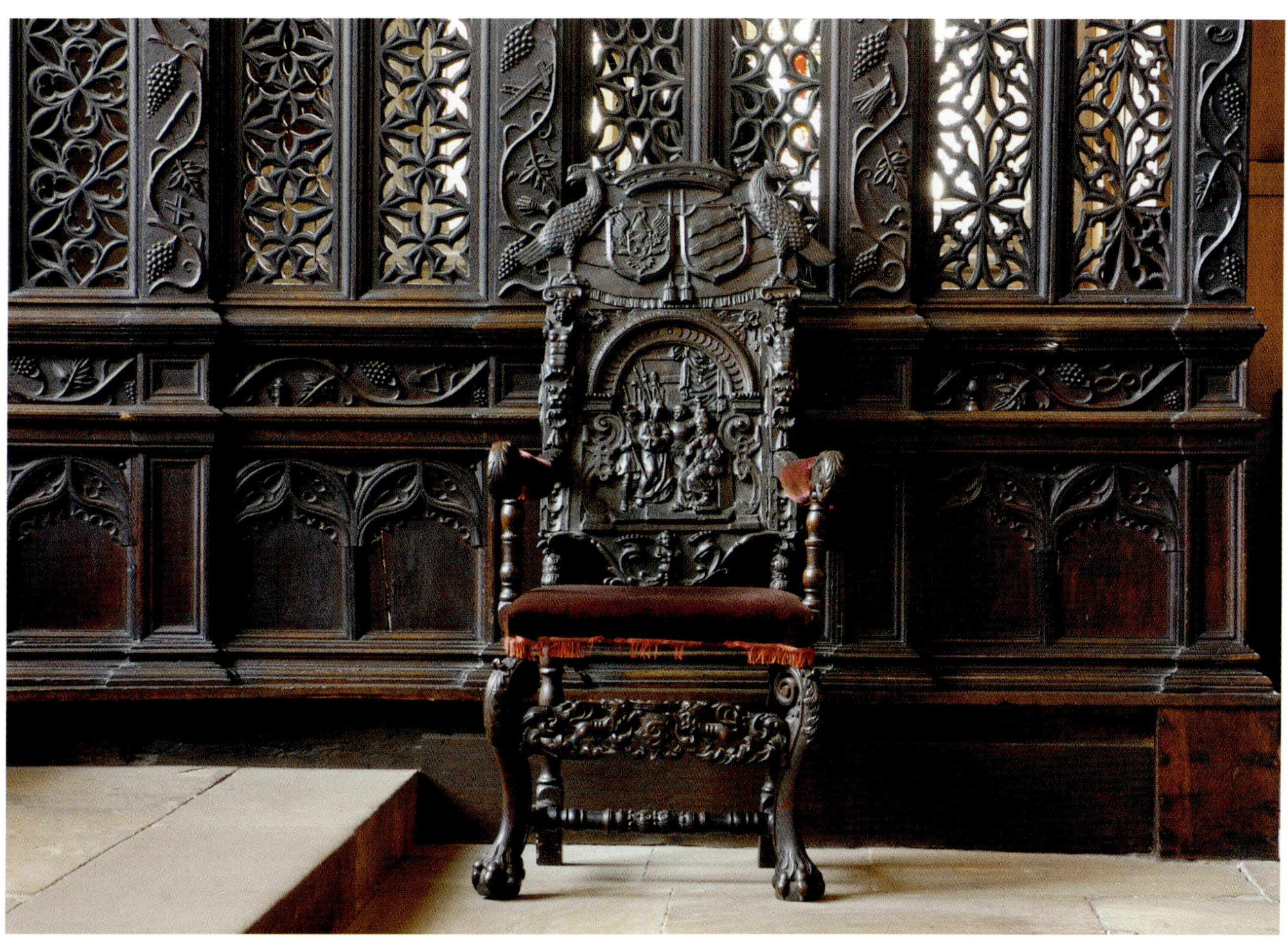

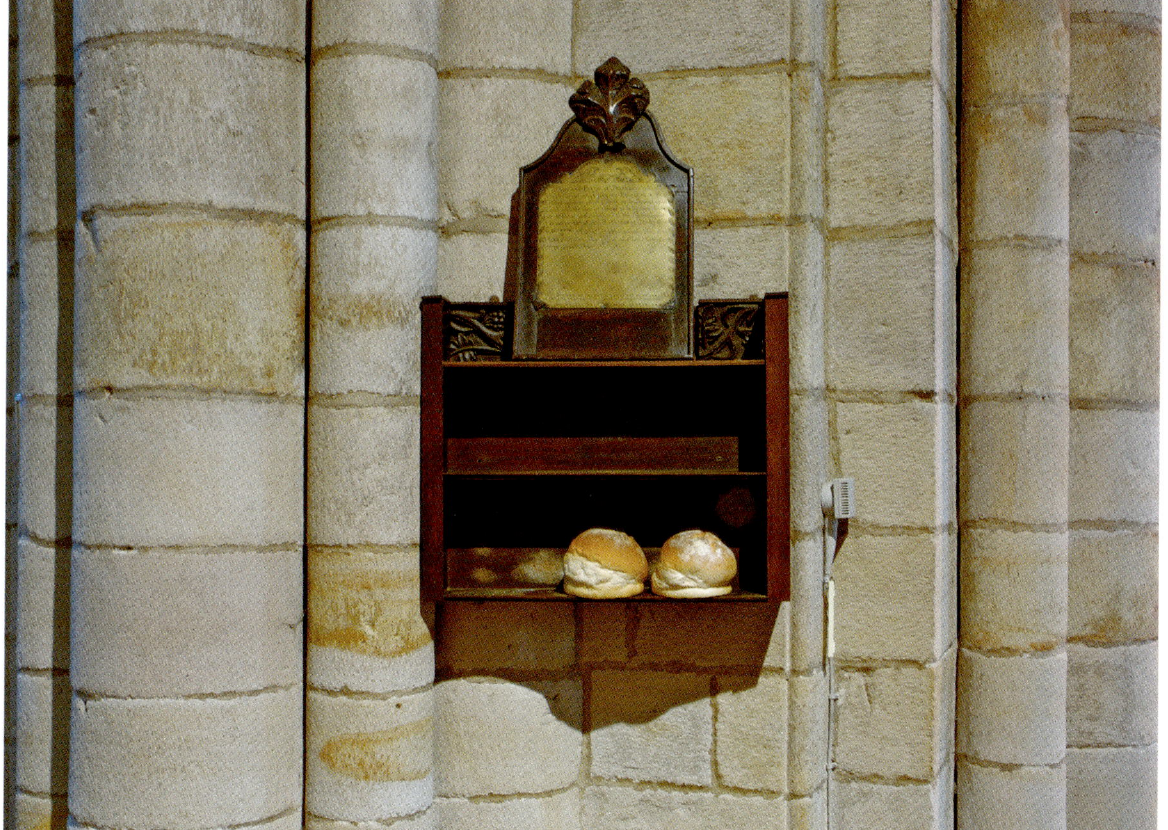



Some of the elaboarately-carved woodwork in Cartmel Priory.



A charitable impulse still thrives in a quiet corner of Cartmel Priory.



When sunlight reflects off the sandbars and mudbanks, Morecambe Bay can be a magical place.

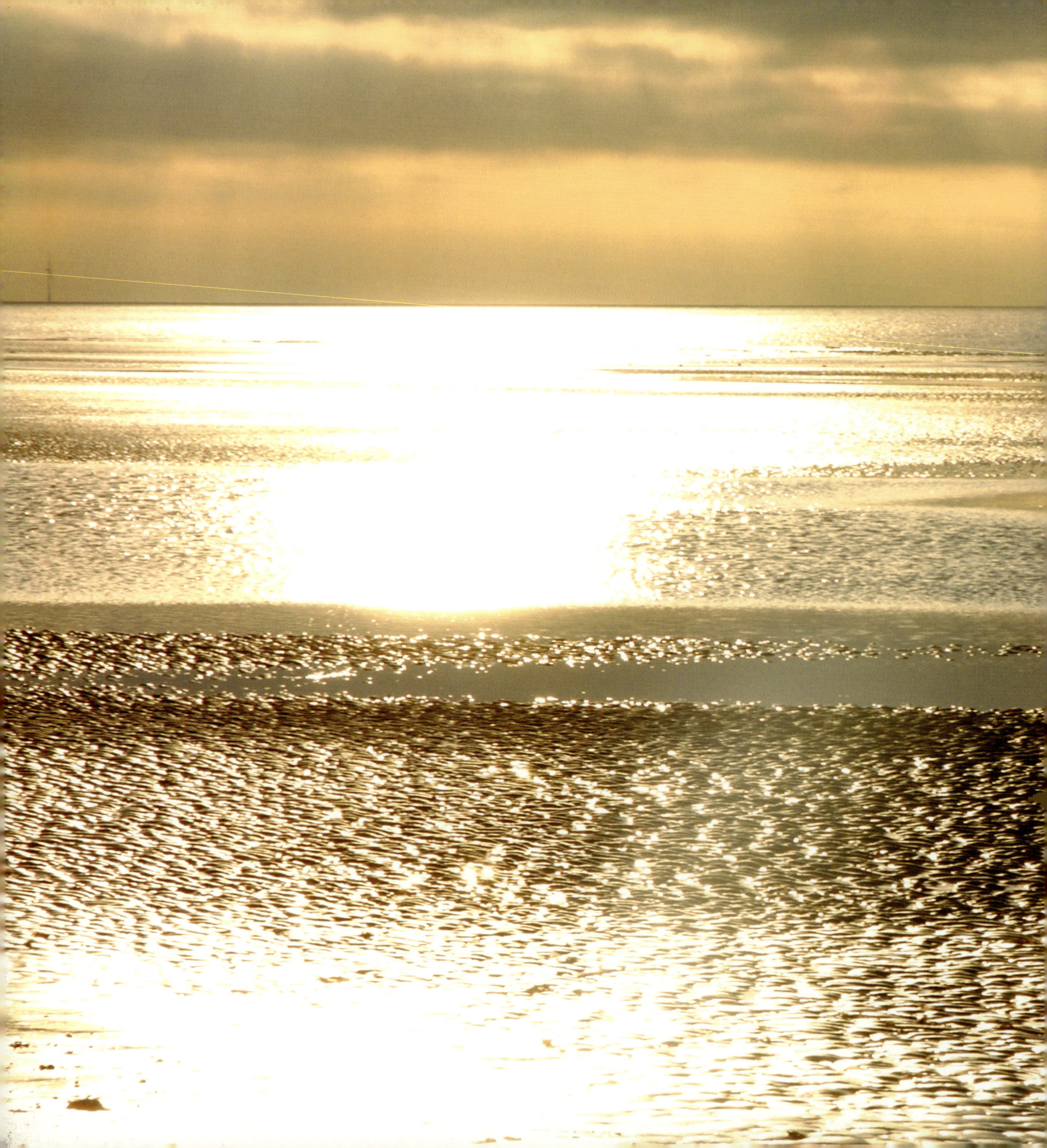

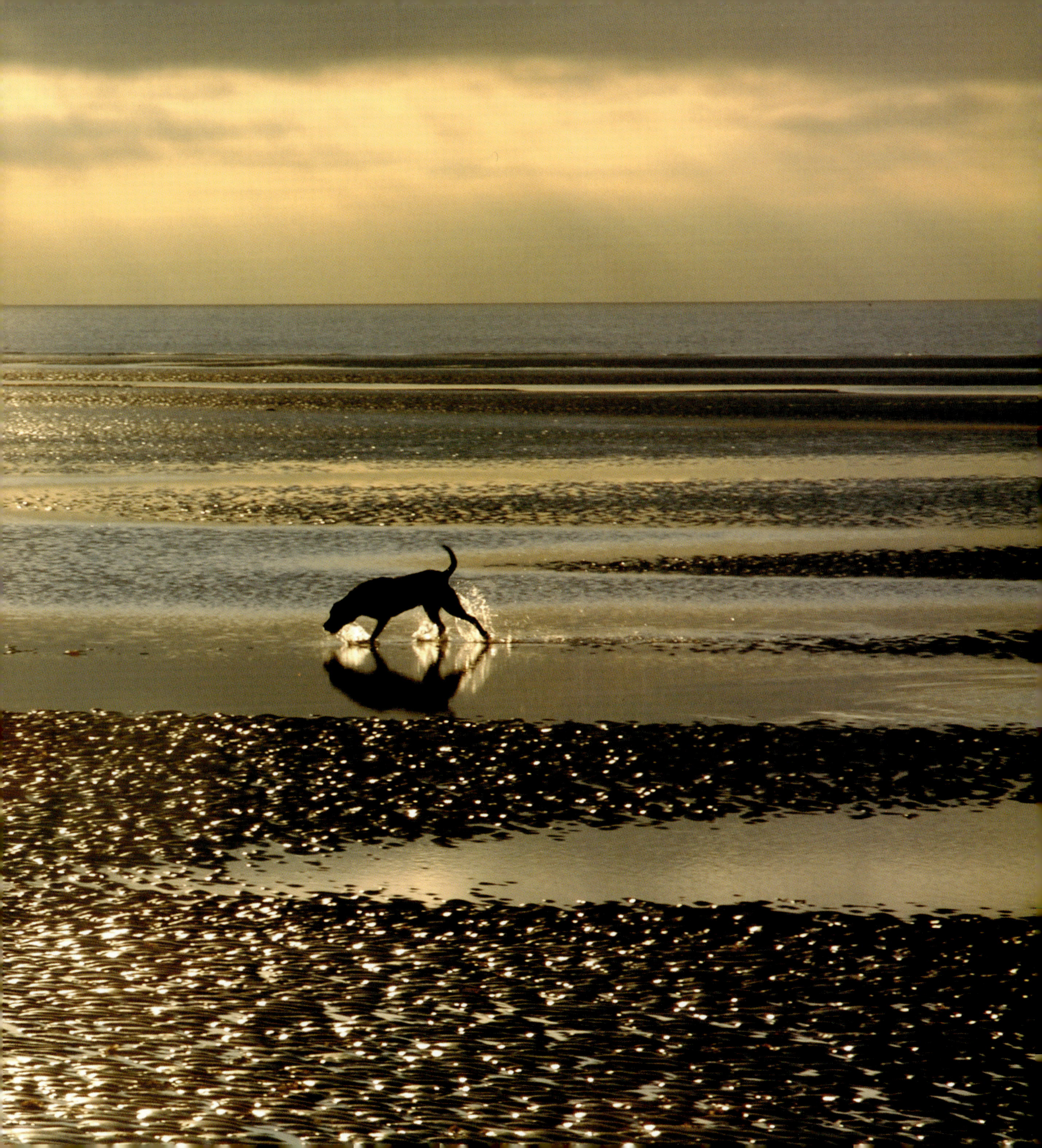

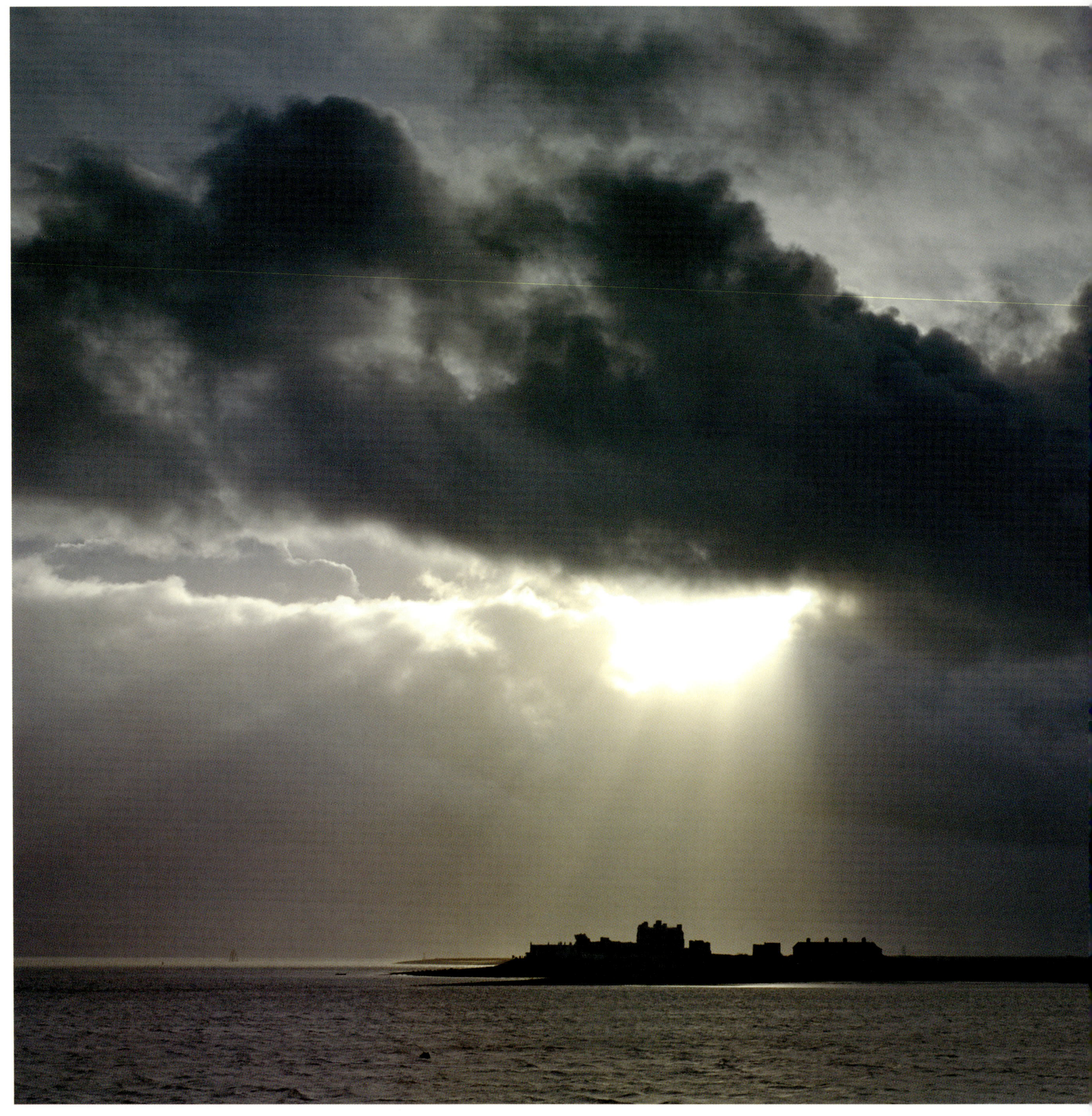

# A SHIFTING SANDSCAPE

Two characteristics combine to make Morecambe Bay so special. It's big – almost 200 square miles (518 sq km) – which makes it the second largest bay in the UK (only the Wash is bigger, and if we narrow the criteria to areas that are continuously intertidal, then Morecambe Bay heads the list). Secondly, the bay is shallow: so shallow, in fact, that when the tide retreats it can go out for seven miles. The water may be shallow, but the sands are deep. At low tide 120 square miles (310 sq km) of the bay are revealed as a 'wet Sahara' of mud-flats, meandering channels, tidal pools, swift currents and areas of quicksand which change position, unpredictably, from one day to the next.

Morecambe Bay is fed by five rivers – the Leven, Kent, Keer, Lune and Wyre – and when the tide turns, the water can roar in faster than a man can run. I've seen the tidal bore racing up the Kent estuary at Arnside. It's a remarkable sight, a force of nature. A skilled surfer could ride in on the wave, though he wouldn't want to be out on the sands to take the full force of this wall of water. As long as people underestimate the power of this tidal bore, and the shifting unpredictability of the sands, the bay will continue to claim lives.

This is low-lying country – making such modest elevations as Hampsfell, Arnside Knott and Humphrey Head seem prominent

Storm-clouds part above Piel Island, near Barrow-in-Furness.

by comparison. Some places along the coastline are lower than the highest recorded tide, which means they have to be protected by sea-walls and embankments.

Many plans have been made for Morecambe Bay down the years – some realistic, some distinctly fanciful. The bay would look very different today if an eighteenth-century land reclamation scheme had gone ahead. The plan included the construction of a road on a raised embankment, to allow bay crossings even at high tide. The embankment would have brought a huge swathe of land into agricultural use: a more important consideration at the time than it would be today. A mile-long breakwater was built out out into the bay, from the Lancashire shore near Jenny Brown's Point, as part of yet another abortive plan to reclaim land from the sea. And there are persistent plans for a massive tidal barrage which could harness the enormous power of the tides – but which would destroy the bay's value as a wildlife reserve.

Morecambe Bay has been silting up over the last millennium, and villages have been lost to the power of the sea. Hert and Fordebodele, for example, survive only as names on old maps, while all that's left of Aldingham, near Ulverston, is St Cuthbert's Church – just yards from the sands, but now protected by a sturdy sea-wall.

The extensive shallows of the bay provided a living – albeit often a precarious one – for those who lived near by. Their way of working, and the tools of their arcane trades, were very different to those employed by the deep-sea trawlermen. Around Morecambe Bay the fishermen went to work on horseback, then with horse and two-wheeled cart, then, in more recent times, with a tractor and trailer.

By agitating wet sand with a 'jumbo' – a plank with long handles – they could bring cockles to the surface, where they could be collected with a 'kraam', a three-pronged rake. The harsh winter of 1962–3 decimated stocks of cockles, which, since then, have proved to be as erratic and unreliable as so many other aspects of life around Morecambe Bay.

Fishermen used to collect mussels from the rocky scars (known as 'skears') off the shores of Barrow and Morecambe – but those rocks are now hidden beneath the sand. Men from Flookburgh caught flukes – flounders – and used horses to haul shrimp nets through the channels. A fleet of almost 200 shrimp boats – known as 'nobbies' – used to ply their trade out of Morecambe. Salmon and sea trout were caught in drift nets suspended in the River Lune.

Fewer people now work on the sands of Morecambe Bay. As a consequence of the tragic deaths in 2004, the cockle-beds were closed. They were re-opened in 2007, with a permit system and other safeguards aimed at averting further tragedies.

The tide-washed causeway from Overton to Sunderland Point, and a rather redundant sign!

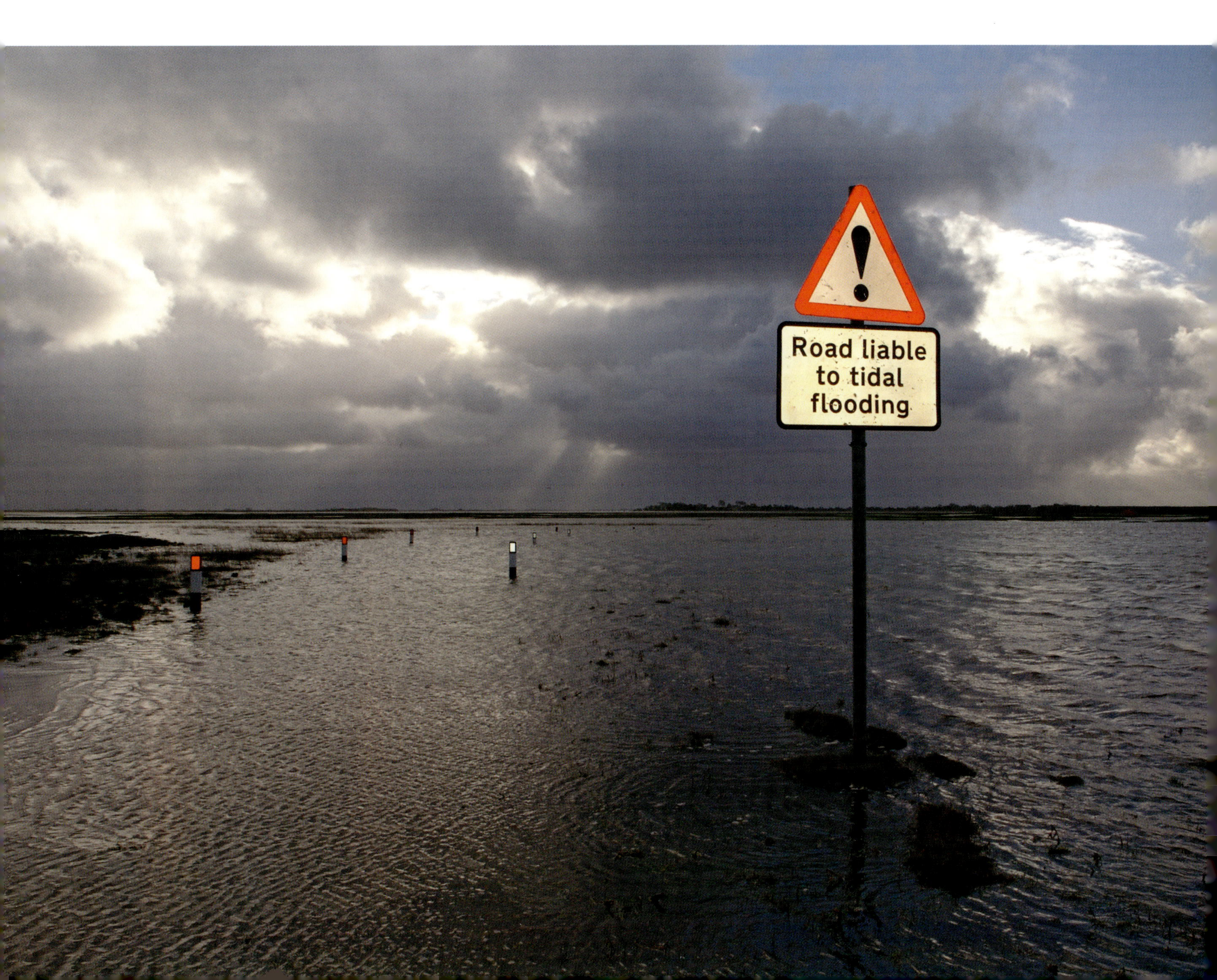
Road liable
to tidal
flooding

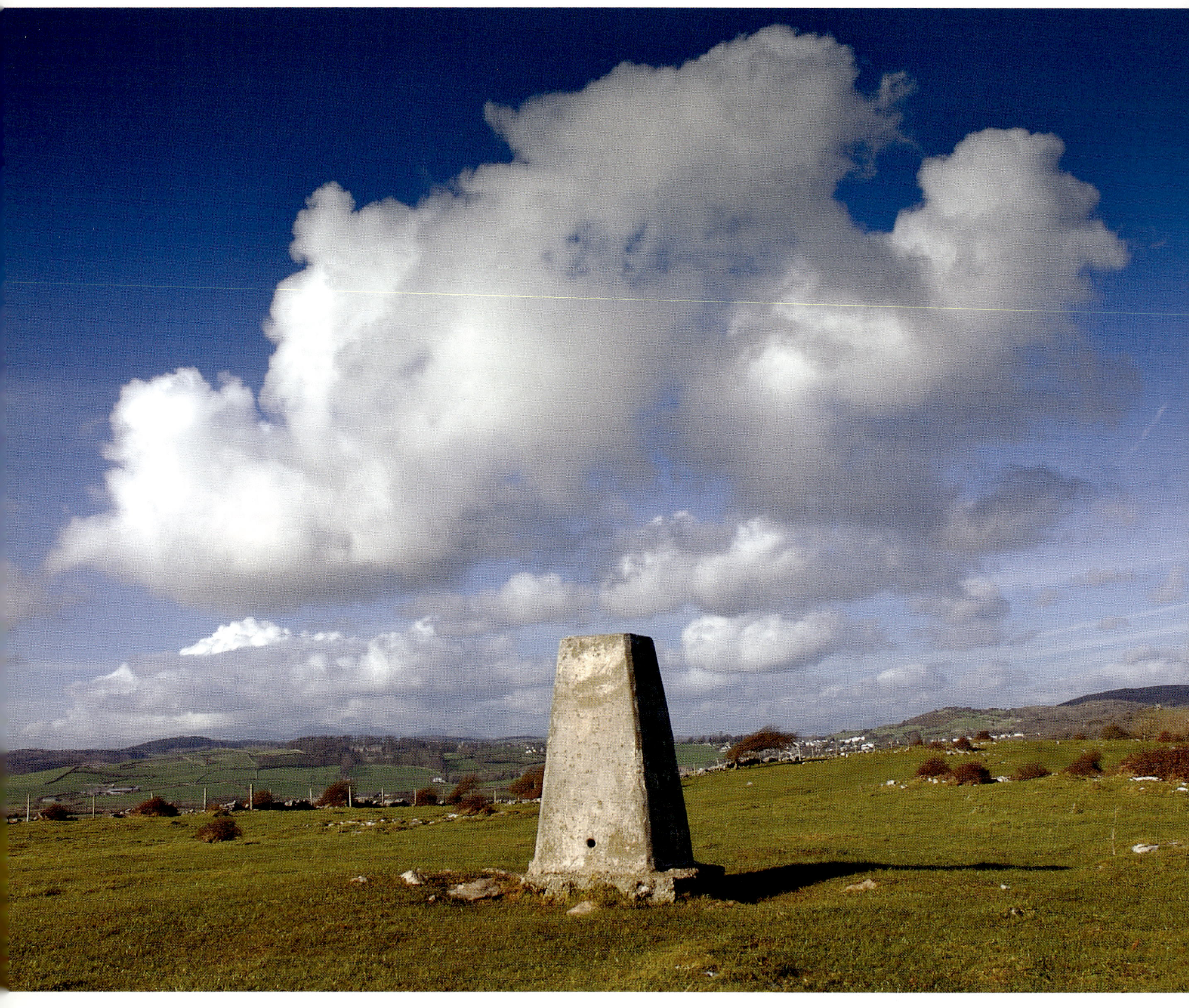

A flurry of clouds surrounds the trig point on the promontory of Humphrey Head.

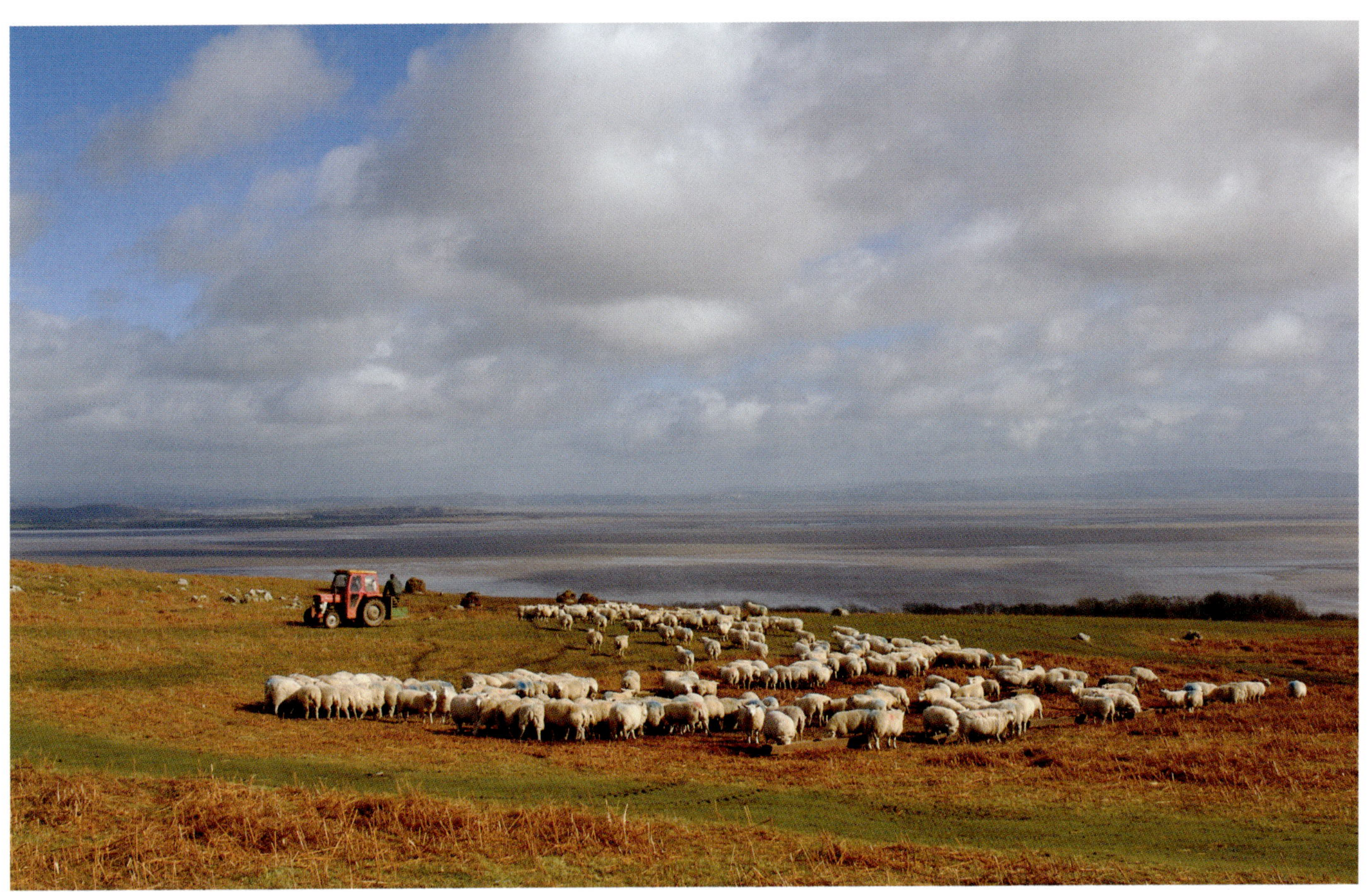

A farmer brings food to his sheep on Birkrigg Common, near Ulverston.

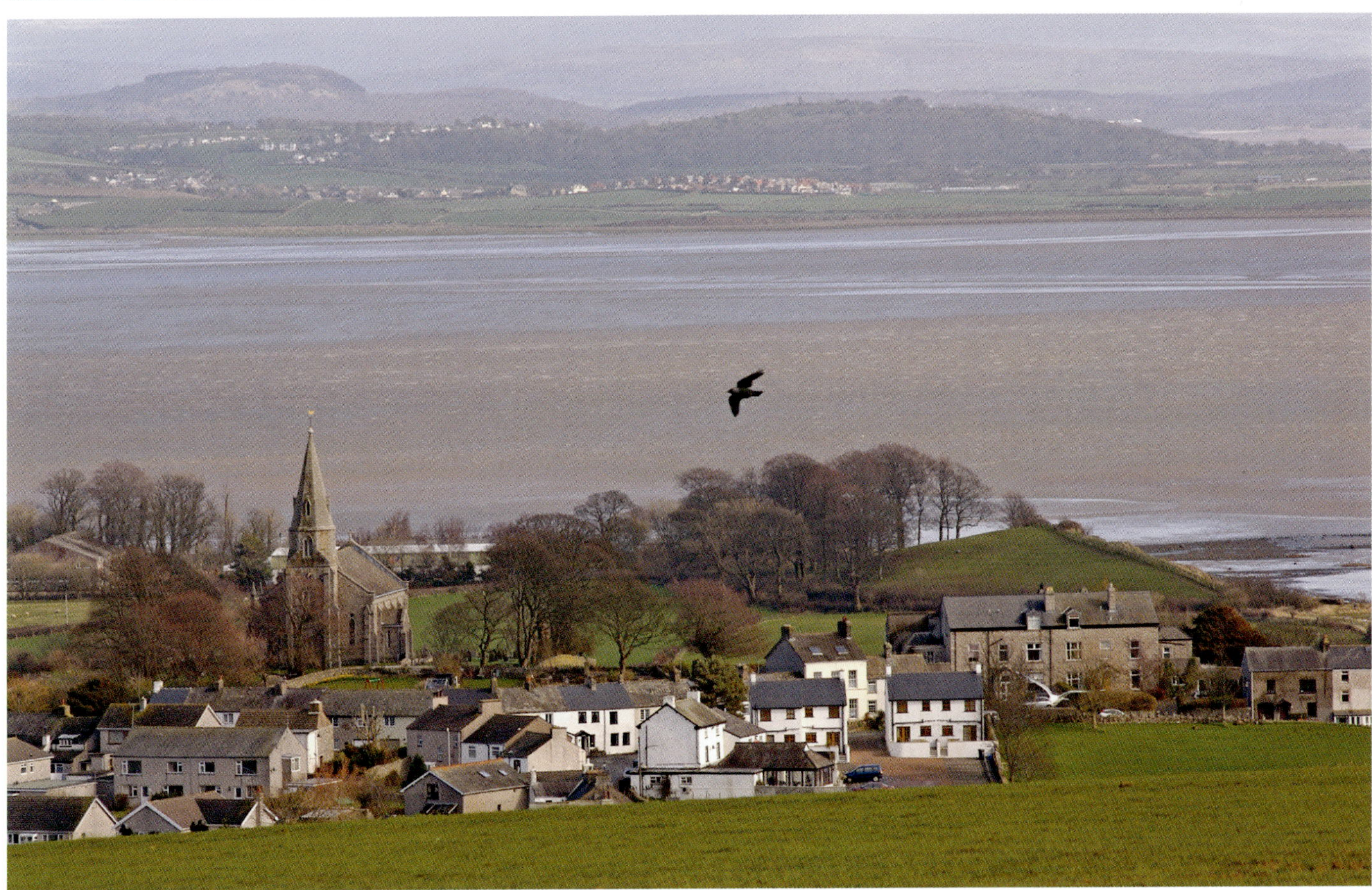

Holy Trinity Church and the village of Bardsea, with the Leven estuary beyond.

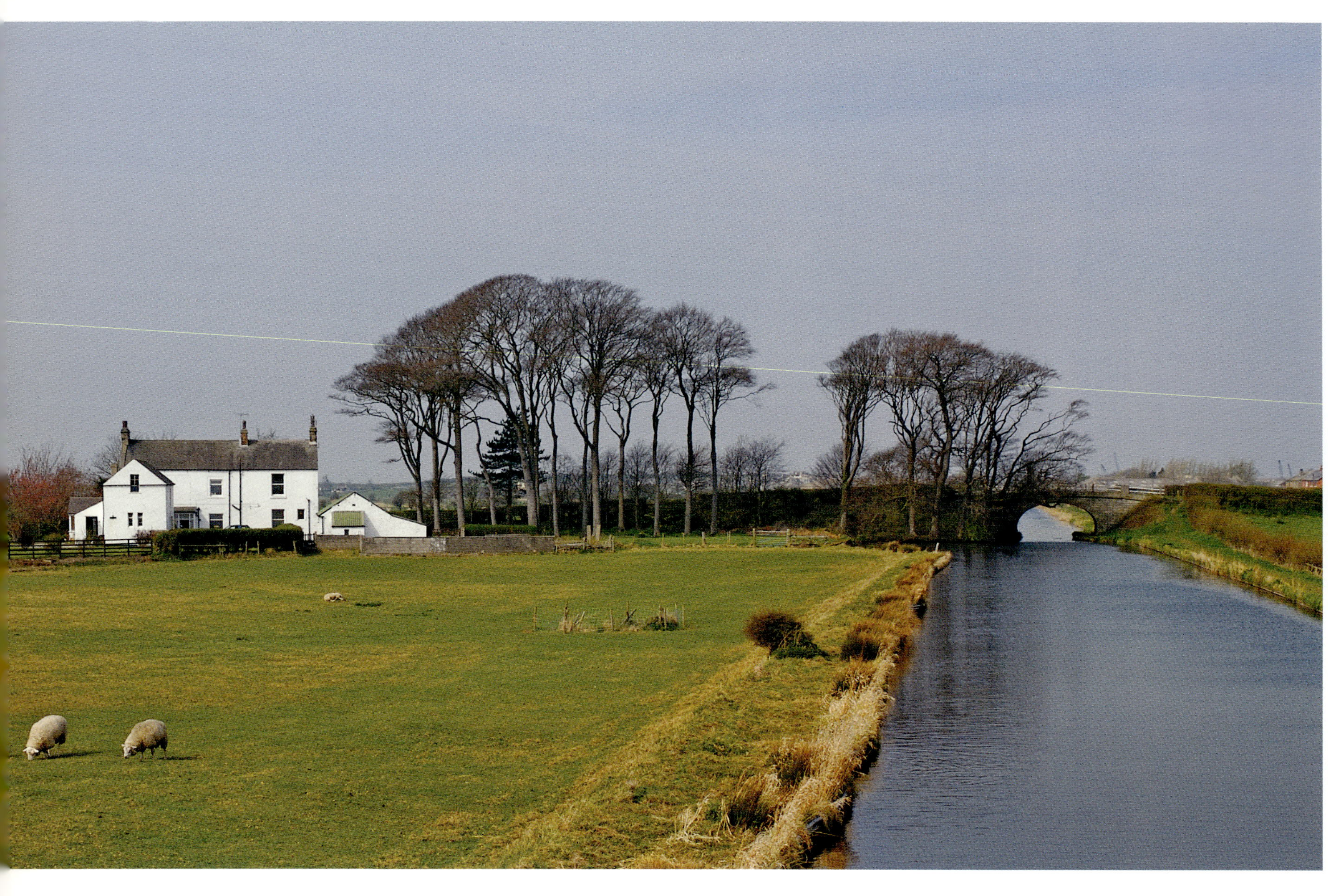

This ruler-straight waterway links the Lancaster Canal with Glasson Dock.

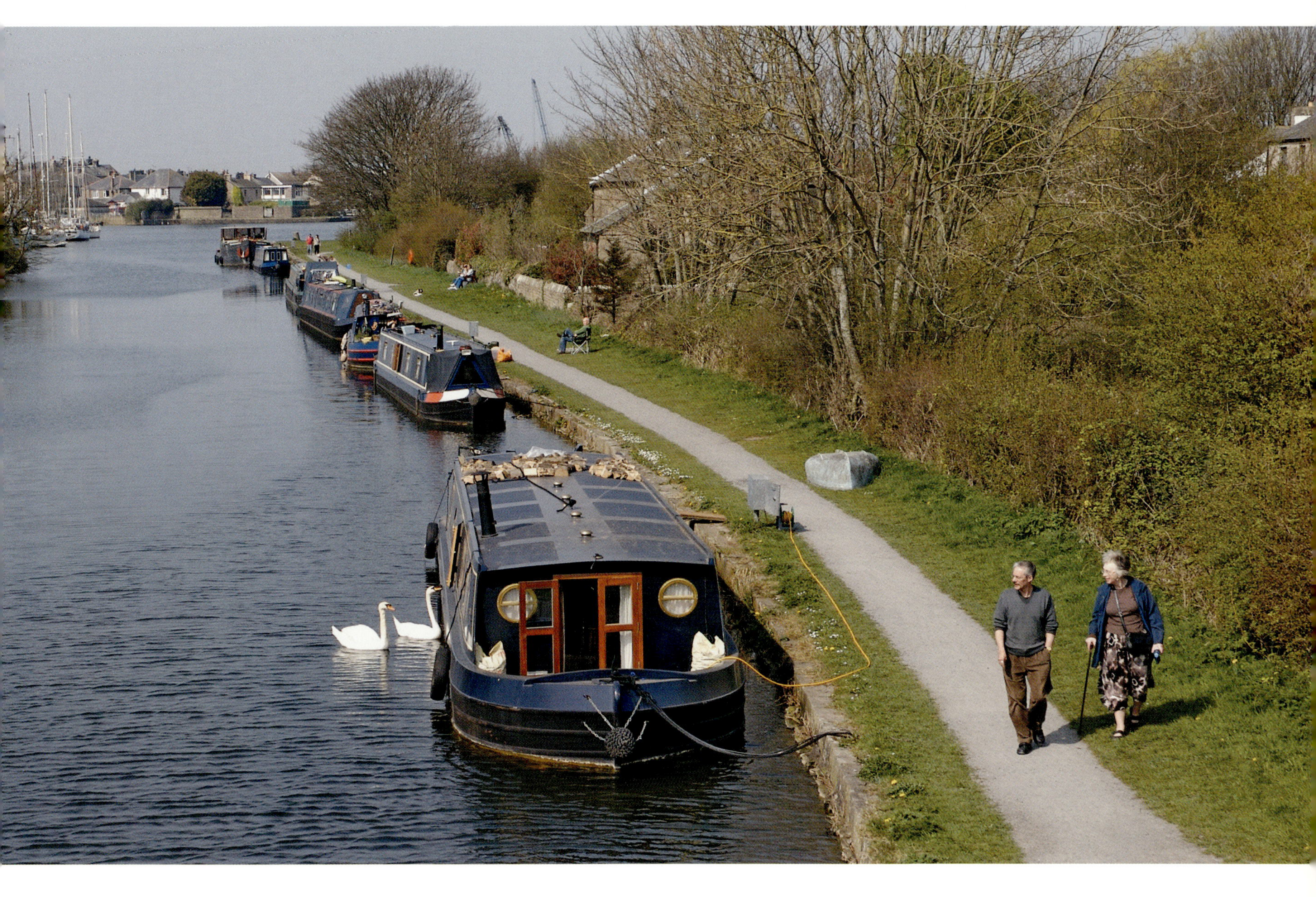

Swans wait to be fed on the approach to Glasson Dock.

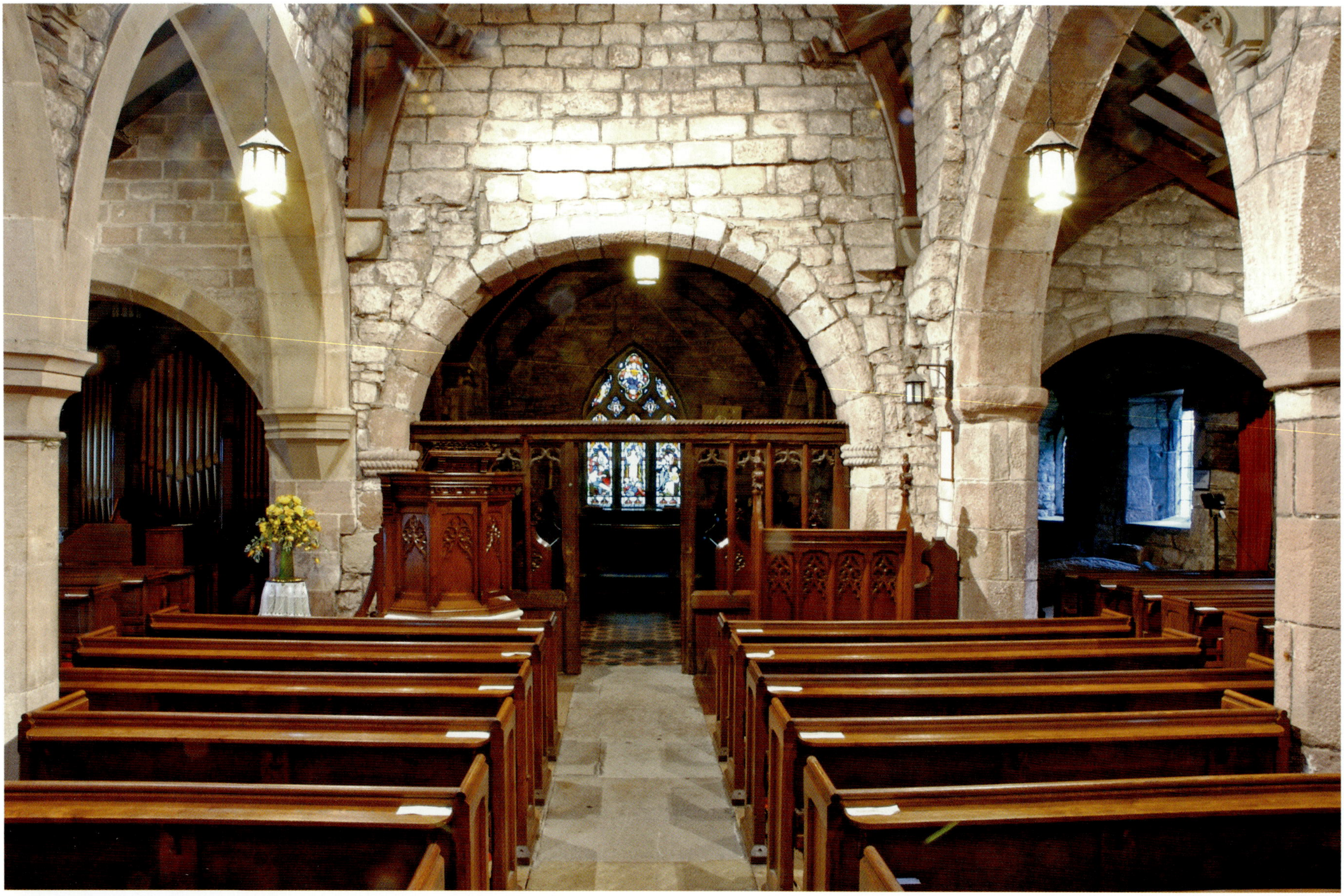

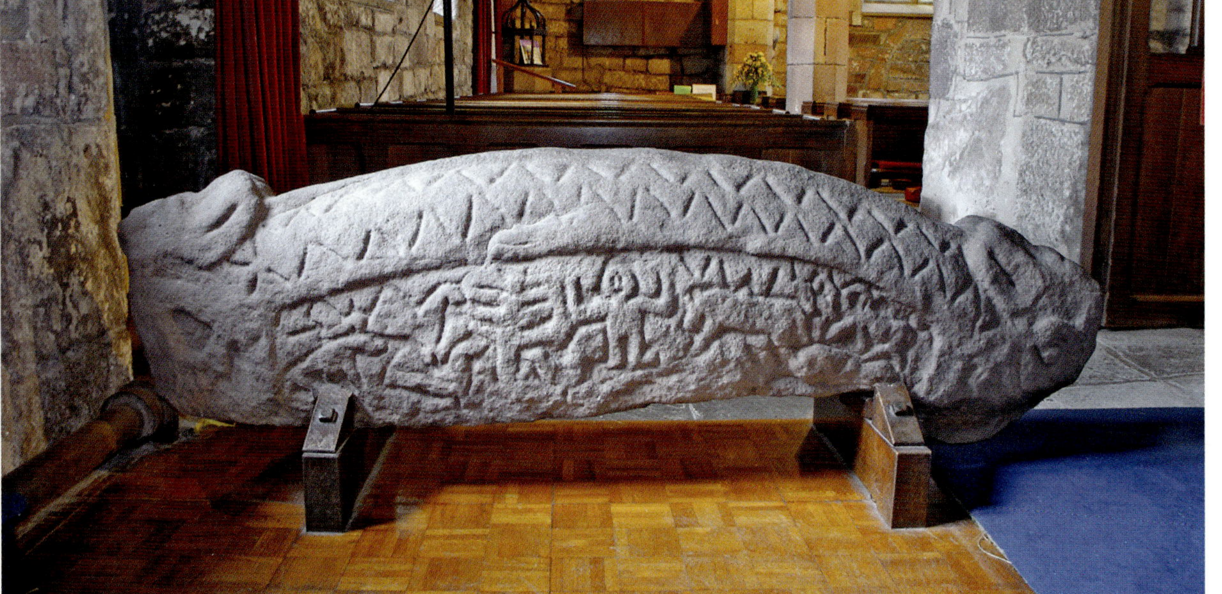

ABOVE
Rough-hewn stonework – the oldest dating back a thousand years – inside St Peter's Church, Heysham

LEFT
This remarkable tenth-century, 'hogsback' grave cover – now in St Peter's Church, Heysham – once marked the final resting place of a prominent Viking.

RIGHT
The Lower Lighthouse, a familiar landmark on the sea-front at Fleetwood.

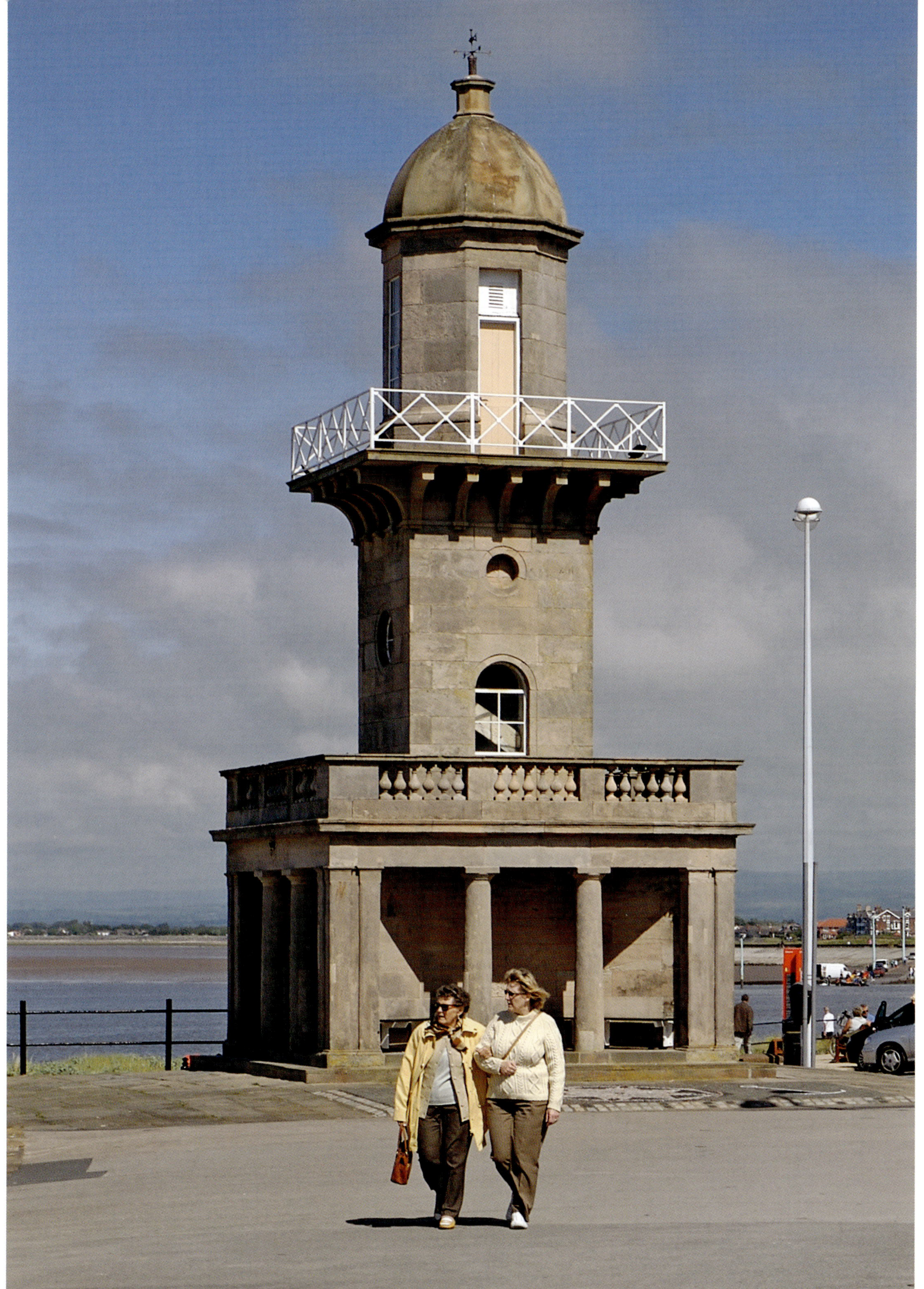

RIGHT
Exercising the dog, and escaping the
crowds, near Grange-over-Sands.

BELOW
Walking the dog on the glistening
foreshore near Bardsea.

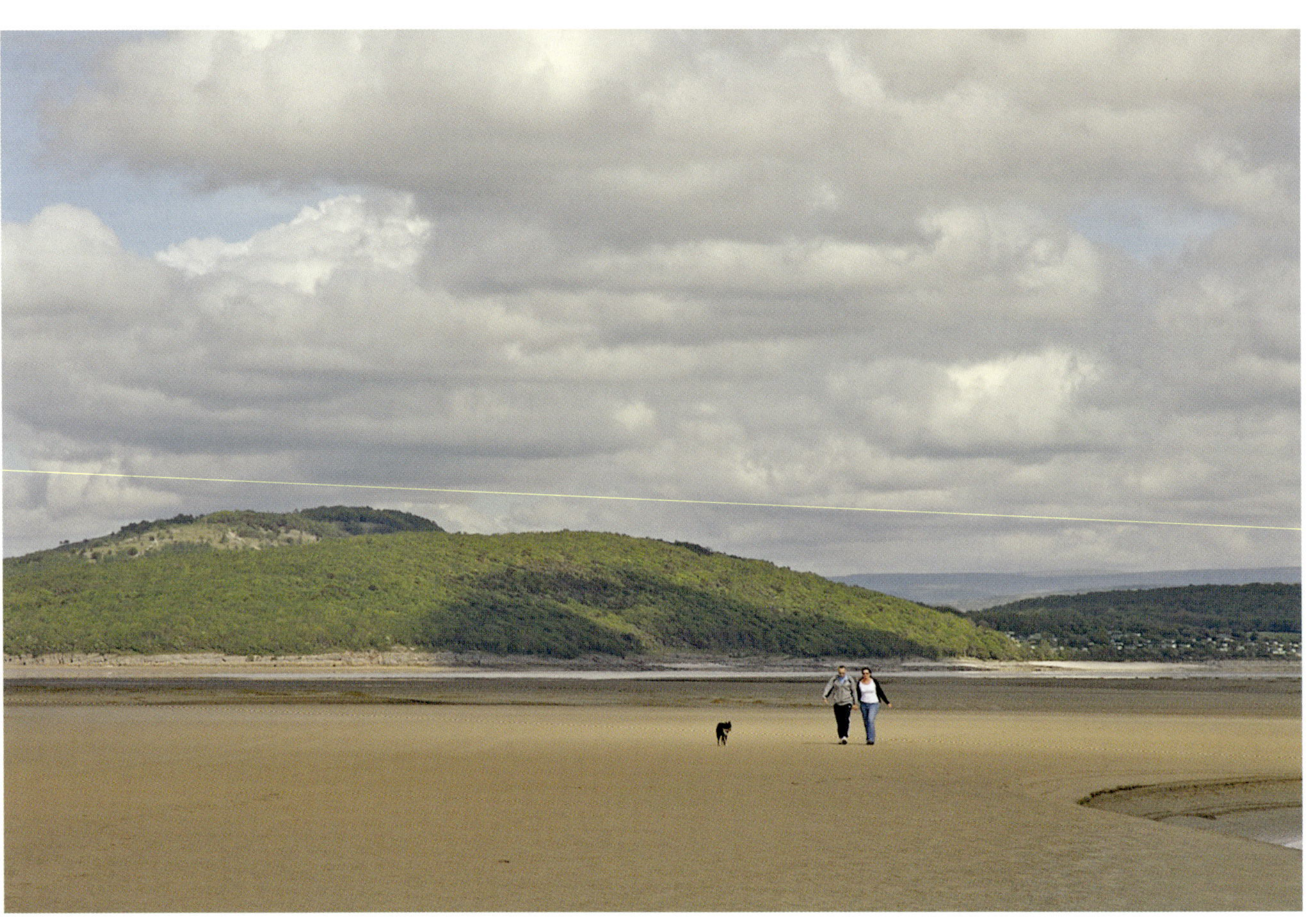

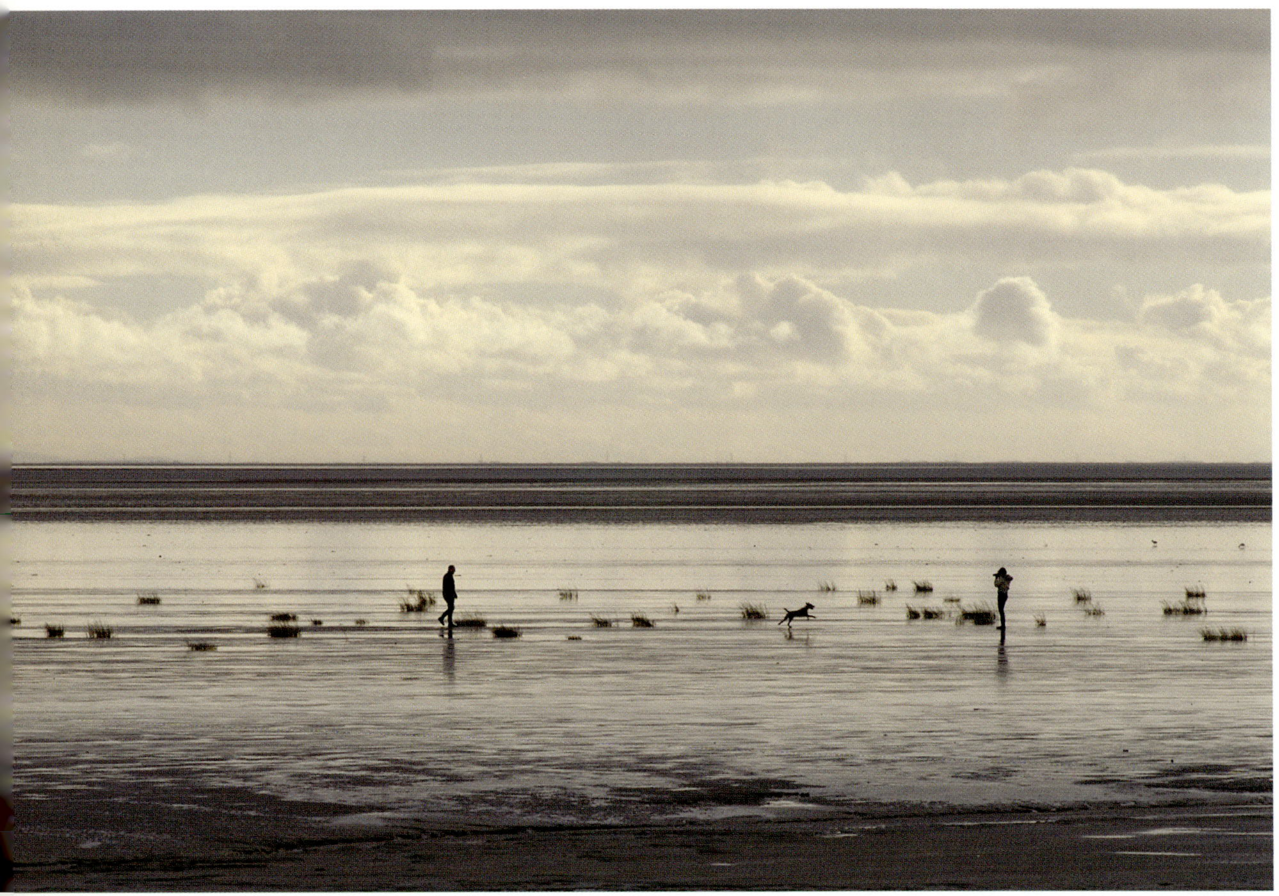

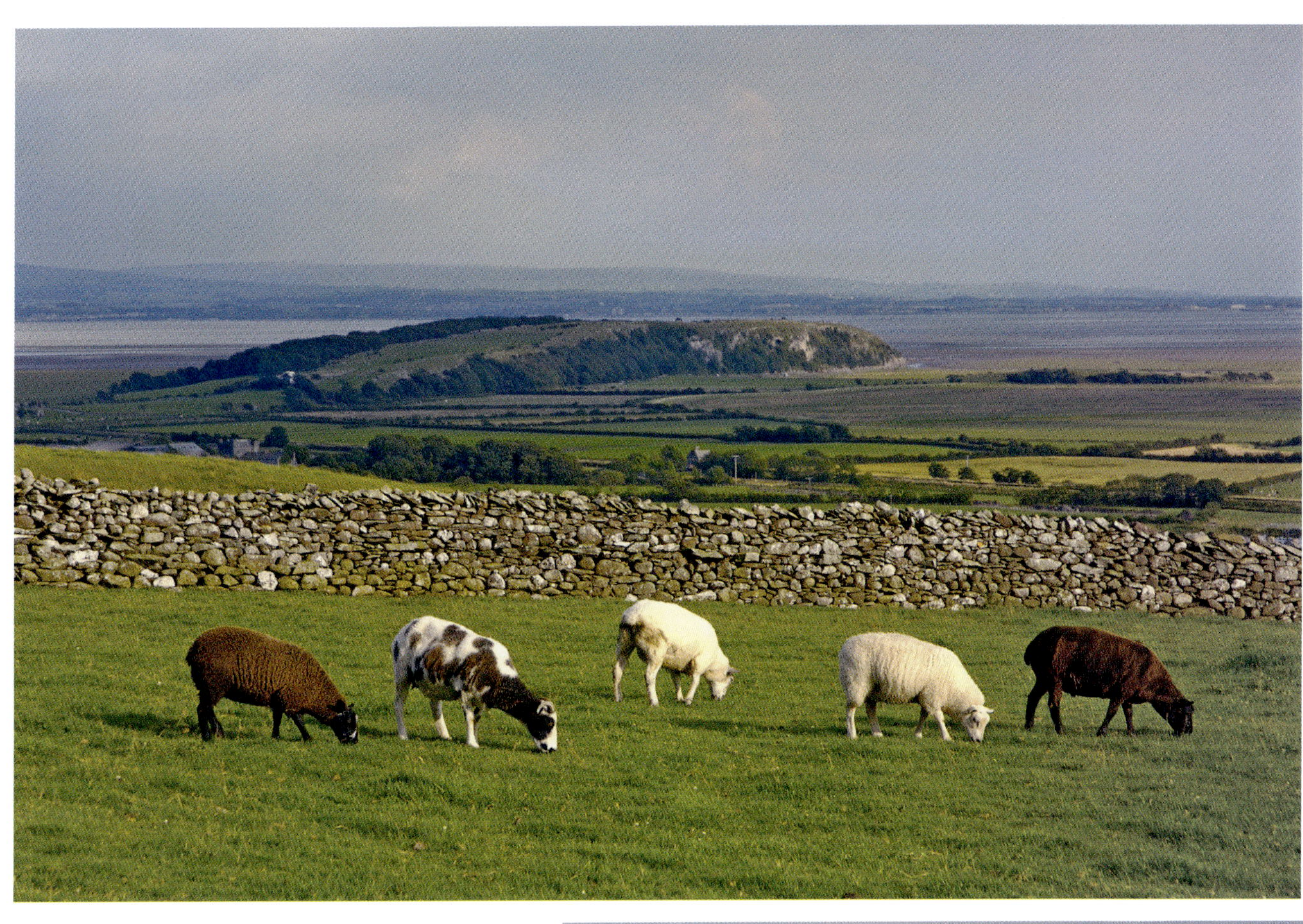

LEFT
Sheep grazing, with the limestone
promontory of Humphrey Head in the
middle distance.

BELOW
Limestone outcrops on Birkrigg
Common, overlooking the Leven
Estuary.

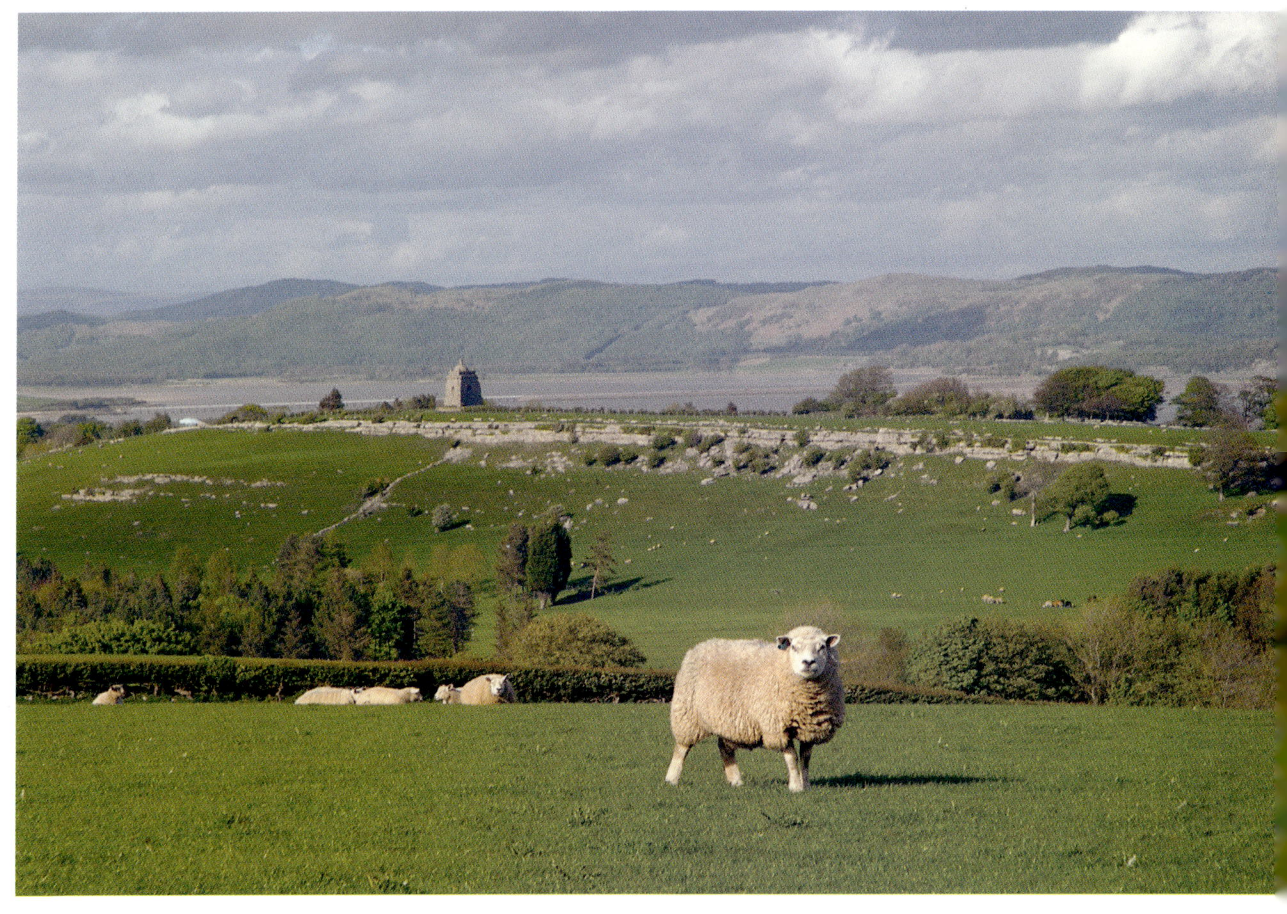

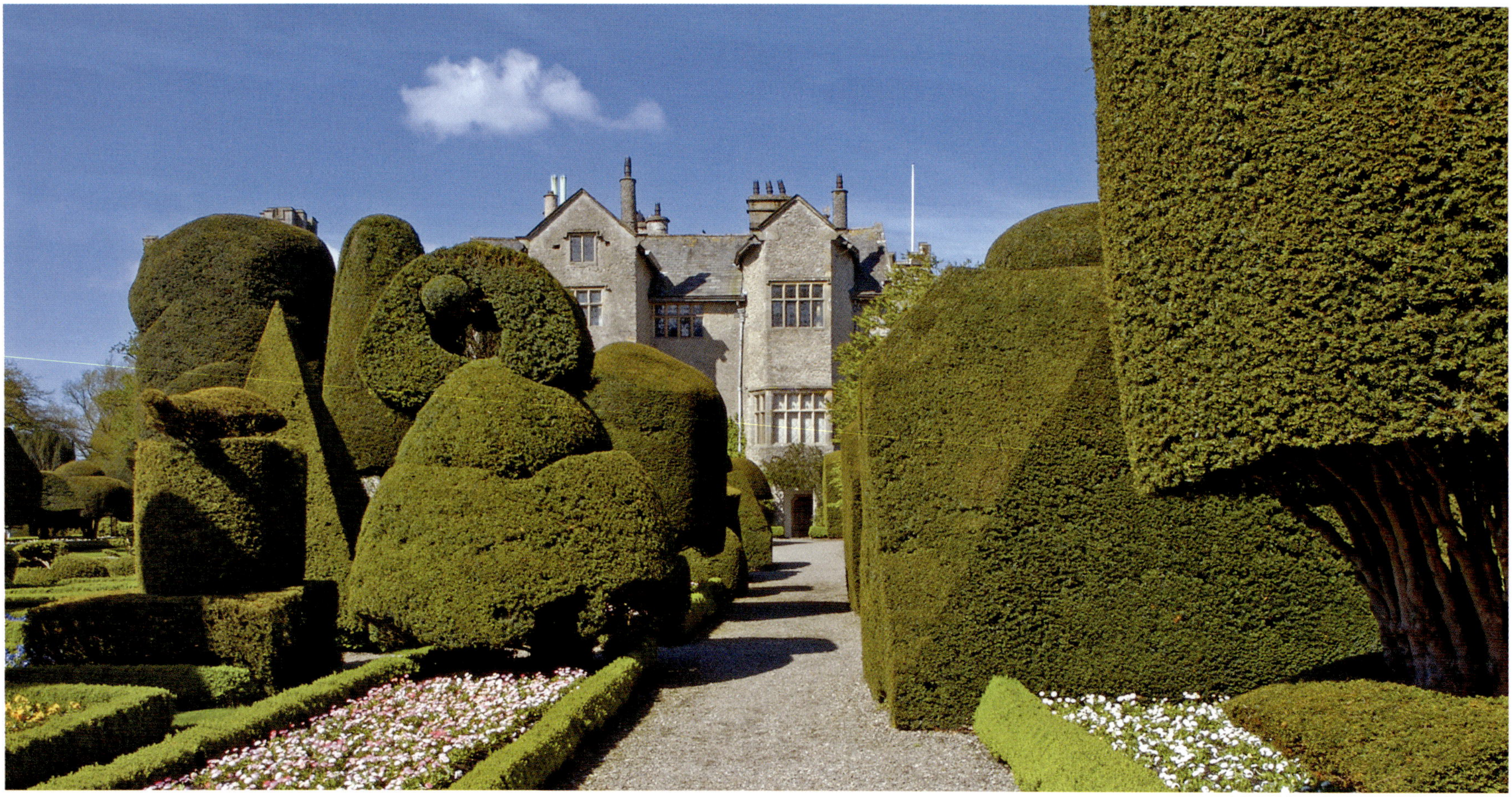

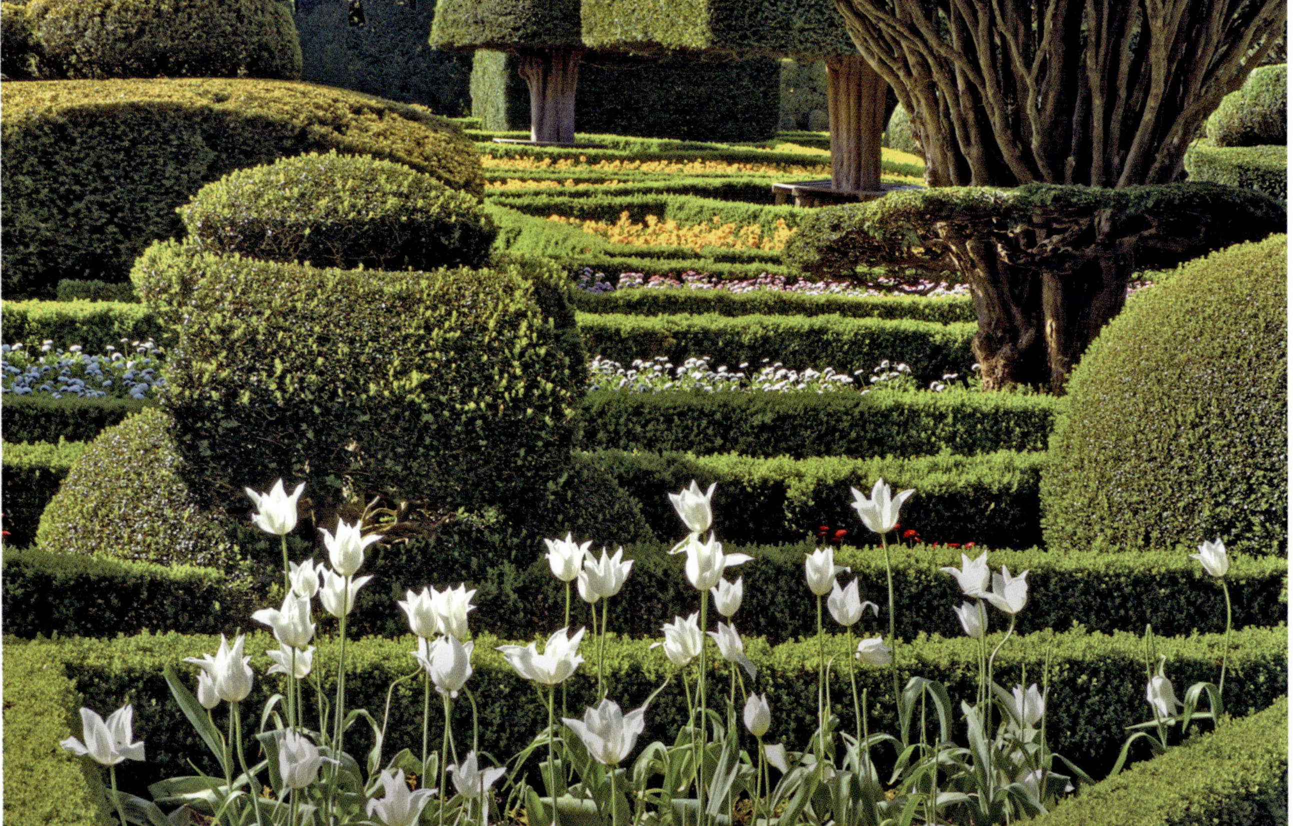

ABOVE
Levens Hall – the Elizabethan house is
almost hidden by exuberant topiary.

LEFT
Shape, texture and colour in the gardens
of Levens Hall.

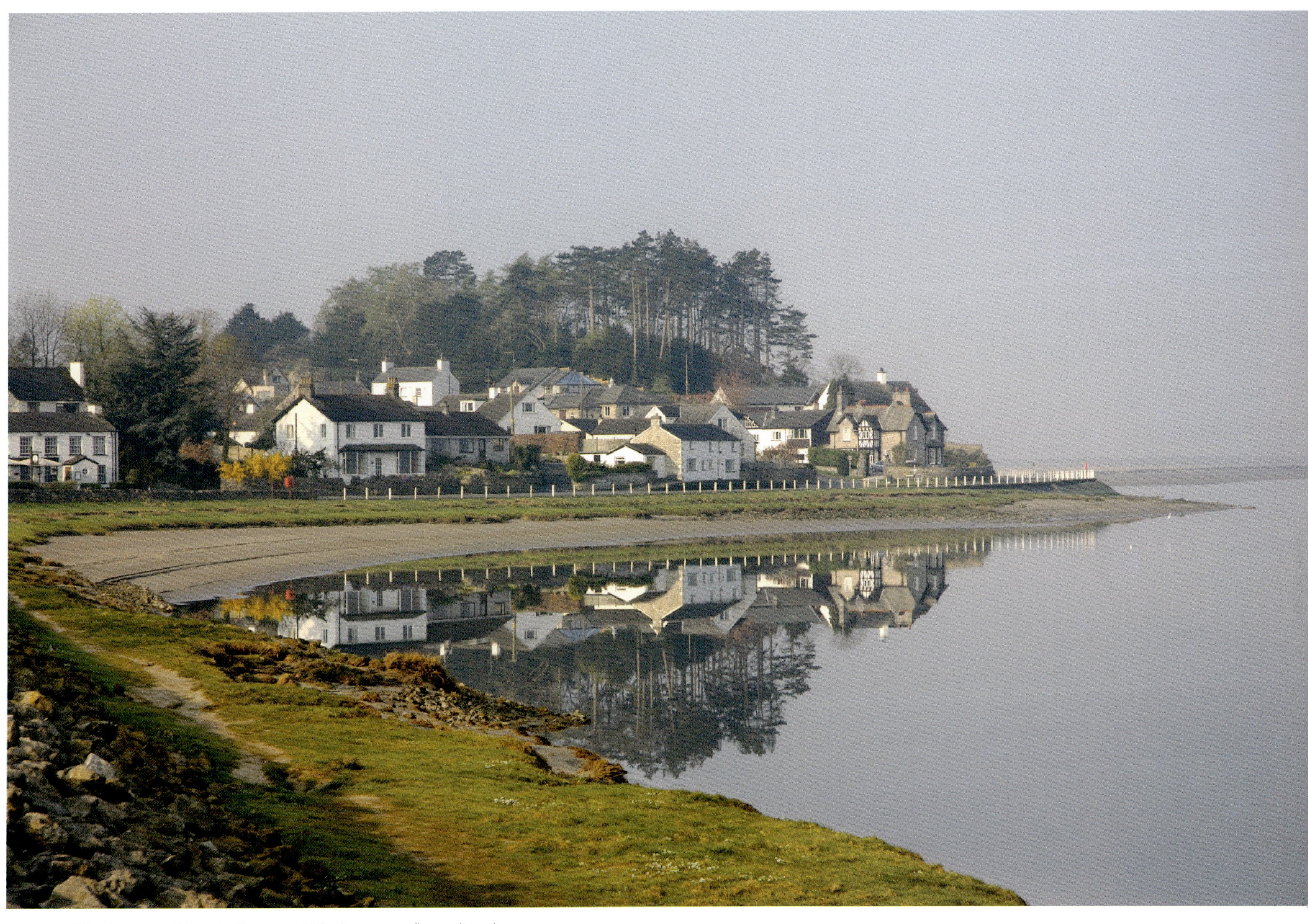

The houses of Sandside, near Milnthorpe, reflected in the
Kent at high tide.

# WILDLIFE

Morecambe Bay boasts an alphabet soup of ecological acronyms. It's a SSSI (a Site of Special Scientific Interest) and a RAMSAR (in recognition of its status as an important habitat for wading birds). It's an EMS (European Marine Site), an SAC (Special Area of Conservation) and a Special Protection Area for Birds. In plain English, the bay's a Mecca for naturalists. People whose palms get moist on finding some rare seaweed. People who know the difference between a dunlin and a drumlin. People who enjoy the evocative cries of redshank and oystercatcher, and who, like me, are happy to share a draughty hide with other binocular-toting enthusiasts, in the hope that something interesting will turn up.

The birdlife is prolific throughout the year, thanks to the bay's variety of habitats: sandflats, shingle beaches, saltmarsh, dunes, rocky 'skears', tidal pools, freshwater lagoons, limestone pavements and deciduous woodland. Migrants arrive each spring, on their way to their breeding grounds, to feed on the lugworms and shellfish which live beneath the sandflats. Many other species stay to nest – including eider ducks, here at the southern limit of their breeding range.

There are nature reserves at both ends of Walney Island. The South Walney Nature Reserve has one of the largest – and noisiest – colonies of black headed gulls in Europe. Birds guard their nests – little more than a scrape in the ground – and repel predators. The scene, multiplied a few thousand times, is mayhem.

Autumn witnesses more movements of migrating birds, refuelling before their long flights south. This is the time of year when most rarities are sighted. But the bay's real importance can best be appreciated in the fastness of winter, when huge numbers of wildfowl are funnelled into the bay from as far afield as Siberia, Greenland and the Arctic wastes of Canada. Waders flock in huge numbers, blackening the sky as the tide turns, forcing them to move from one sandbar to another. Thousands of knot and dunlin twist and turn through the air in perfect synchronicity, as though possessed of a single mind. Their evocative cries fill the estuaries.

I always find room in my camera bag for a pair of binoculars, so wandering around the creeks, sandbars and shingle beaches of Morecambe Bay gives me the opportunity to see if I can still tell the difference between a turnstone and an oystercatcher. My best birding moment – and certainly the most surreal – was when I rounded the tip of Sunderland Point to find a little egret wading through the shallows. This is a bird I usually associate with the heat and dust of Andalucia, rather than a grey day on the Lancashire coast.

While bird-watchers have their favourite haunts – such as Walney Island, Humphrey Head and Jenny Brown's Point – the jewel in the crown is the RSPB reserve of Leighton Moss. With luck you may be able to spot rarities such as bitterns, avocets and bearded tits from the walkways and observation hides.

If you can tear yourself away from Morecambe's traditional attractions, you can spot plenty of birds simply by standing on the stone jetty and gazing out to sea (the statue of Eric Morecambe on the promenade even has a pair of binoculars slung around his neck. Yes, the one with the glasses – not the one with the short, fat, hairy legs – was a keen bird-watcher, and one of the hides at Leighton Moss is named after him).

This huge lime tree at Holker Hall, more than 400 years old, has been recognised by the Tree Council as one of our fifty Great British Trees.

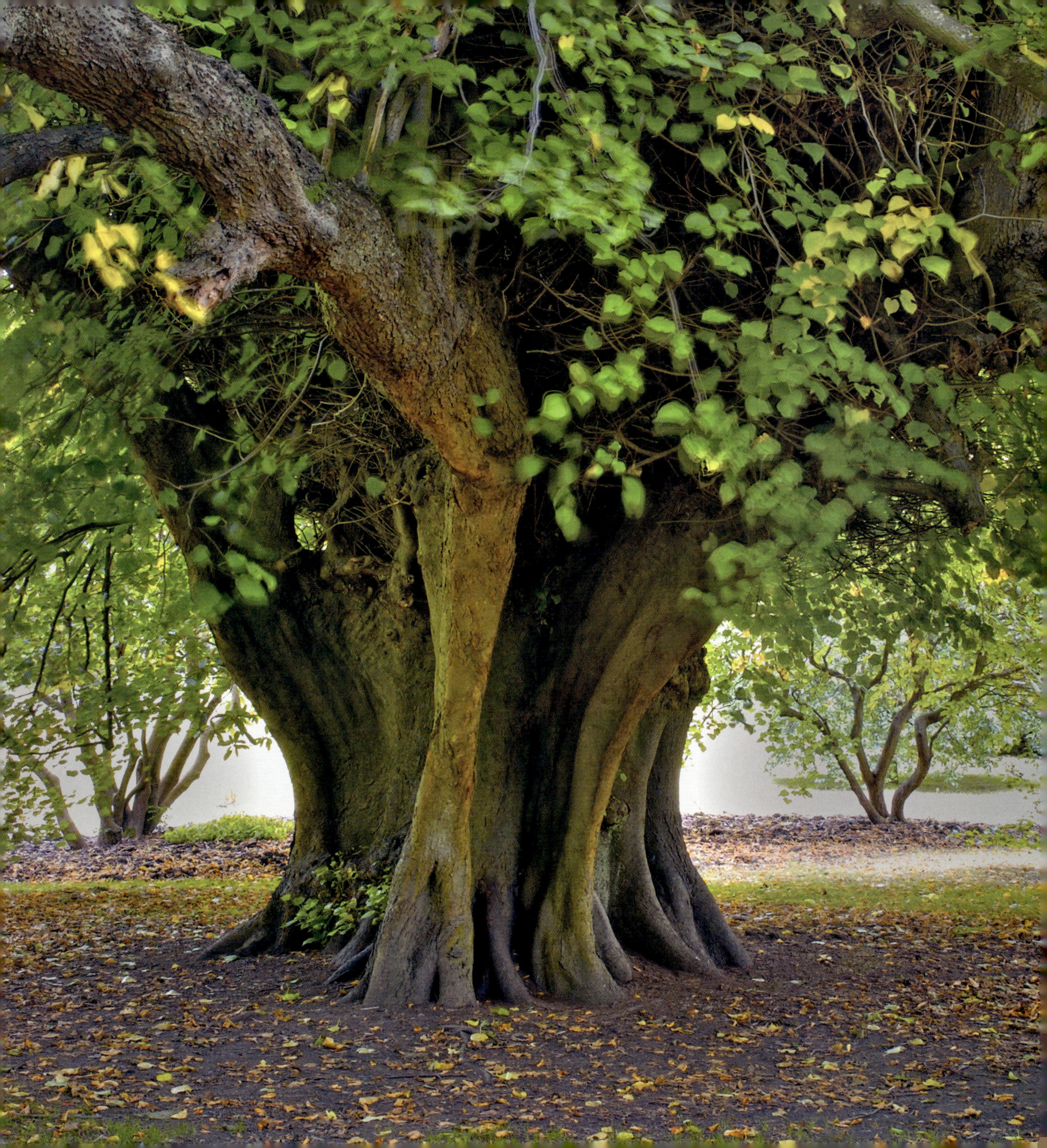

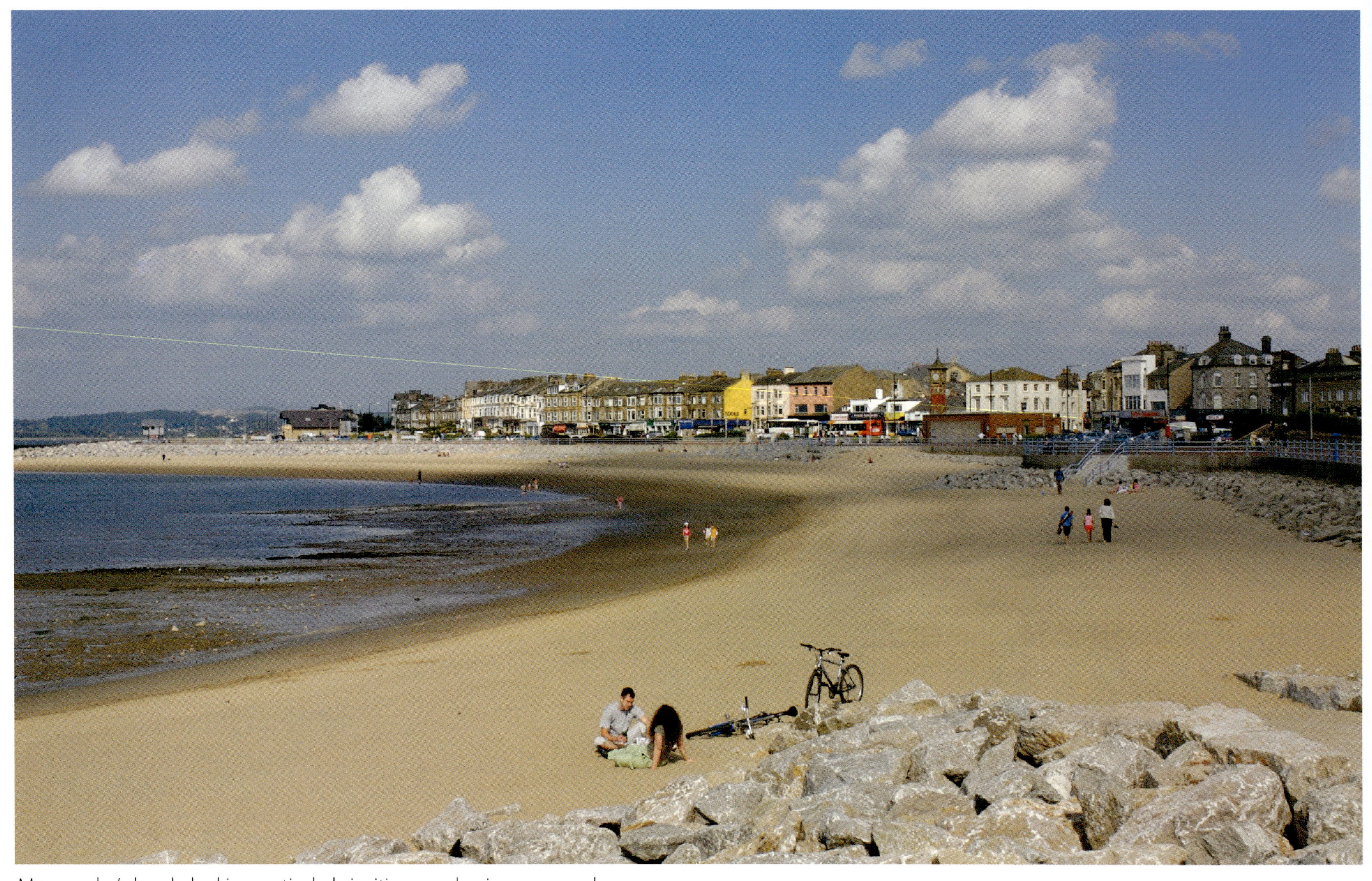

Morecambe's beach, looking particularly inviting on a benign summer day.

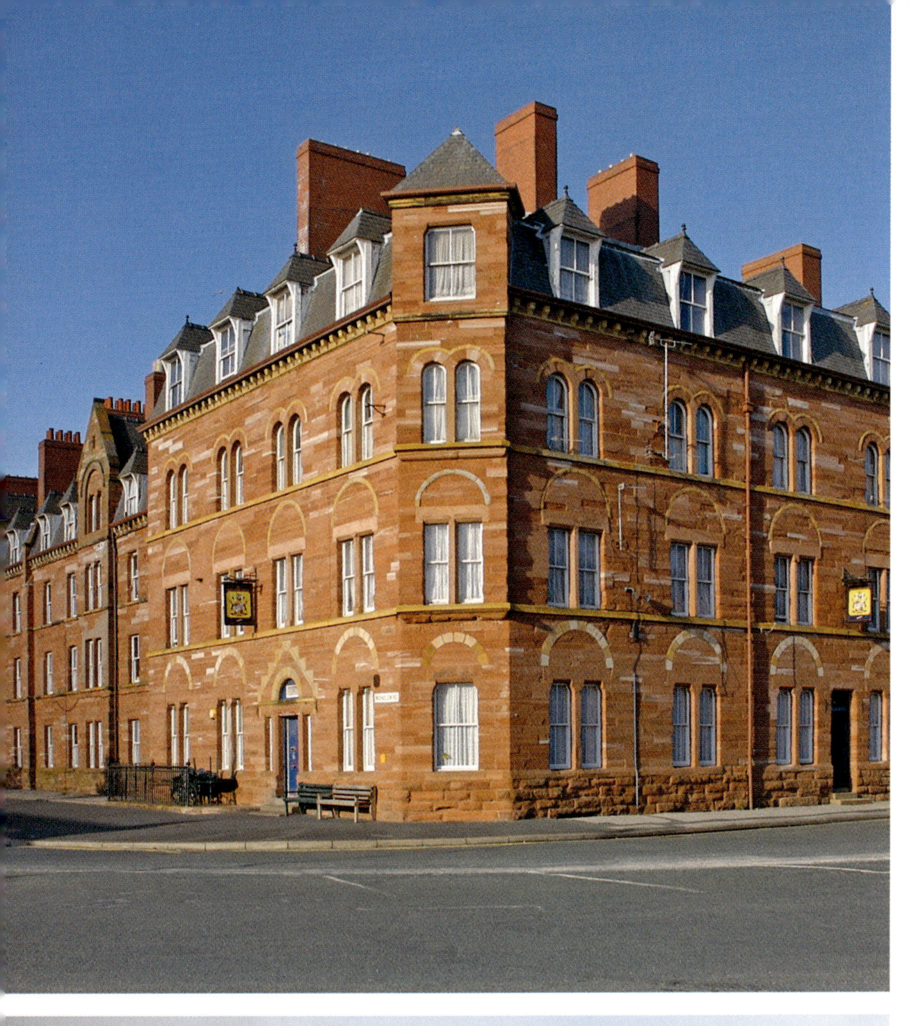

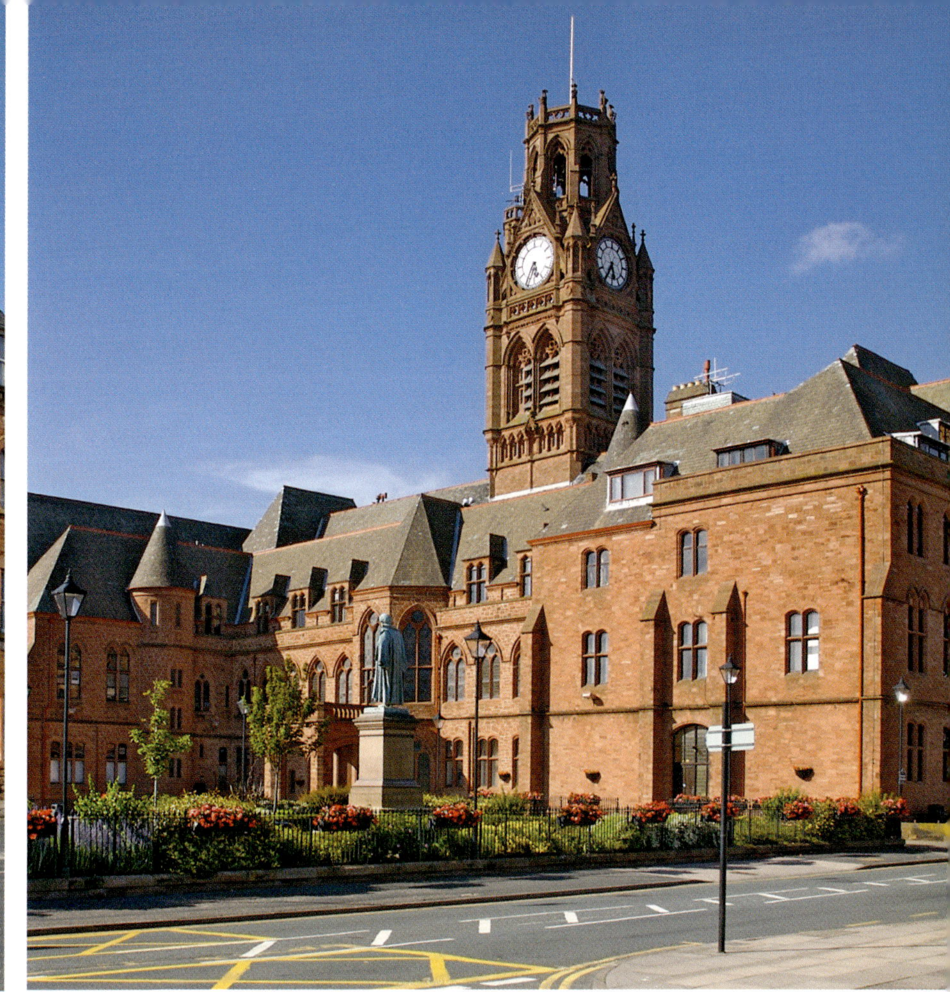

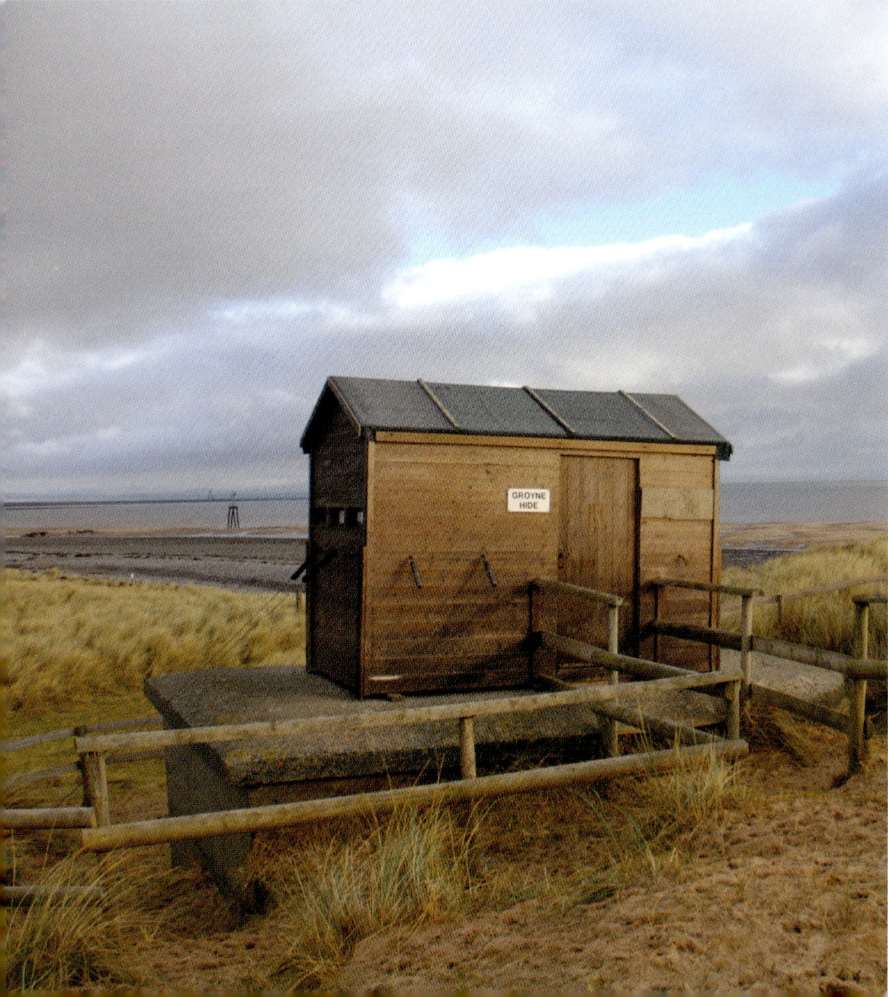
GROYNE
HIDE

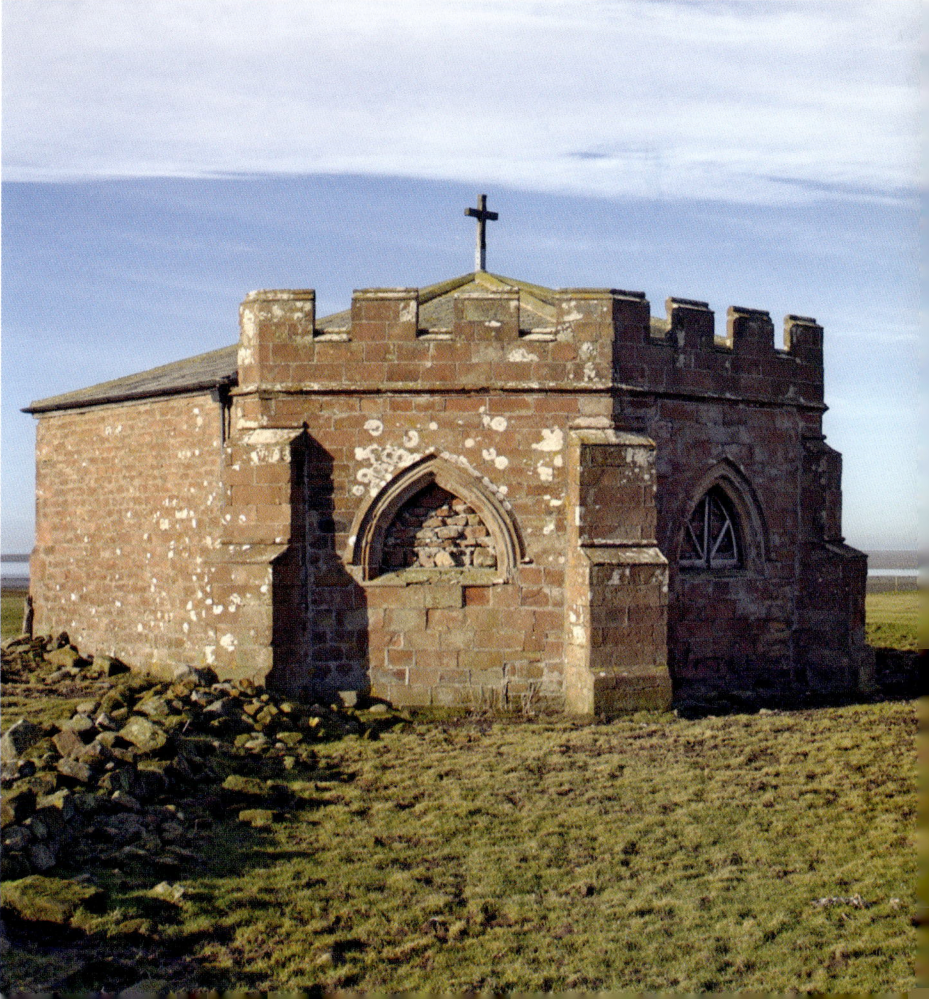

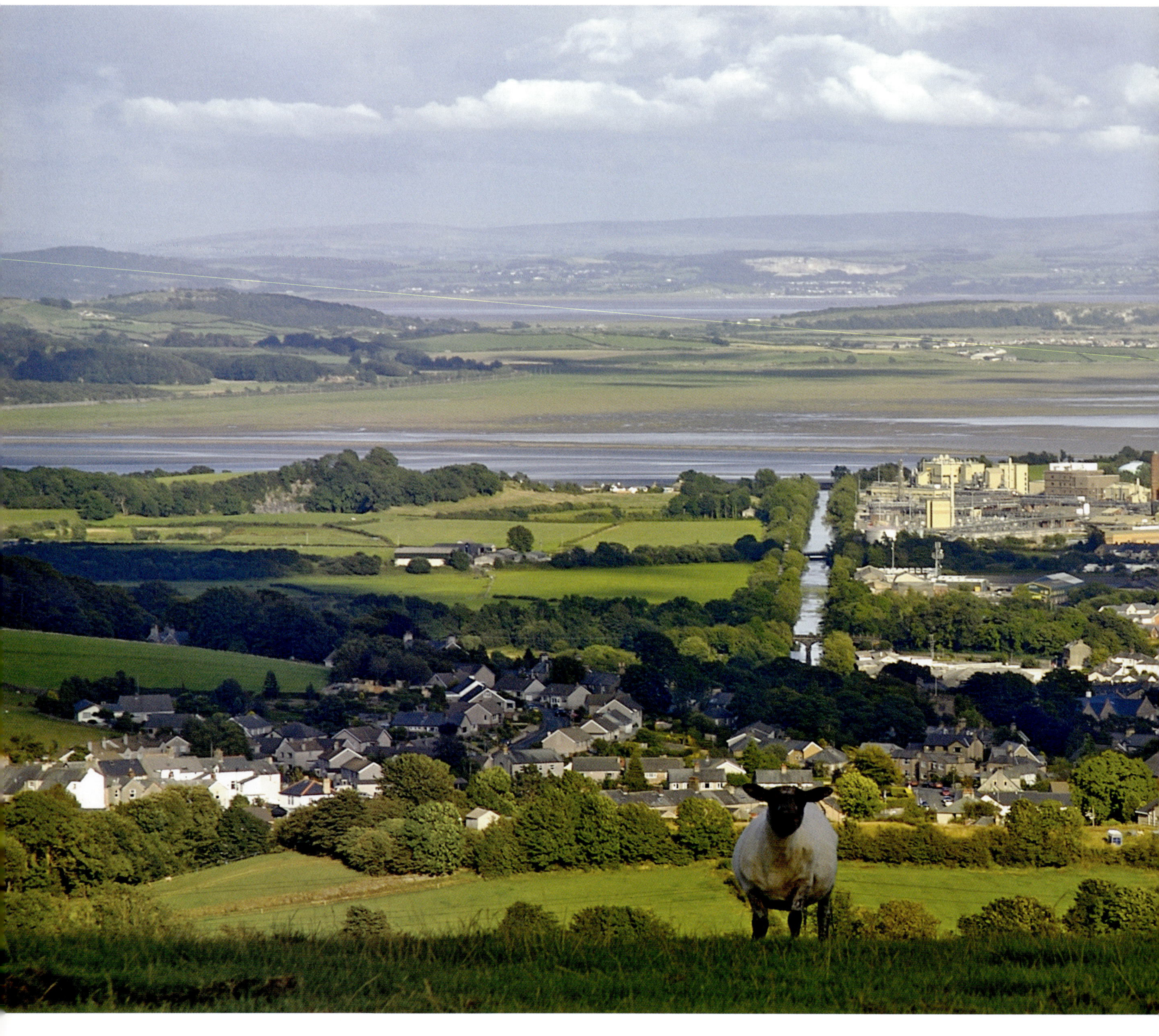

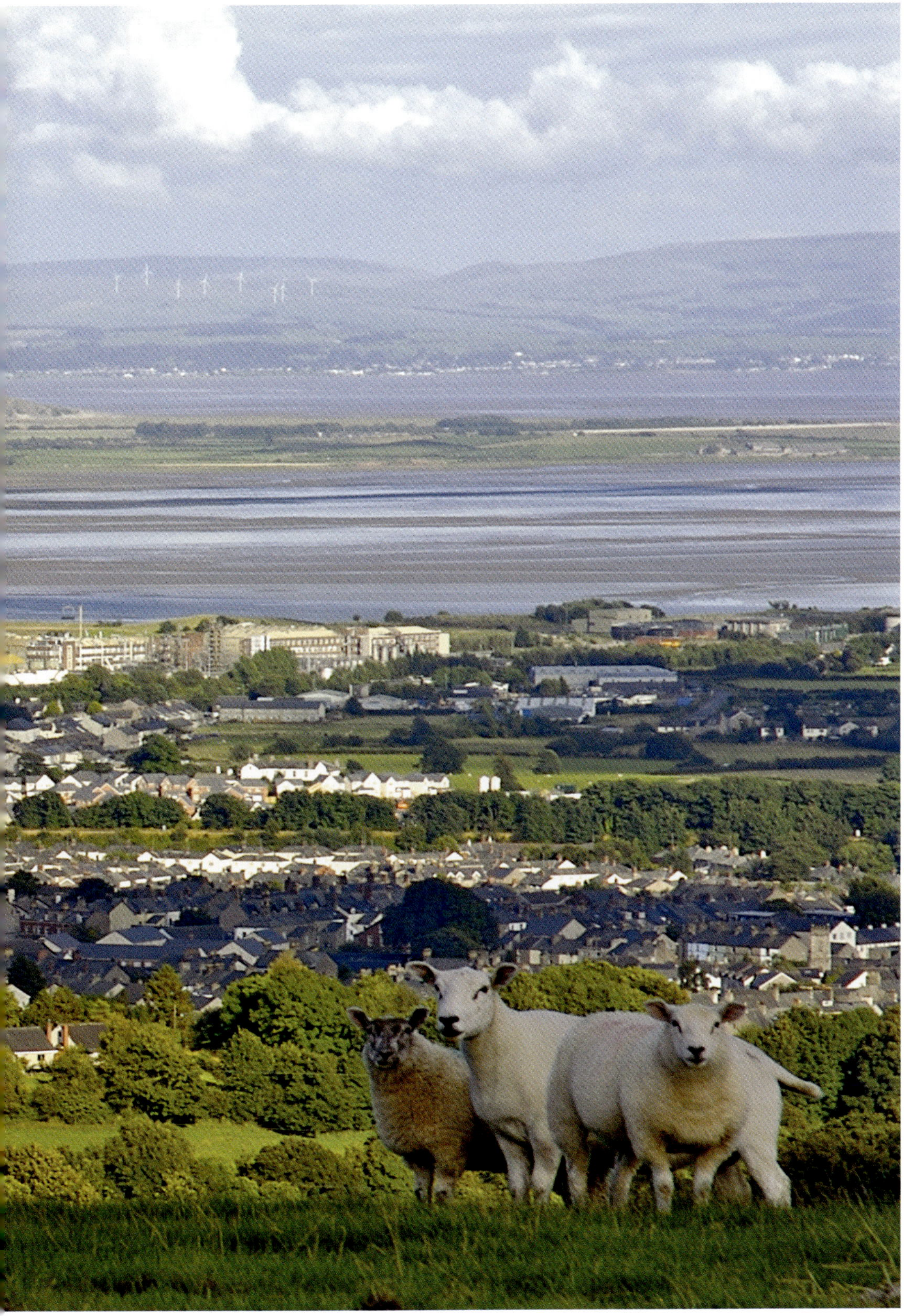

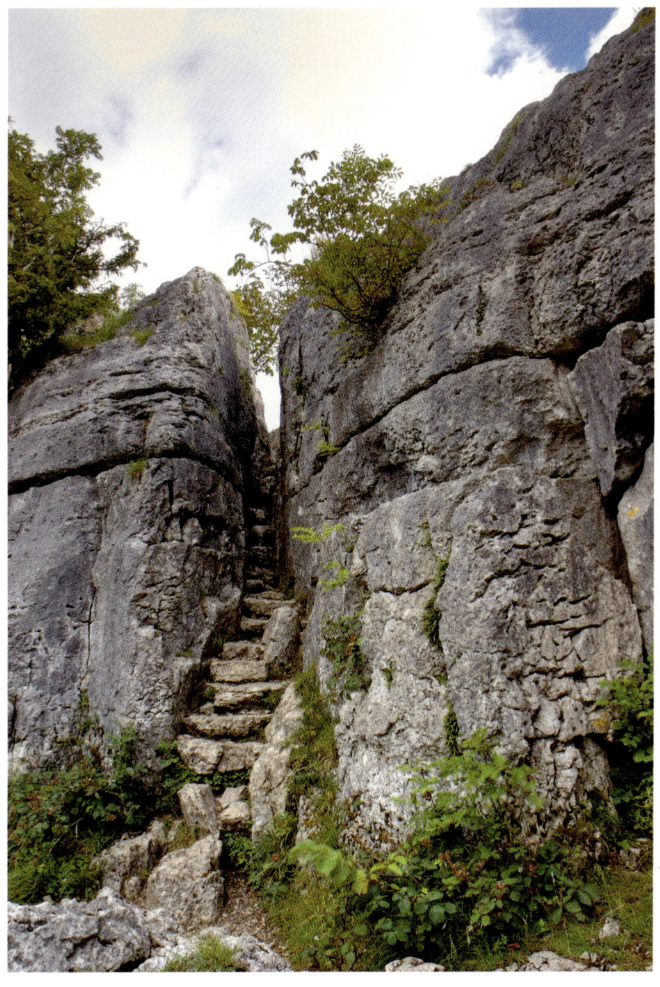



ABOVE
The 'fairy steps' near Beetham: if you can climb them
without touching the sides, the fairies will grant your wish.
I couldn't, and they didn't . . .

LEFT
Ulverston, with its short and straight canal heading out into
the Leven estuary.

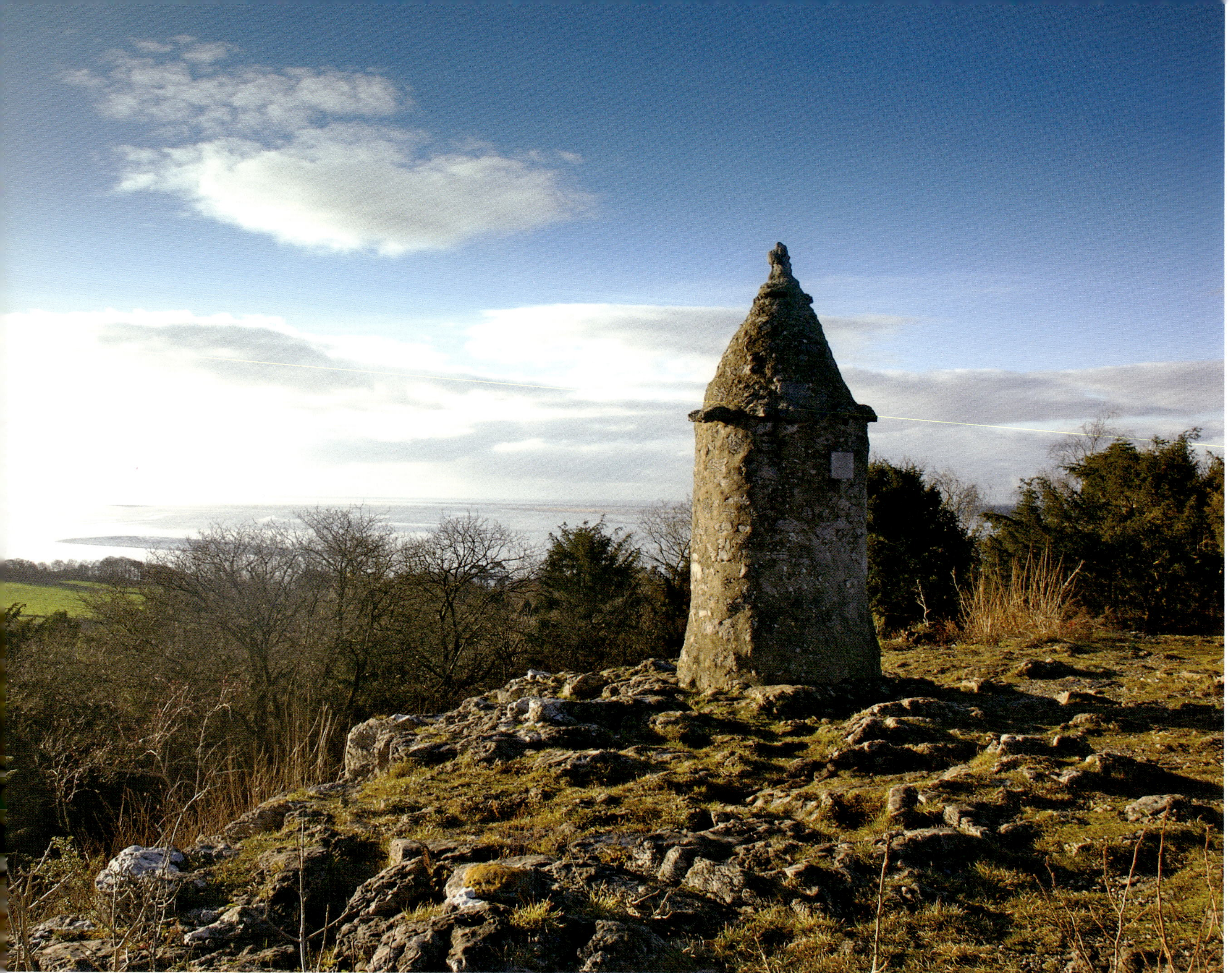

The view from the top of Eaves Wood, near Silverdale, and the 'Pepperpot', built in 1887 to mark Queen Victoria's Golden Jubilee.

RIGHT
One of the many seagulls to be found around Morecambe Bay.

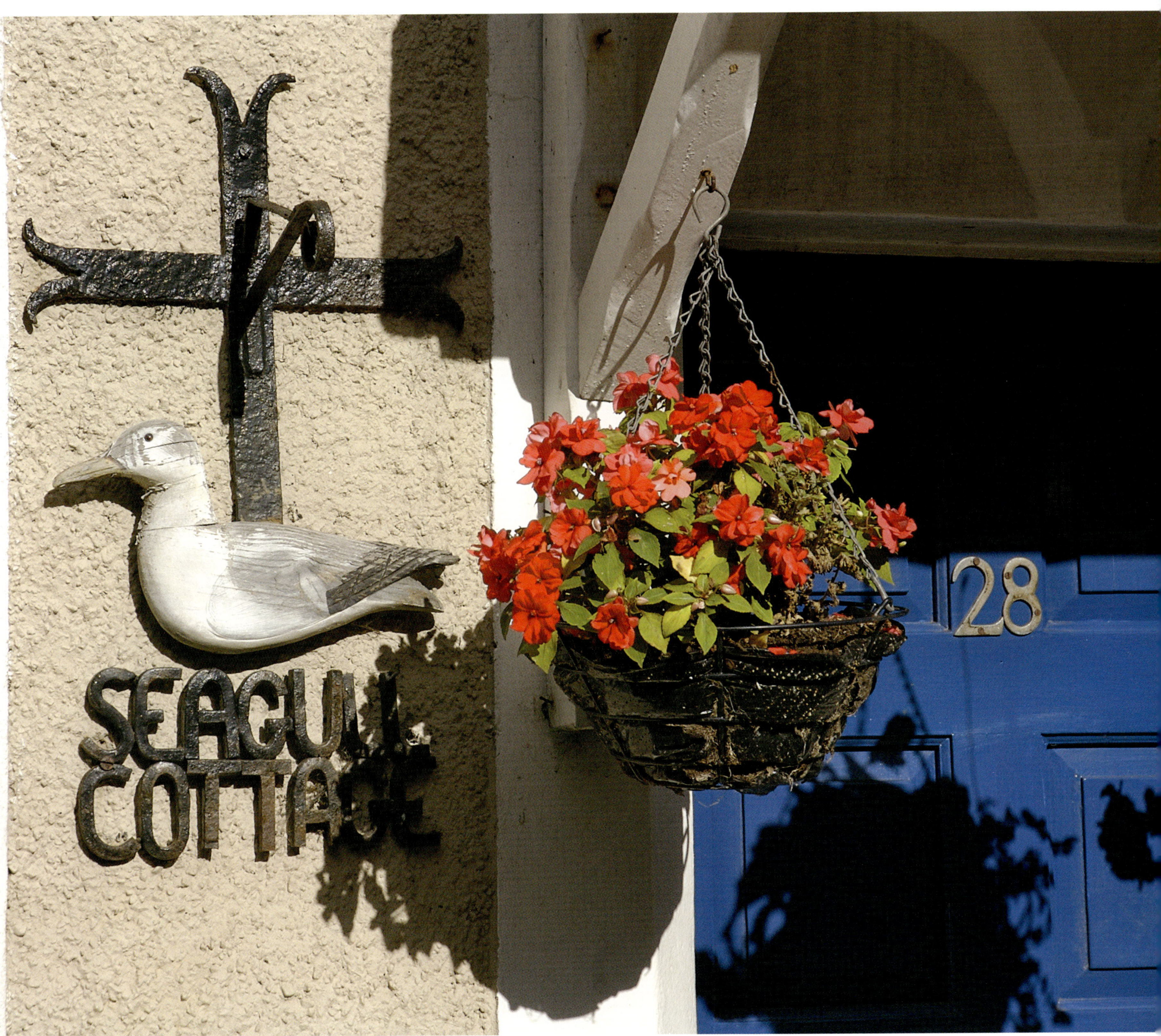
SEAGULL
COTTAGE
28

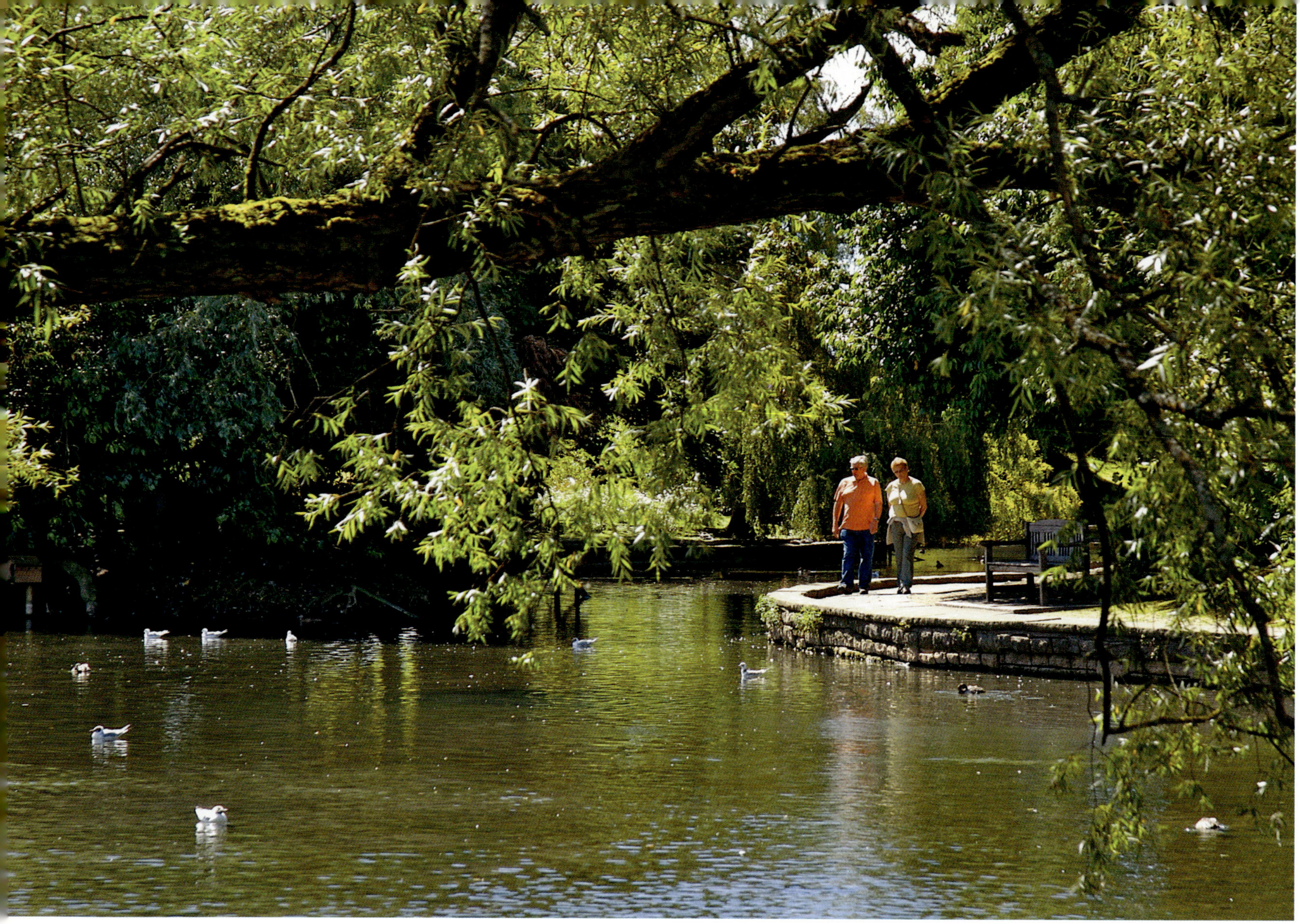

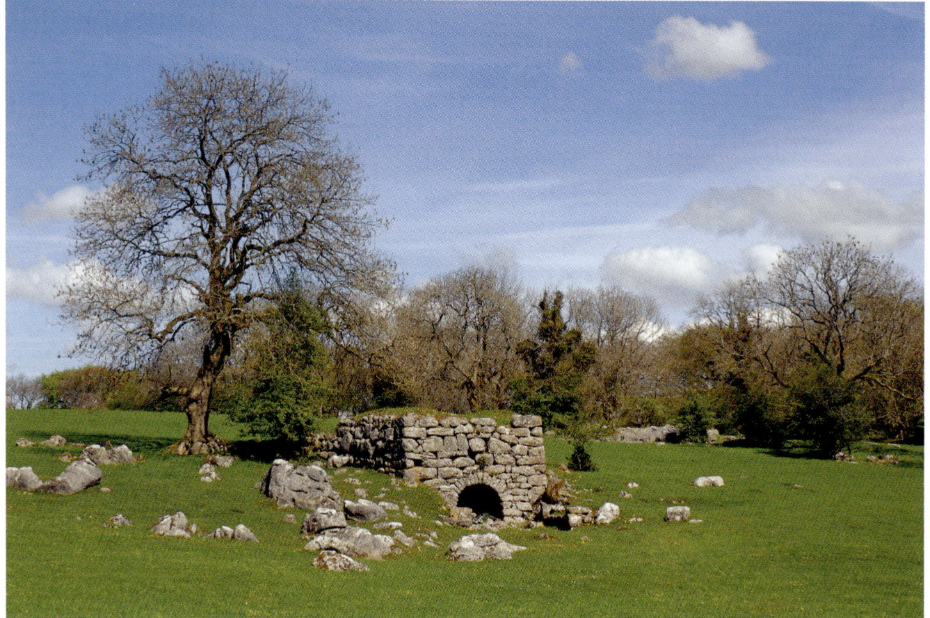

ABOVE
A quiet corner of Grange-over-Sands, where seagulls fraternise
with many species of exotic wildfowl.

LEFT
Limestone was burned in this kiln, near Yealand Conyers, to
produce quicklime for 'sweetening' acidic soils.

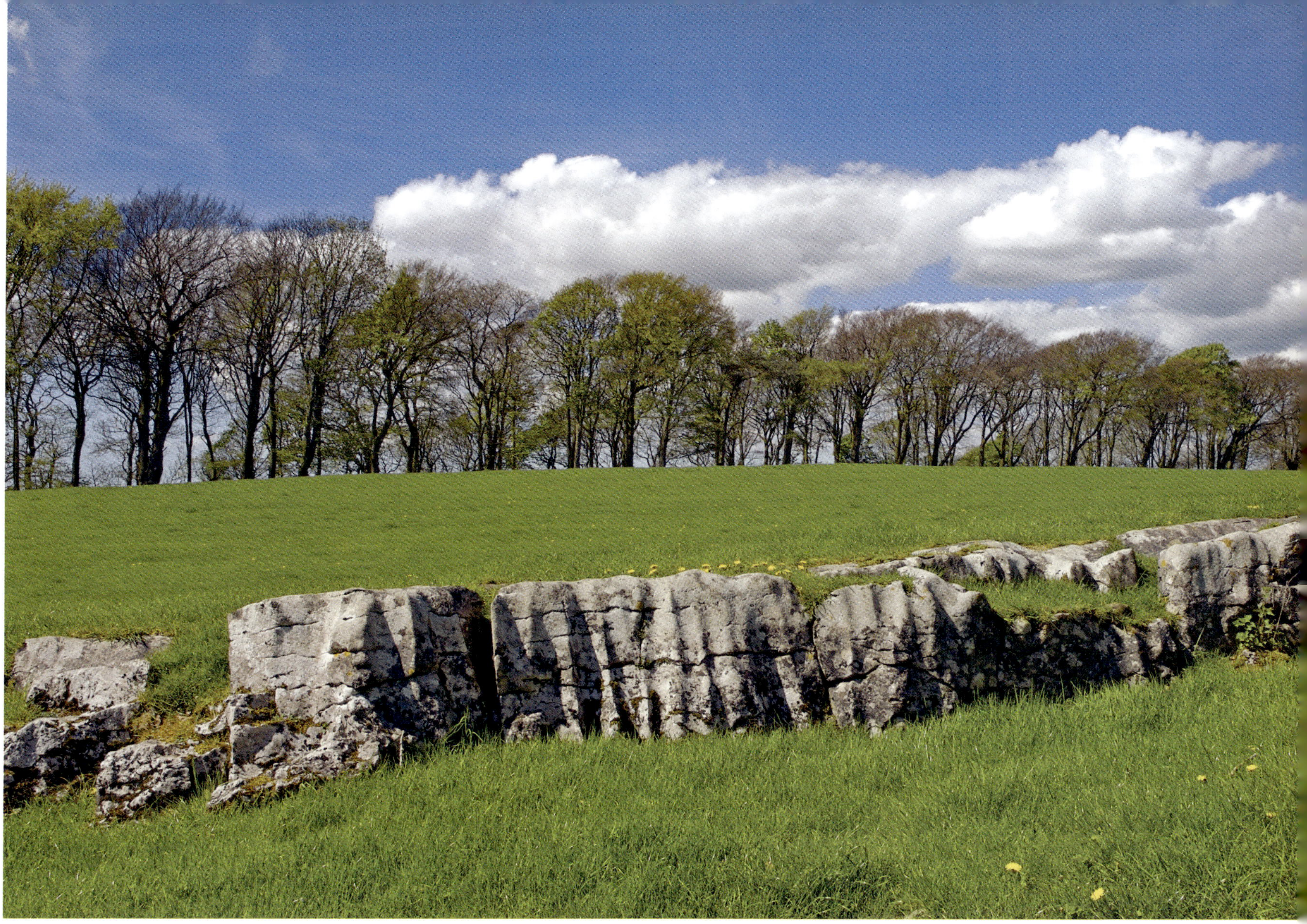

ABOVE
Knuckles of rock in the limestone country around Arnside
and Silverdale.

RIGHT
Approaching the aquaduct which carries the Lancaster
Canal over the River Lune.

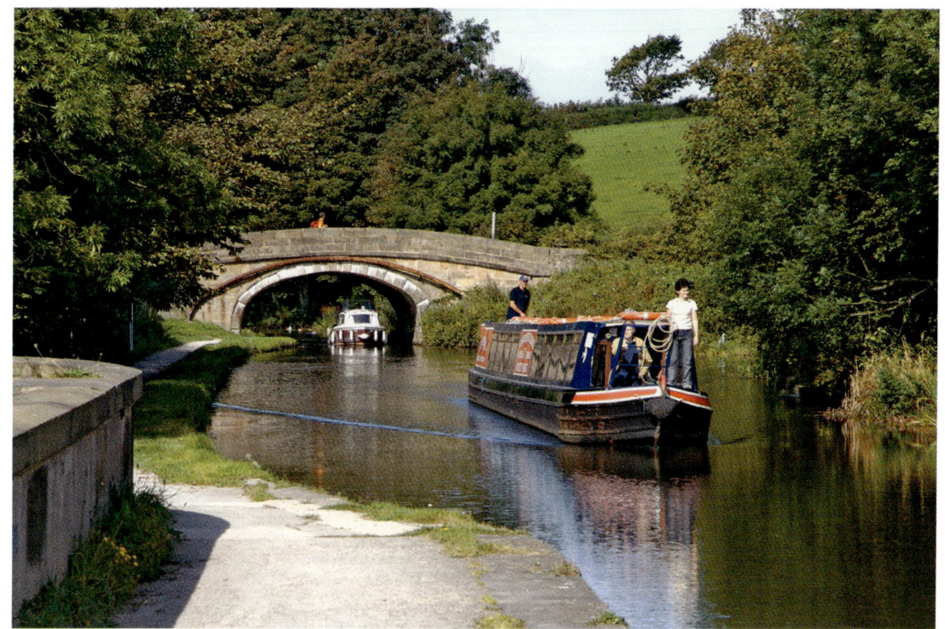

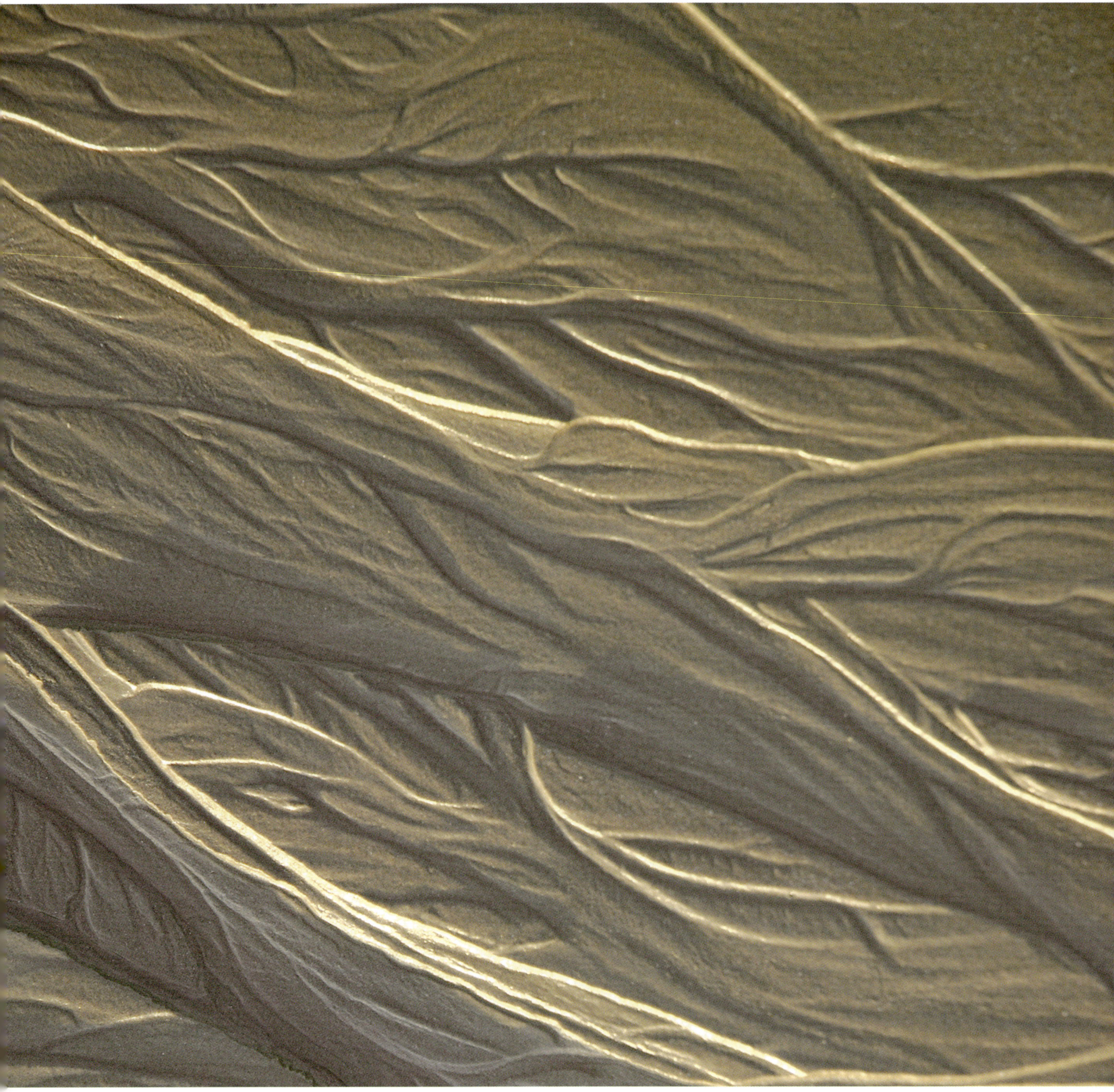

# CROSSING THE SANDS

With the water being shallow, even at high tide, there are few places in Morecambe Bay where breakers crash against the shore. The sands are dangerous precisely because the dangers aren't immediately apparent; an early writer called them 'deceitful'. People have crossed 'The Sands' for centuries, so we shouldn't be surprised that many of them were lulled into a false sense of security. They didn't come this way from choice (they would have gone by road if a good route had been available), but because it was a short-cut. The overland alternatives, across boggy ground, added many miles to their journey.

In AD79, according to Ptolemy, Agricola's army was guided across the sands by local fishermen. Robert the Bruce came this way during the Great Raid of 1322, when he plundered his way through Cumbria, and decimated most of Furness (though the abbot of Furness Abbey paid a huge ransom to stop his abbey being destroyed). Having crossed the sands, the Scots meted out much the same punishment to the people of Lancaster.

The monks of Furness Abbey, Cartmel Priory and Conishead Priory crossed the sands to visit their farms and other properties (a 'grange', as in 'Grange-over-Sands,' was a monastic farm or granary). To ensure safe passage the monks employed local guides (and a coroner to investigate drownings, which suggested that safe passage was not always ensured). The first written account of sand-guides was in 1501; after the dissolution of the monasteries, a generation later, the guides were retained by the Duchy of Lancaster.

Remarkably, the role has continued in an unbroken lineage of almost 500 years – from monastic times to the present day. Cedric Robinson is the present incumbent. Since 1963 he has held the official title of Queen's Guide to the Sands (and Guide's Farm, at Kents Bank, the property that goes with it). He is retained in the

The mud of Morecambe Bay: sometimes dangerous, sometimes just photogenic.

ancient post at the princely sum of £15 a year, and takes thousands of people on the crossing every year.

Furness, comprising the northern shore of Morecambe Bay, has always been rather remote ('Furness' means 'far ness'). The Lakeland hills formed a natural barrier to the north, while the sea created an obstacle to the south. A milestone in Cartmel reveals the distance to Lancaster: a mere 15 miles 'over sands'. The long way round, via the bridge over the River Kent at Kendal, was 36 miles. That would have represented a significant difference for a man, or a horse, or a horse-drawn carriage. For livestock too, since Scottish drovers would drive their cattle across the sands to sell them in English markets. From Cartmel to Ulverston, across the Leven estuary, was 7 miles; by land it was 11 miles. No wonder most travellers opted to tackle the sands. Those continuing up the Cumbrian coast would cross the Duddon Sands, circumnavigate the mass of Black Combe, and, at Ravenglass, wade through the shallower waters of the rivers Esk, Mite and Irt.

John Wesley crossed the sands from south to north, in search of Cumbrian souls to save. Heading for the port of Whitehaven, he waded through the estuaries of the Kent, Leven, Duddon and Esk. He found the route arduous. 'I can advise no stranger to go this way,' he confided to his journal. 'He may go round by Kendal and Keswick, often in less time, always with less expense and far less trial of his patience.' George Fox, founder of the Quakers, went in the opposite direction. He was marched under armed guard from his home at Swarthmoor Hall, near Ulverston, to face a charge of treason at Lancaster Assizes.

Right up until the mid-nineteenth century, the 'main road' from Lancaster to the Furness peninsulas continued to be across the sands of Morecambe Bay. It was marked as such on the map included in Thomas West's influential *Guide to the Lakes* (published in 1723): a long, curving route from Hest Bank, on the Lancashire coast, to Kent's Bank, near Grange-over-Sands. From here the road passed through Allithwaite and Flookburgh, before crossing

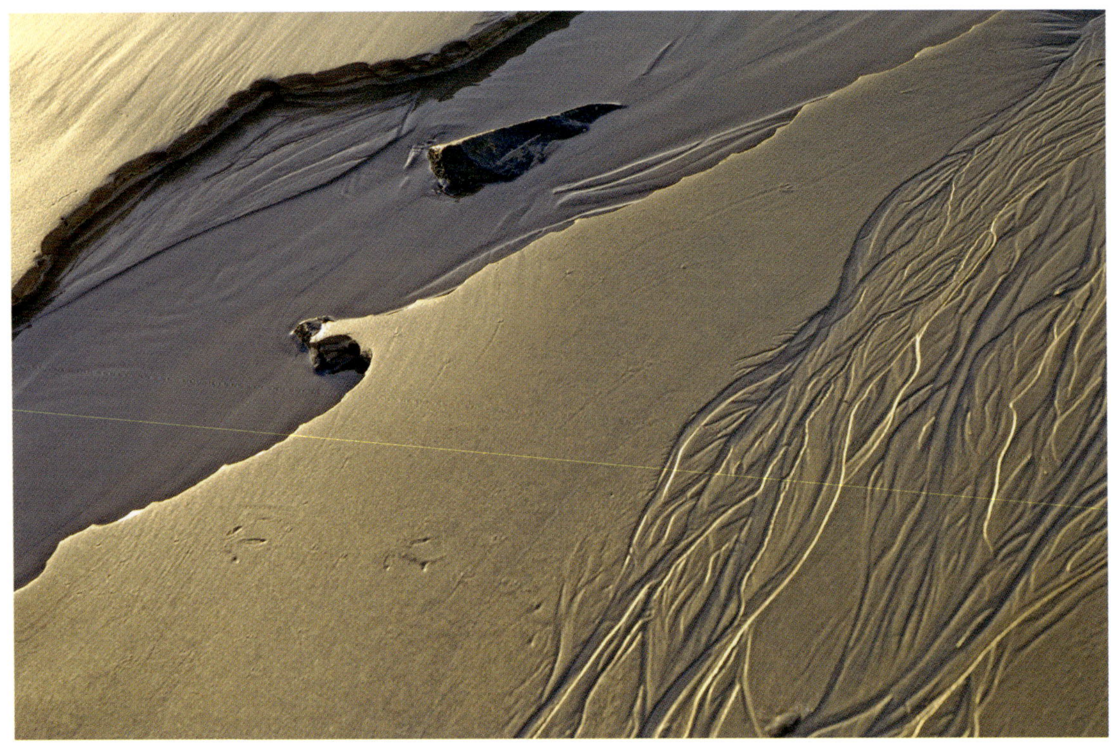

The mud of Morecambe Bay.

another expanse of sand, the Kent estuary. West was enthusiastic about crossing the bay. 'On a fine day,' he wrote, 'there is not a more pleasant sea-side journey in the Kingdom.'

If the map appeared to present a definitive route across the sands, the reality was rather different. The best route would differ from one day to the next. It was the guide's responsibility to find it – with a combination of local knowledge and by using poles to test the state of the sand – and then mark the most viable route with small branches (known as 'brobs'), pressed far enough into the sand to withstand a couple of tides.

John Lucas, a local historian and contemporary of West, was more concerned with the dangers. 'Where one day is a fair ford, is perhaps the next day deep and impassable; and where it may to all appearance be safely rid, there frequently happen deep places which are always dangerous and sometimes fatal to passengers. Often as the tide flows in the banks are so seered that they collapse in chunks hundreds of yards long, and the roar of the demolition may be heard a mile away.' In one collapsing sandbank, the body of a man was discovered, dressed in clothes that belonged to the previous century. Lucas noted that the man 'had his horse-whip still securely gripped in his lifeless hand'.

William Wordsworth called the bay 'a plain from where the sea has retired', and watched 'coaches, wains and travellers, horse and foot' taking to the sands. *Crossing Lancaster Sands* by coach was famously recorded by J.M.W. Turner (1775–1851), in a painting now hanging in the Birmingham Museum and Art Gallery, but still used as a local postcard. Experienced guides were on hand to negotiate, for a fee, the safest route across the sands (though Thomas Hodgson, a sixteenth-century guide, was said to have looked on impassively while a group of travellers drowned).

Those who could afford to travel in comfort would make the trip in horse-drawn carriages. In 1757, a regular service was started between Lancaster and Ulverston, using coaches drawn by six horses. The coach operators assured the public that they had 'produced sober and careful drivers who are well acquainted with the sands'. If coach travel was more comfortable, it was not always safer. Local newspapers reported each new tragedy with journalistic relish, and the graveyards are full of people who died by drowning. Of course, the many thousands of safe crossings each year didn't make headlines, and we can assume, from the amount of traffic, that most crossings took place without major incident or accident.

It wasn't until 1820 that a viable turnpike road was constructed around the Kent estuary. This route – linking Milnthorpe and Heversham via Levens Bridge – knocked a few miles off the road journey around the bay. Nevertheless it was

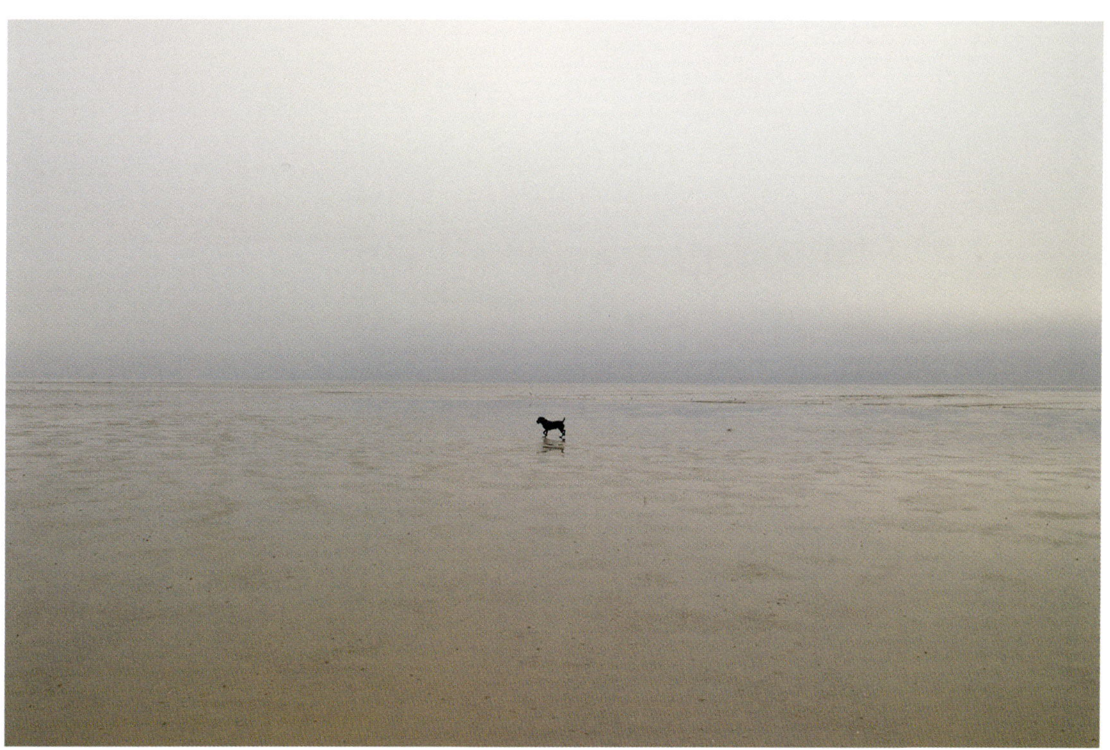

A dull day.

still further to travel than across the sands and, in any case, tolls had to be paid. The sands route remained in regular use for a few more years. The event that had the greatest effect on cross-bay traffic was the Furness Railway, built like a tourniquet of steel around Morecambe Bay.

As early as 1837, George Stephenson had surveyed the route for a proposed railway line from Preston to Carlisle. His preferred route, across the broad Kent estuary, was abandoned, however, for a more direct (but expensive) line across Shap Fell. It was Barrow's rapid and unprecendented rise as an industrial powerhouse, a few years later, that forced the railway engineers to look again at Morecambe Bay.

The Furness line was originally built for transporting iron ore, slate and other goods (human cargo being carried only on Sundays). A causeway was constructed from the village of Rampside, near Barrow, along which rails were laid to Roa Island. This branch provided a link to the pier at Roa Island, where ships could moor both at high and low tide. The first locomotives arrived by tugboat.

William Wordsworth complained vociferously that trains ran so close to Furness Abbey (it could have been worse: the original plans showed the line running straight through the ruins). Though the line reached Ulverston in 1854, progress further east was slow. The notoriously unstable sands of the Leven and Kent estuaries were major obstacles for the railway engineers when they attempted to span them with viaducts.

It took them four years to anchor the fifty piles across the Kent, by sinking them through the sand and down to bedrock. Since the viaduct was a fixed structure, ships could no longer navigate the upper reaches of the river. In any case, the building of the viaduct caused the estuary to silt up. The first train crossed the bay in 1857 (the line's formal opening having been delayed – twice – by ships colliding with the piers of the Leven viaduct). The Furness line was continued, to link up with the West Coast line at Carnforth, immediately transforming this unassuming little town into an important railway junction. The station later became the setting for the famous 1945 film *Brief Encounter*.

The Furness line escaped the attentions of Dr Beeching's infamous axe during the 1960s, when so many branch lines were unceremoniously closed. It remains one of the most scenic railway lines in the country, as well as being a vital resource for local people. Those who cross the sands on foot today are doing so for recreation (and often to raise money for their favourite charity), rather than from necessity, and they do it under the the watchful eye of Cedric Robinson.

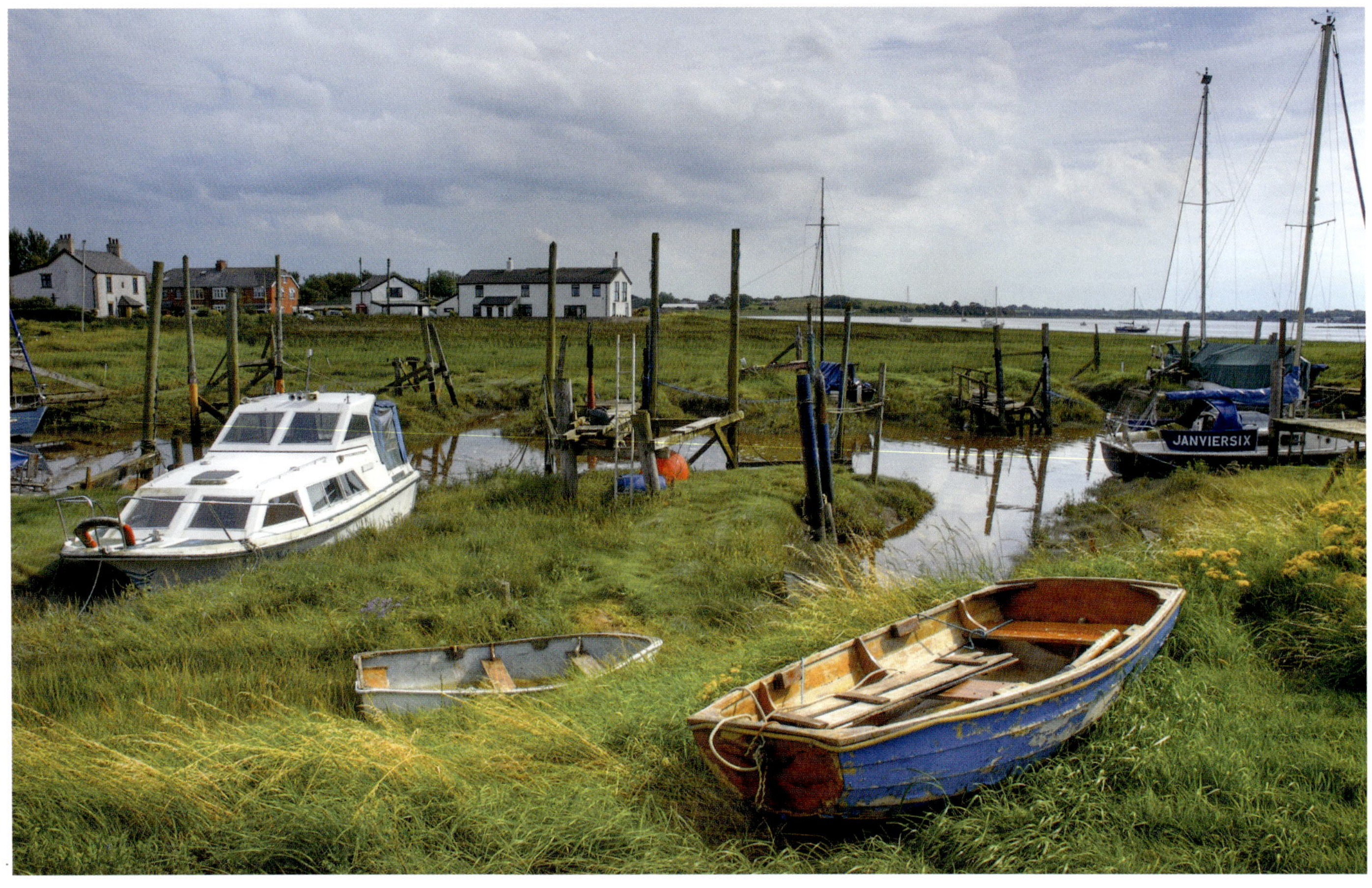



ABOVE
Boats and walkways at
Wardley's Pool, a muddy creek
on the eastern bank of the
River Wyre.

RIGHT
Work in progress at Skippool
Creek, on the opposite side of
the Wyre.

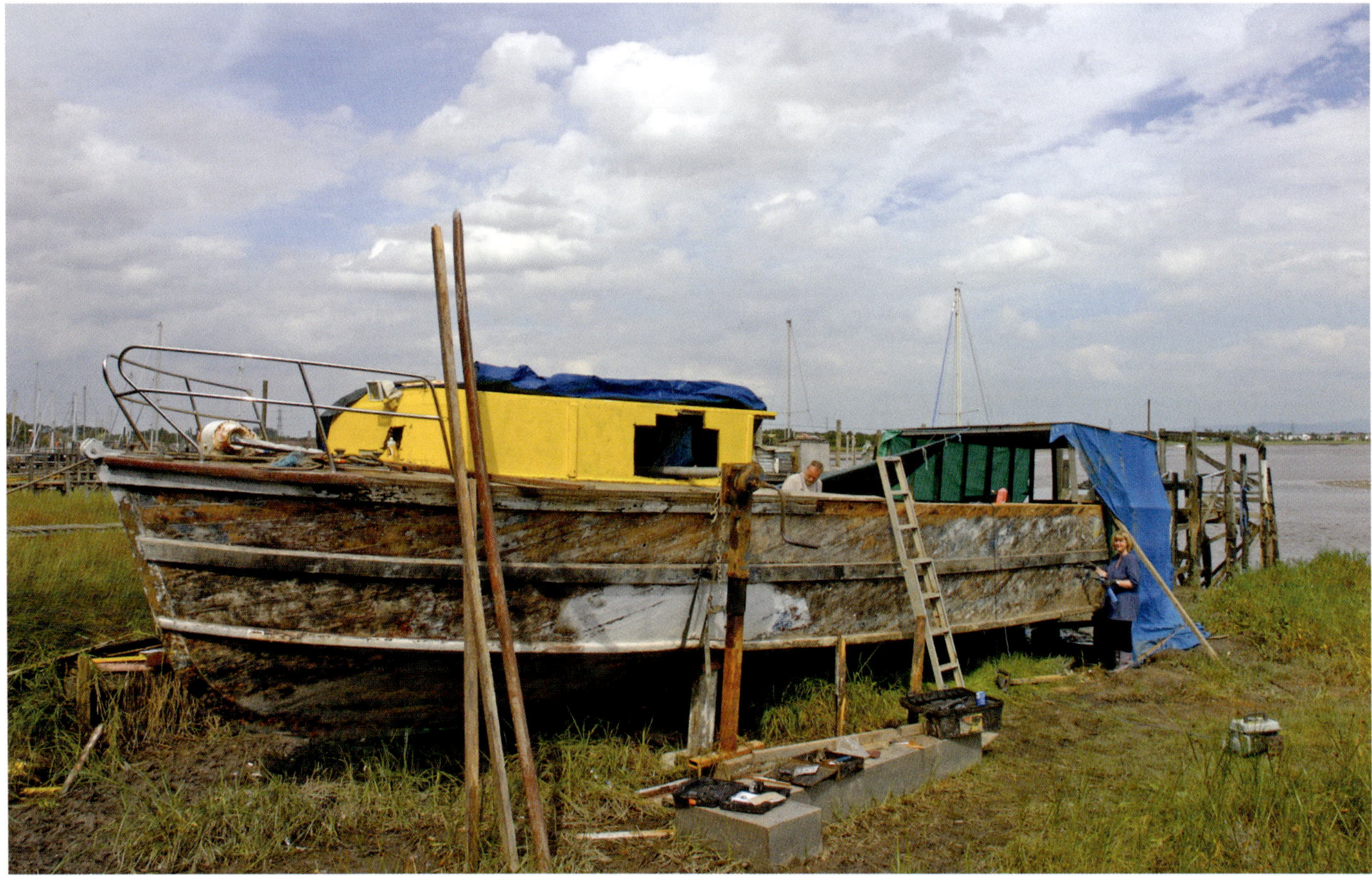

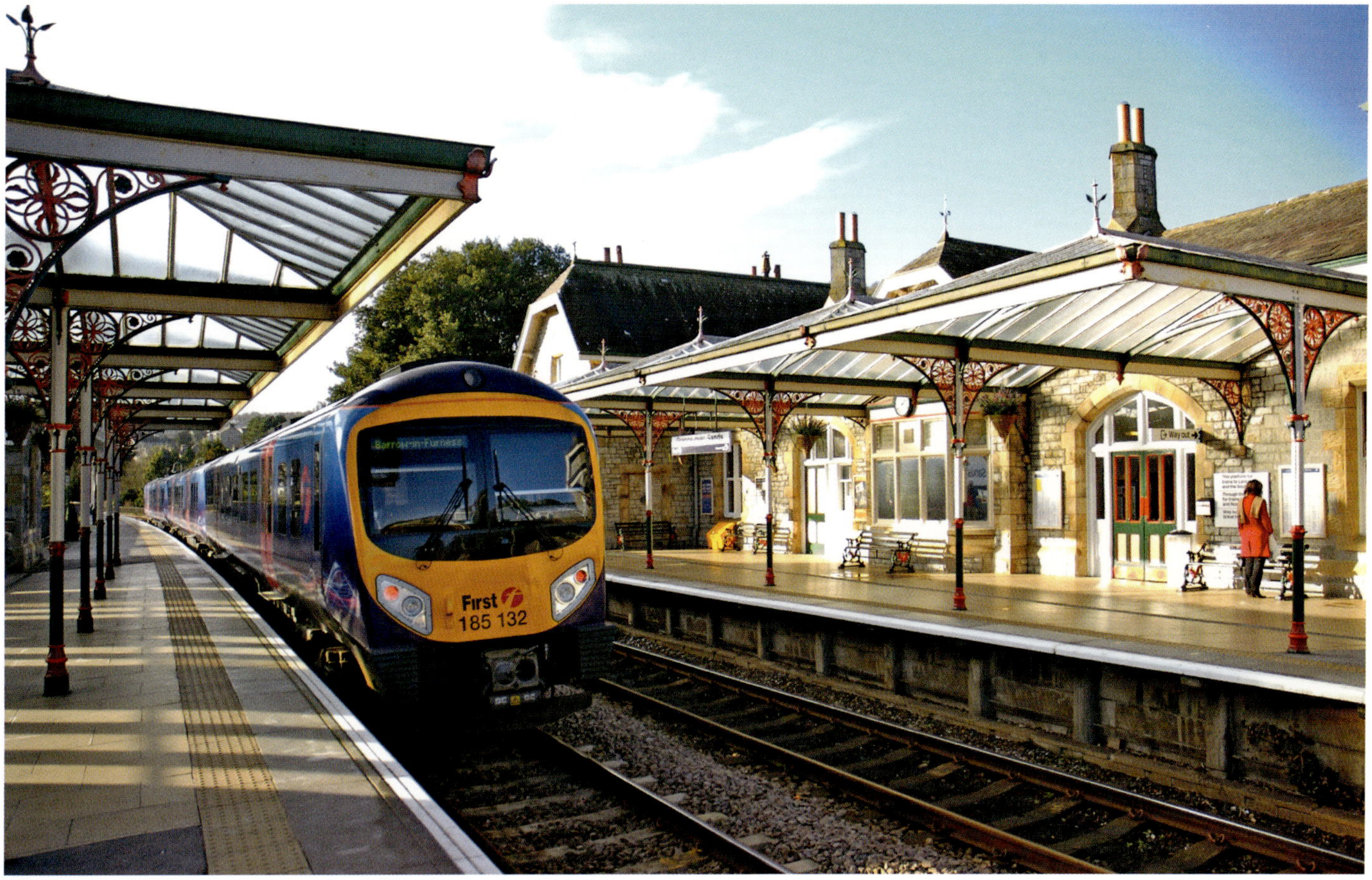

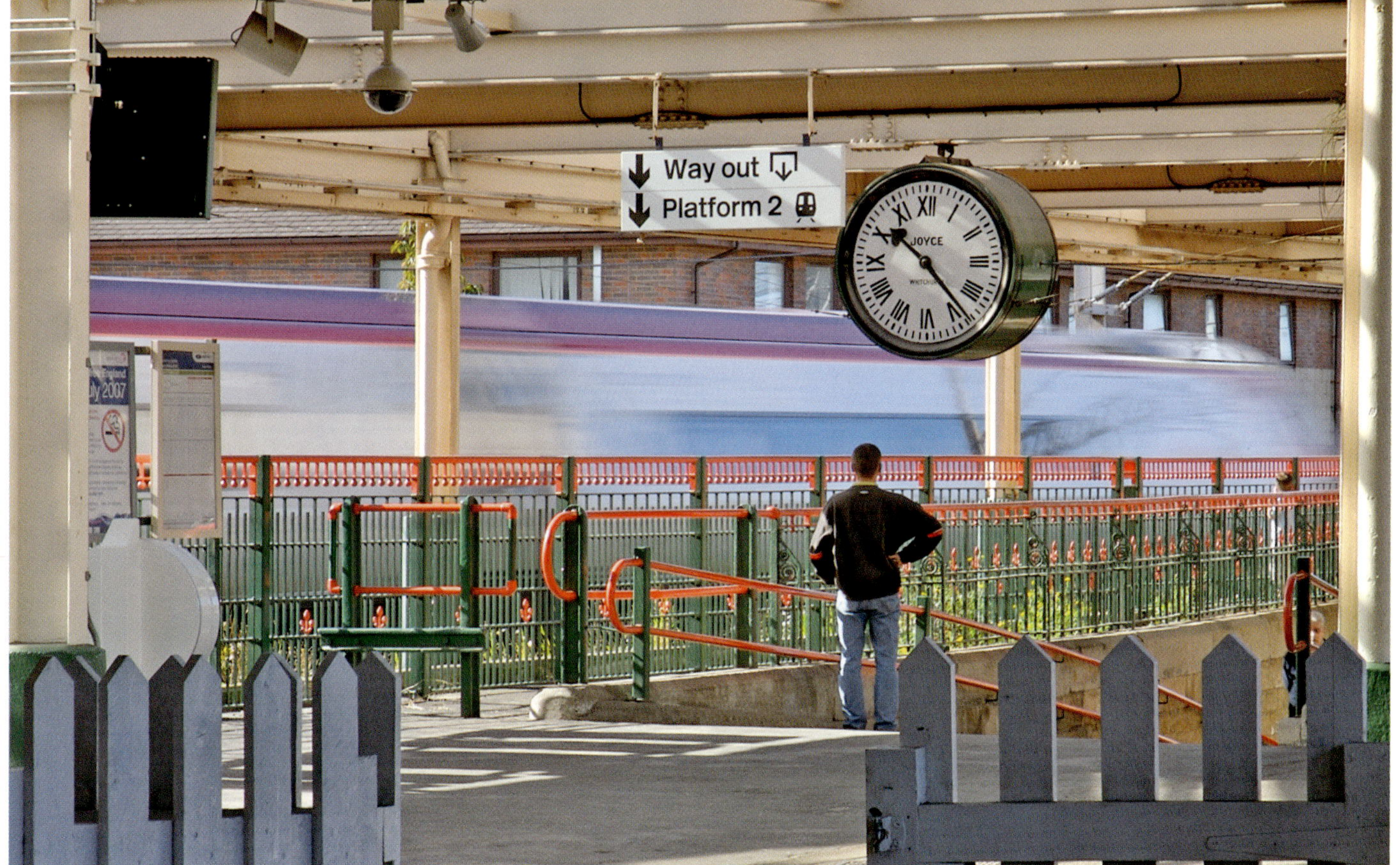


ABOVE
The railway station at Grange-over-Sands, restored to the way it looked when it was built in 1864.

LEFT
A train is just a blur as it races through Carnforth station, past the clock which famously appeared in the film *Brief Encounter*.

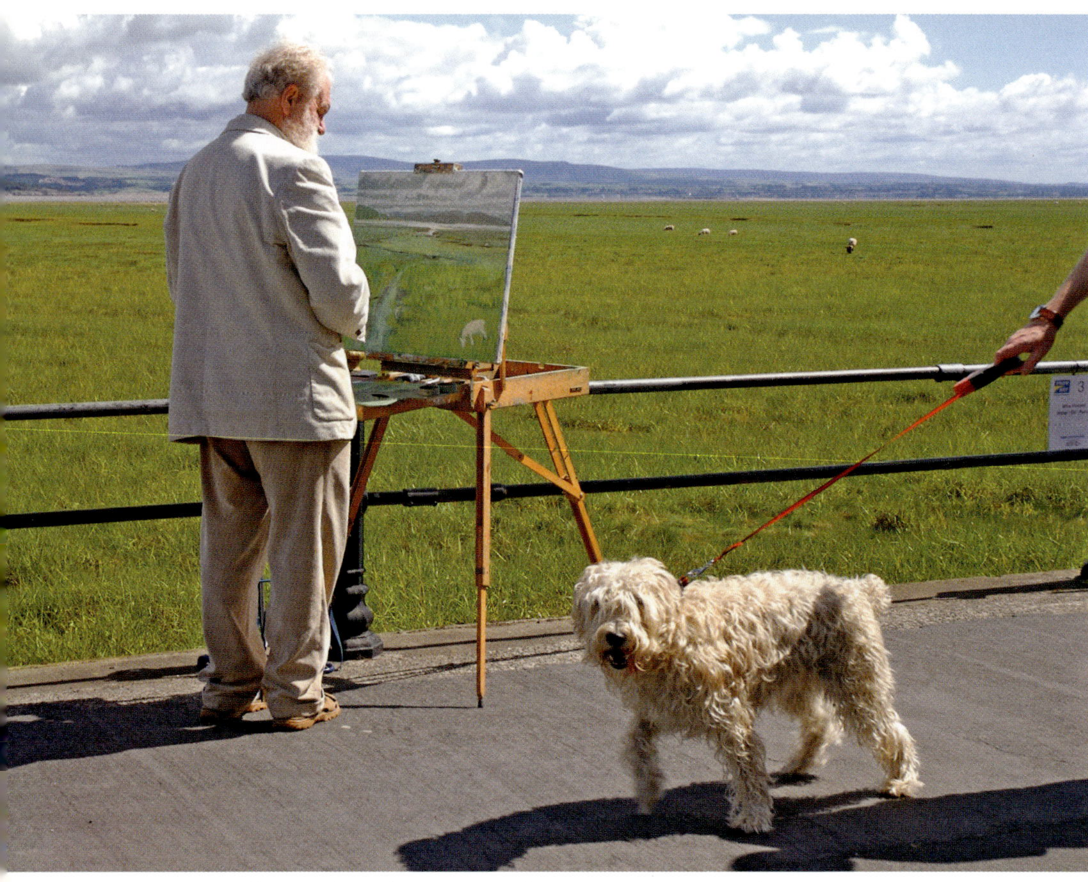

An artist sets up his easel on the promenade at Grange-over-Sands.

RIGHT
The view from Hampsfell: across the Kent estuary to Arnside Knott and beyond.

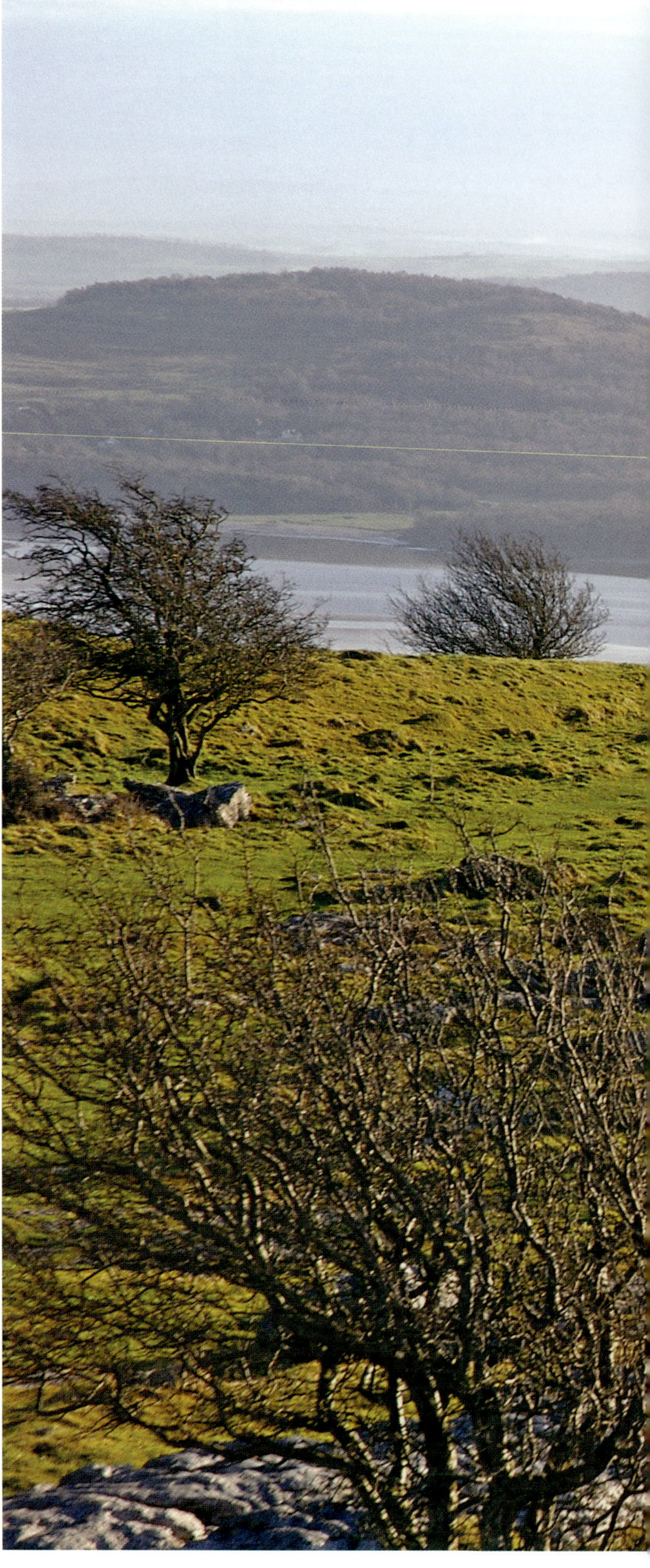

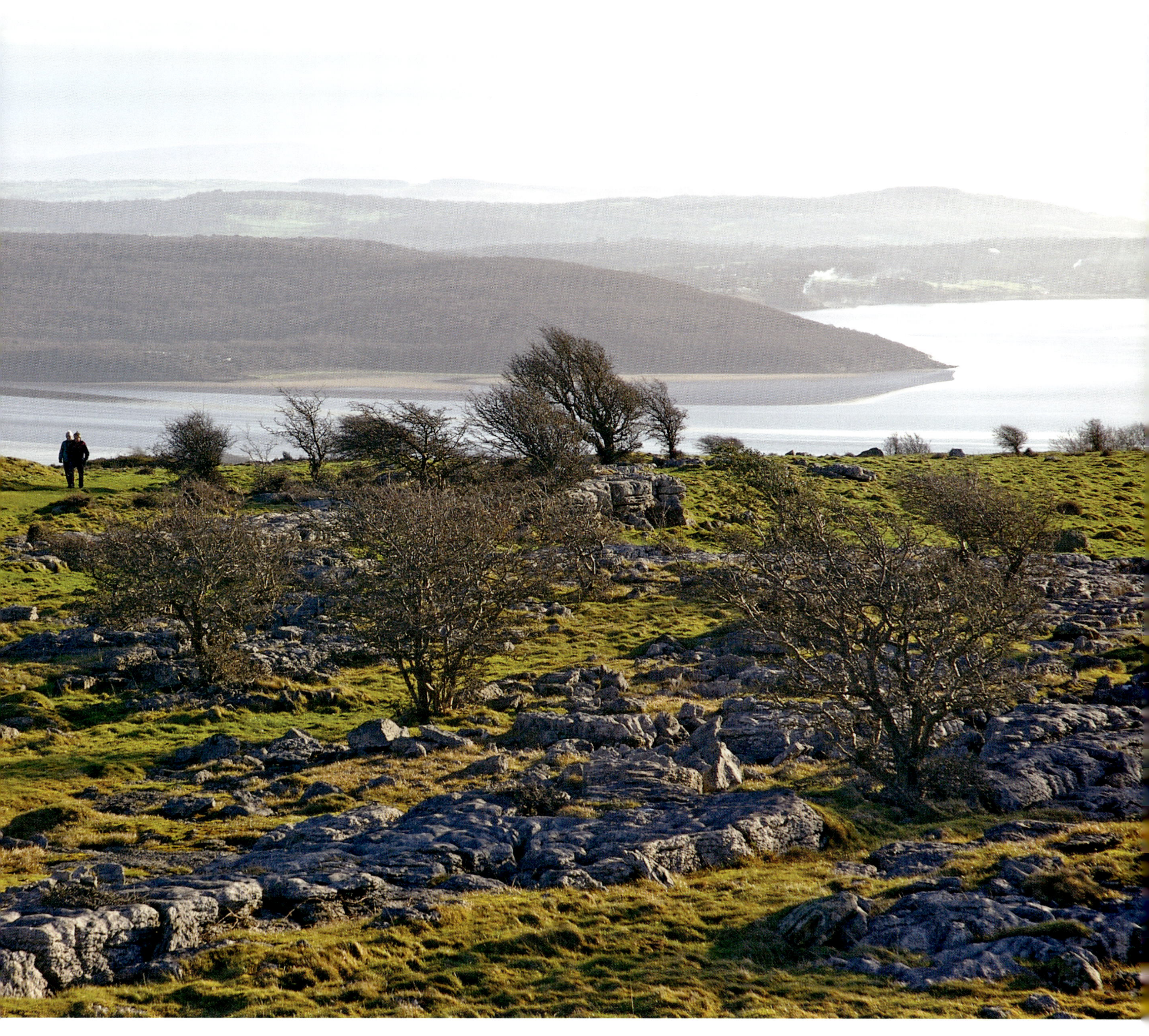

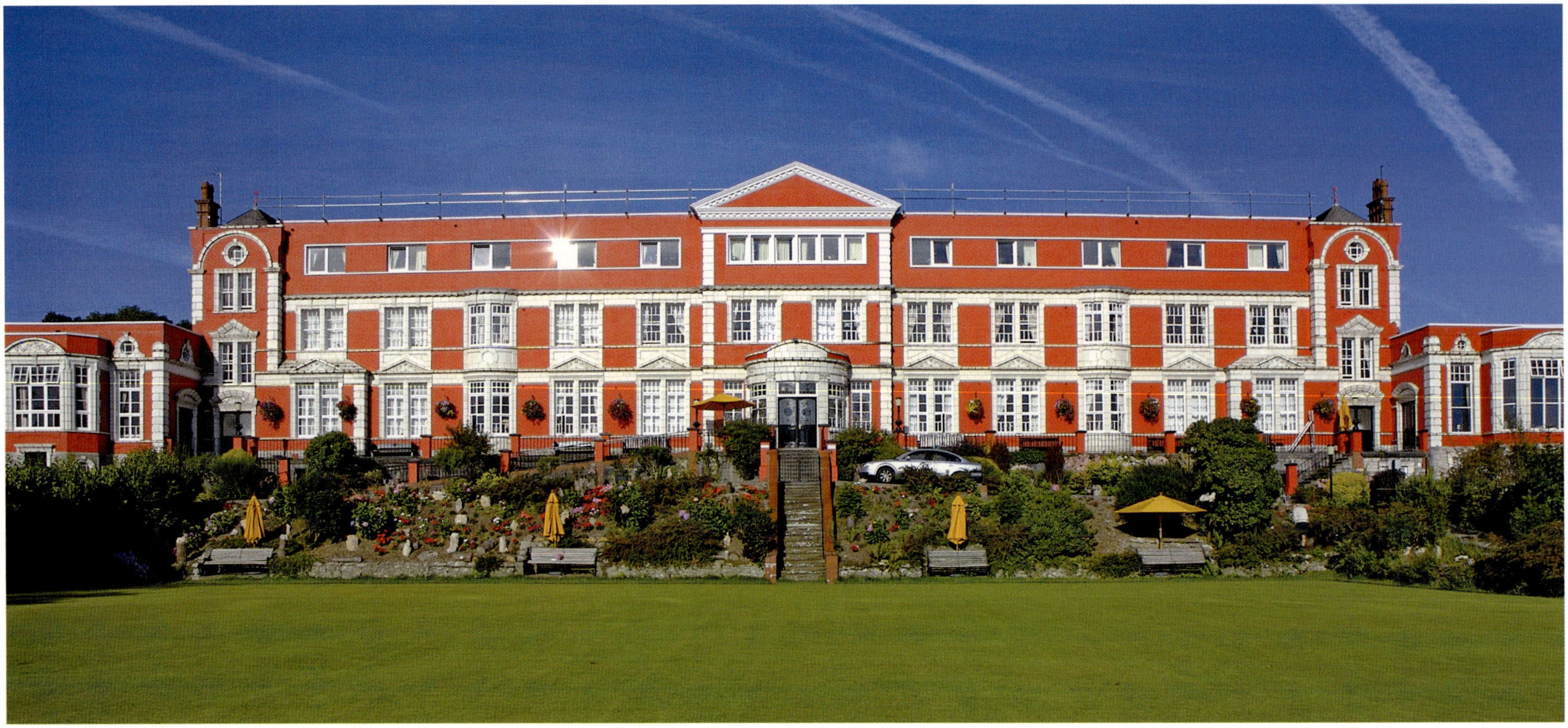

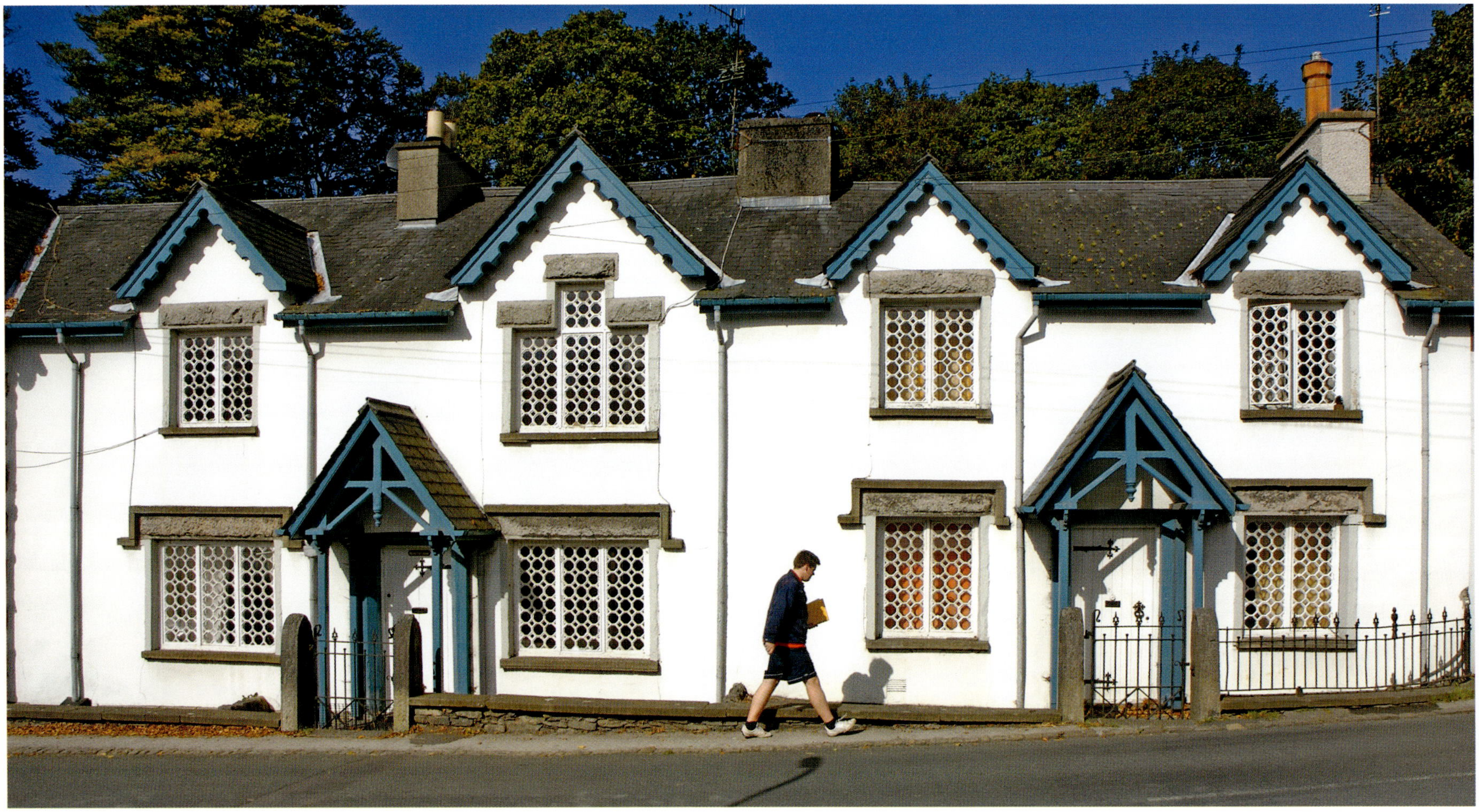

LEFT ABOVE
Hotels in Grange-over-Sands were built on a grand scale, to match
the town's aspirations as a genteel resort.

LEFT BELOW
All the houses in the estate village of Holker – under the aegis of
Holker Hall – share an architectural style.

BELOW
A terrace of houses in Salthouse Road, Barrow-in-Furness, built
during the 1850s to house railway workers.

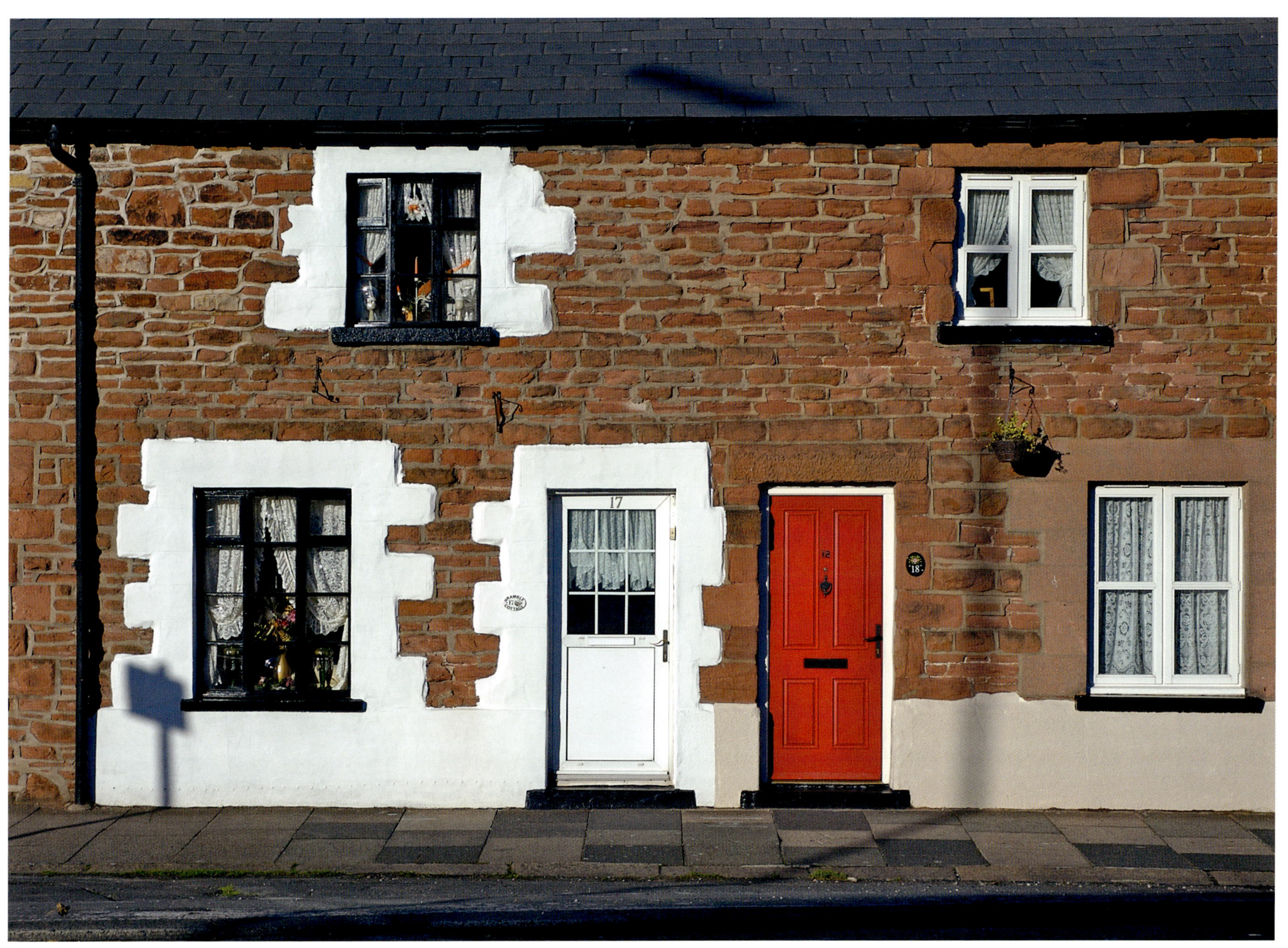

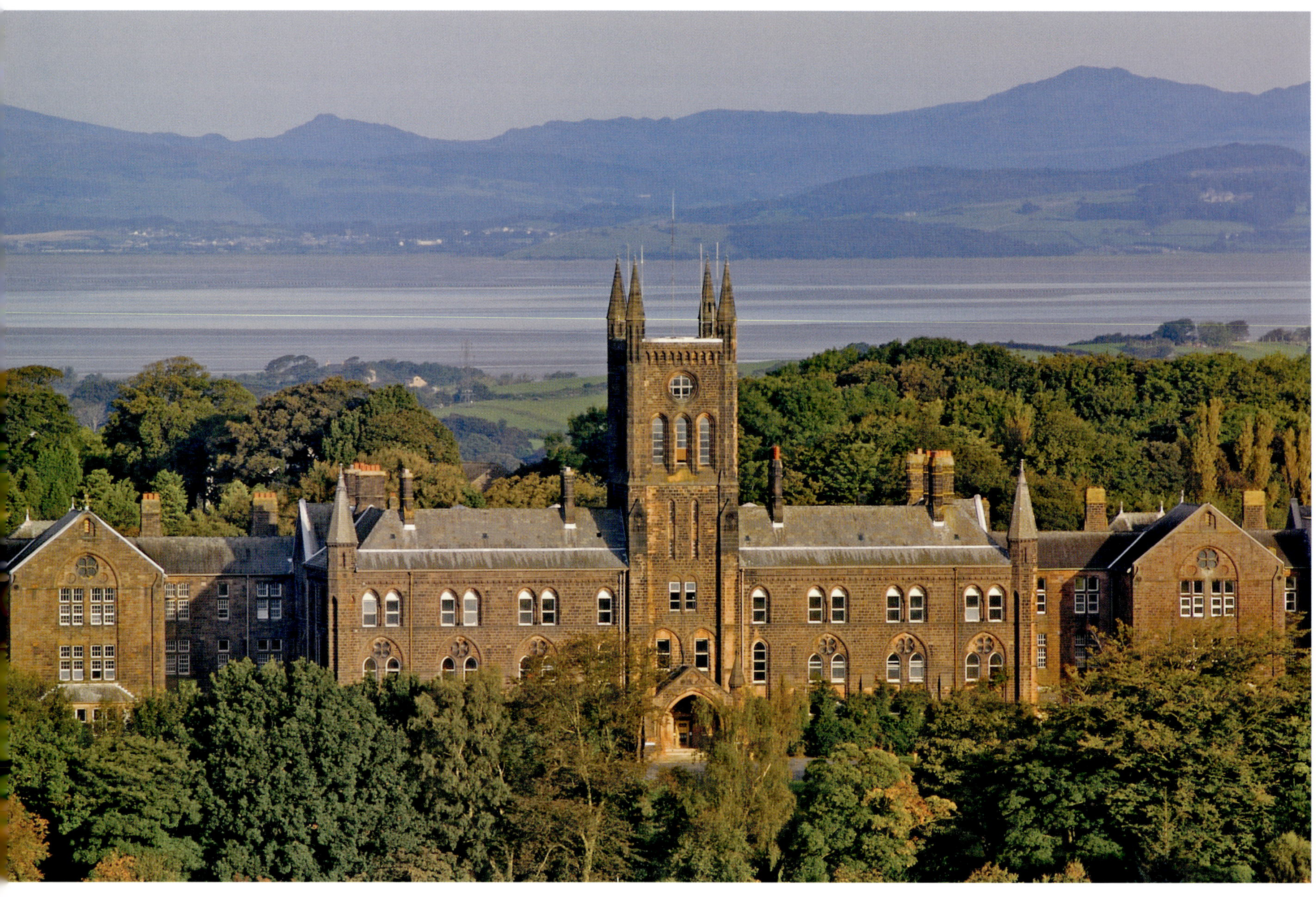

The only shot taken from the 'wrong side' of the M6 motorway: the old
Lancaster Moor Hospital, built in 1883, with Morecambe Bay beyond

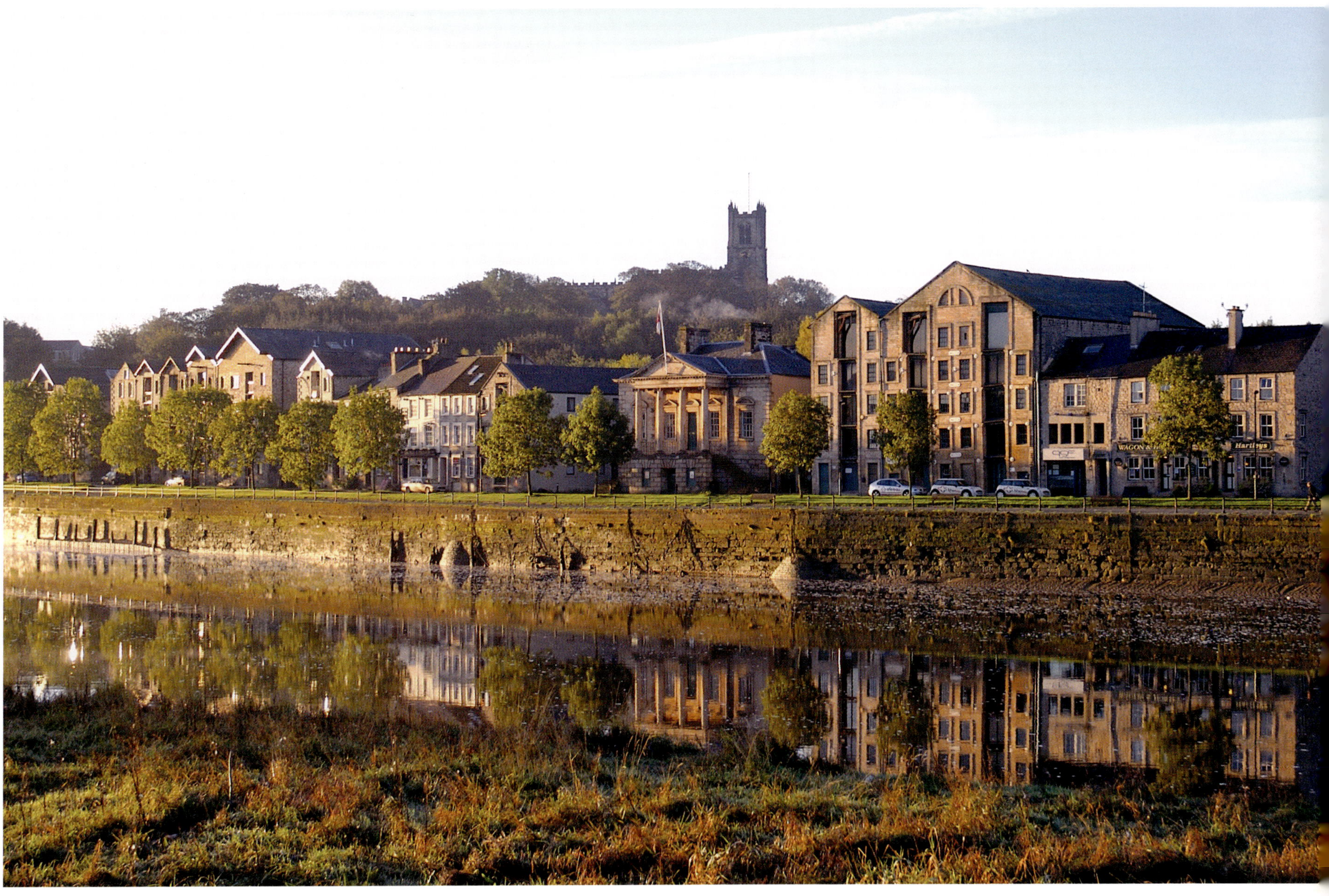

The River Lune and St George's Quay in Lancaster, with most of the old
warehouses now converted into waterside apartments.

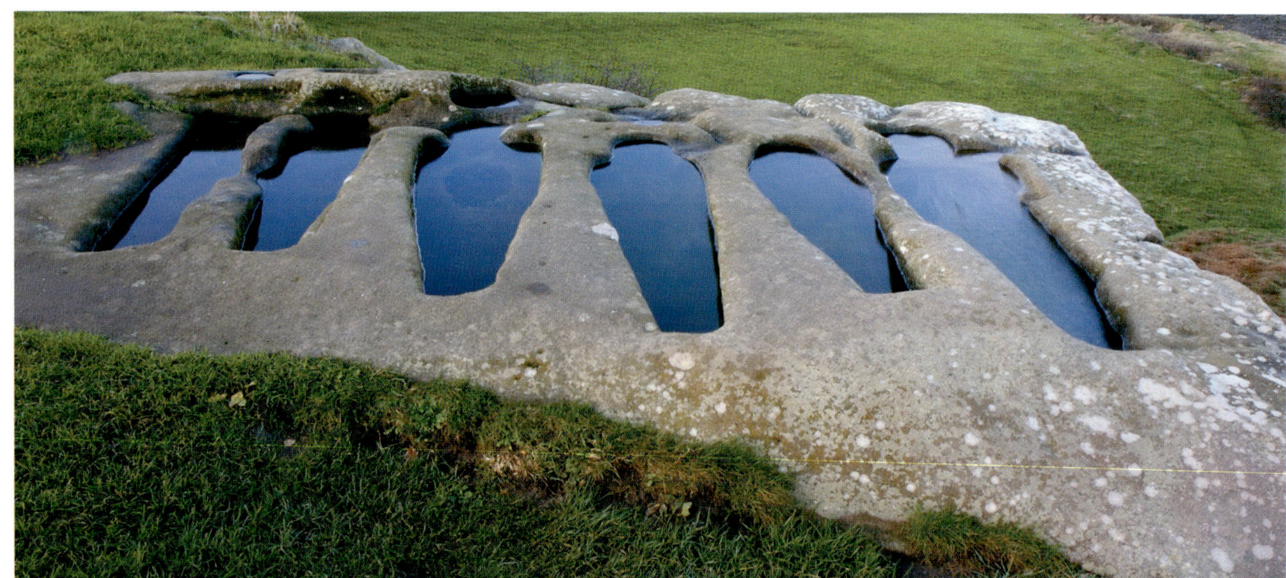

LEFT
The remarkable rock-hewn graves at Heysham Head.

BELOW
The evocative remains of St Patrick's Chapel, on Heysham Head, built more than twelve centuries ago.

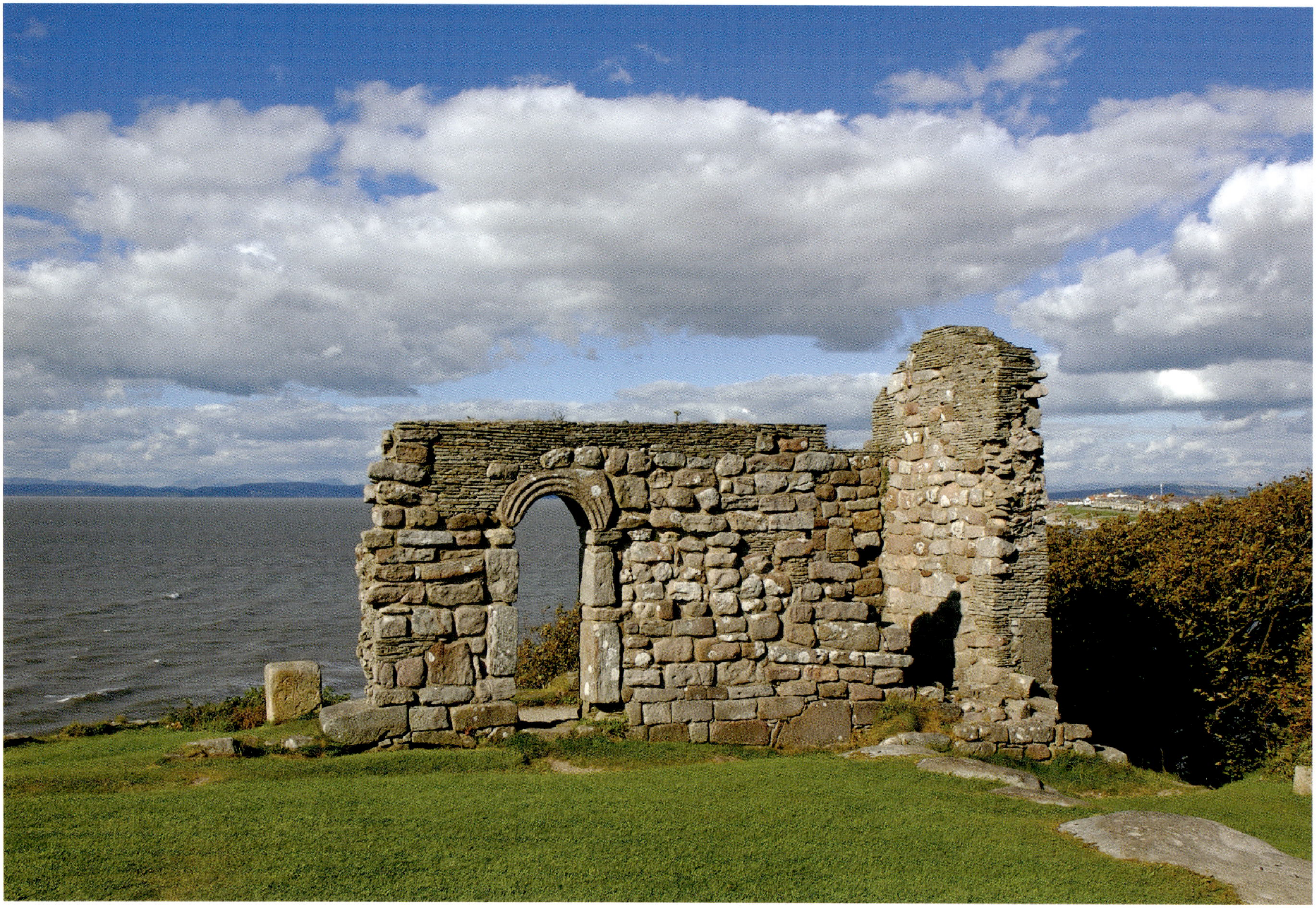

The sixteenth-century Judges' Lodgings: the oldest town house in Lancaster and once the home of witch-hunter Thomas Covell.


Manor House Farm, a handsome house in Slyne, north of Lancaster, the porch embellished with a 1681 datestone.

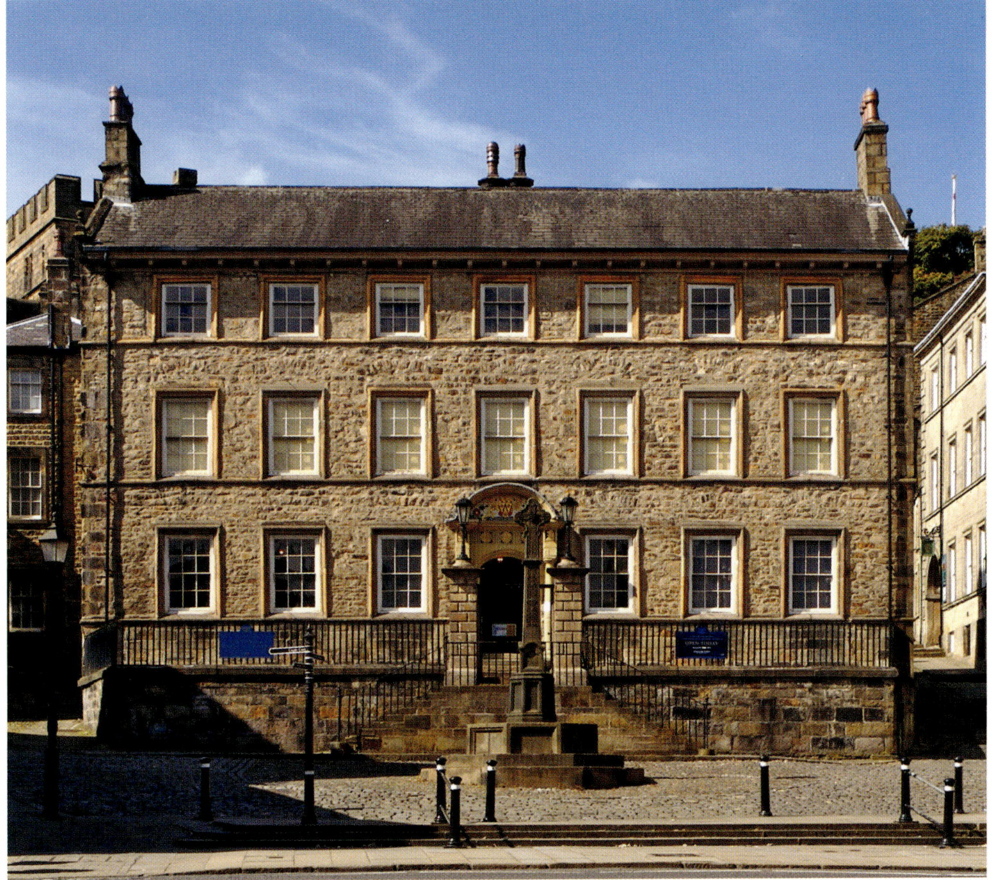

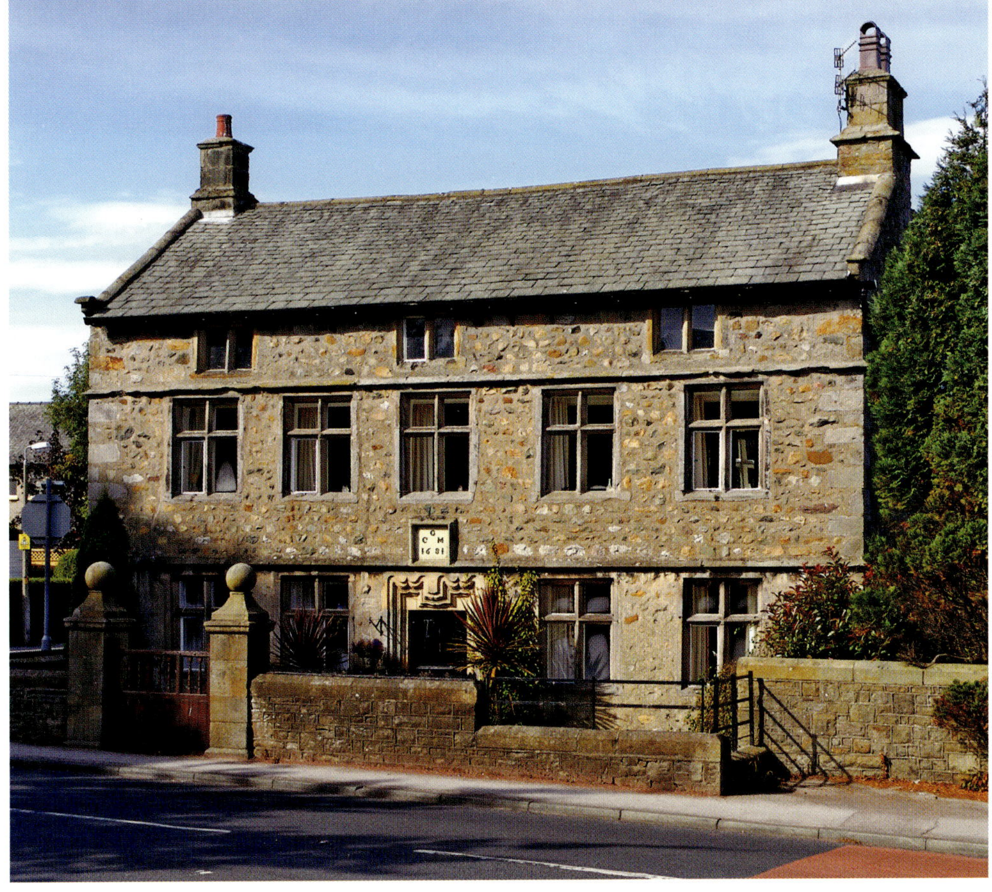

With its houses painted in a variety of
pastel colours, locals have their own
name for Soutergate in Ulverston. They
call it 'Balamory'.

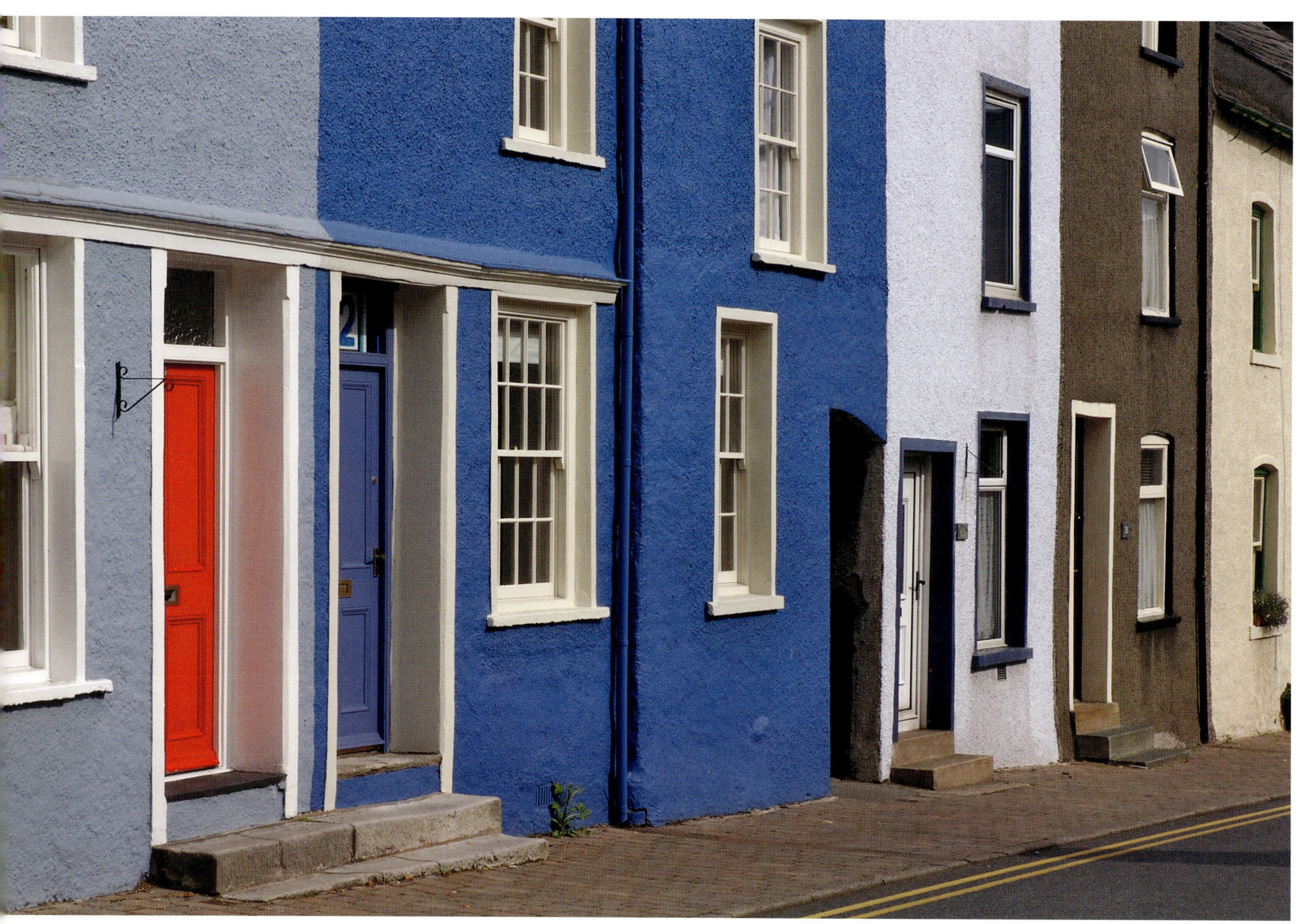

Bold shapes, rich colour: they like the
smell of fresh paint in Ulverston.

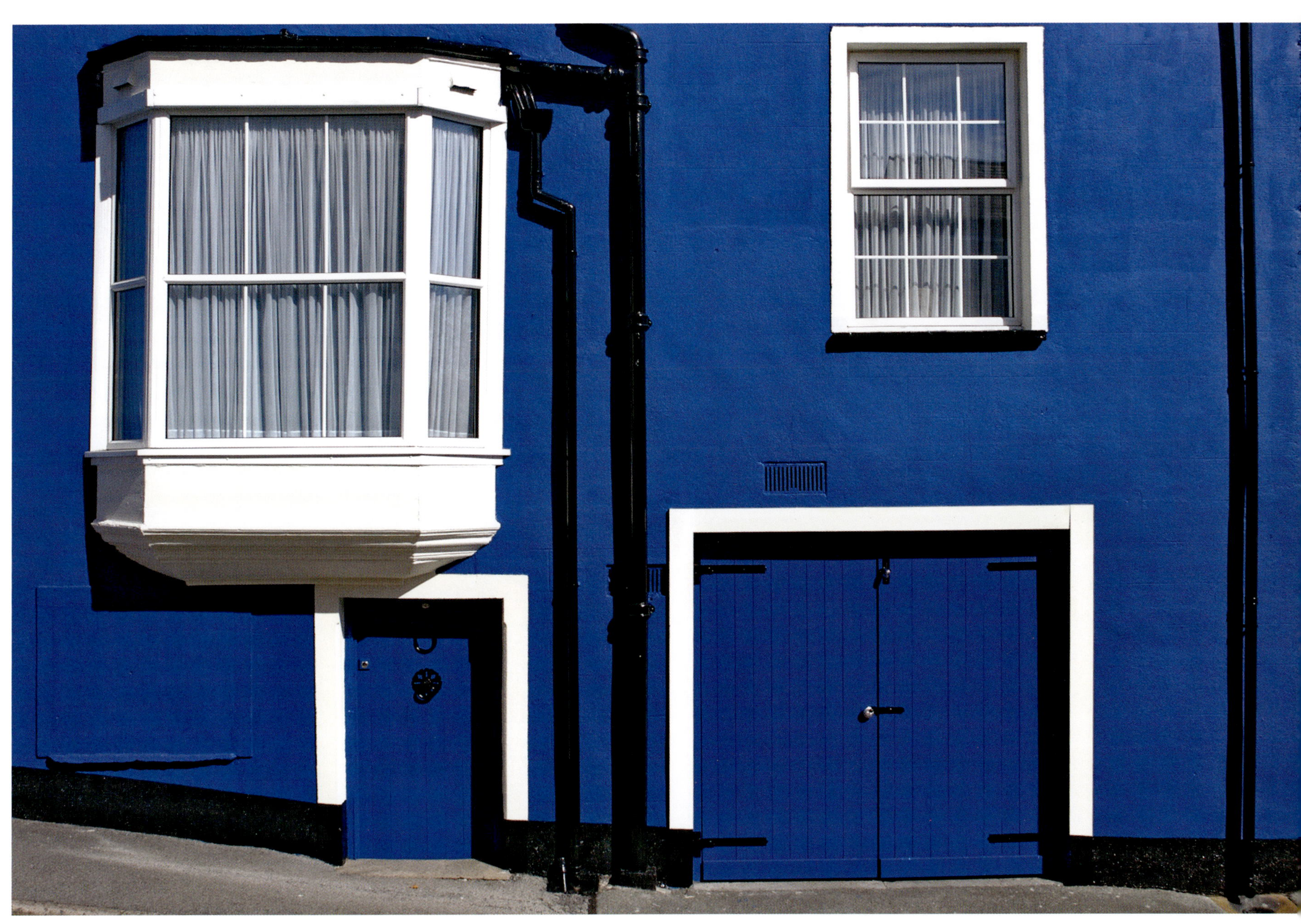

Until the boundary changes of 1974, Furness extended north to include the lakes of Coniston and Windermere. It was also in Lancashire. Well, sort of. The region, known as North Lancashire or Lancashire-North-of-the-Sands, was separated from the rest of Lancashire, somewhat incongruously, by a strip of Cumberland.

Furness is currently being touted, perhaps optimistically, as the 'Lakeland Peninsulas'. It obviously irks the tourism promotors that visitors flock to the Lake District National Park instead of exploring the attractions that the Cumbrian coast has to offer. Someone else (probably not in the tourism business) has described Furness as 'the largest cul-de-sac in England.'. And it's not hard to see why: when you're scrunching along the shingle banks of Walney Island, you can feel a long way from what we like to call 'civilization'.

In monastic times, when Furness Abbey prospered near by, Dalton was the most important town in Furness. The baton was passed to Ulverston – which was mentioned in the Domesday Book – once it had developed as a port. Both towns were eclipsed, however, by the expansion of Barrow-in-Furness: a rise that, by any standards, was meteoric.

Iron ore – haematite – had been mined for centuries throughout the limestone areas of the Furness peninsula. The monks of Furness Abbey had their mines and bloomeries, though it wasn't until the nineteenth century that ore was mined on any industrial scale. The growth of Barrow was linked inextricably to the profitability of the mines, and the man behind both projects was Henry William Schneider. He was born in London in 1817 in a wealthy family with many mining interests, both here and overseas. Keen to expand their business interests, the family looked to the northern counties. When Henry took a holiday in the Lake District, he combined business with pleasure by making a detour to Furness to investigate local mines and assess their prospects.

A number of companies were already involved in small-scale mining, carting iron ore to ports at Conishead Bank, Greenodd and Ulverston. Convinced that good deposits of iron ore lay beneath land owned by the Earl of Burlington, near Park, Schneider hired geologists, at great expense, to survey the area. Exploratory shafts were sunk, but with little success. Schneider sunk a lot of money into the project too – money made from other, more successful, ventures.

By 1850, when the royalty on the Park mine was about to lapse, Schneider was close to abandining the project altogether. With his budget running out, he was only persuaded to continue by his miners, who offered to put in an extra week's work without pay. At a depth of 36 feet – eureka! – a large deposit of ore was struck. In the years which followed, Schneider dined out on this story of the 'free week', which underpinned all his subsequent successes at Barrow. Park became the biggest and most profitable mine in Furness, producing about 1,000 tons of top-quality ore per day.

In 1853 Schneider went into partnership with Richard Hannay, a wealthy Scottish landowner. It was a good match: Schneider with a potentially profitable business and Hannay with money to invest. Both men built up considerable fortunes from their joint venture. They saw that Barrow – at that time just a village on the Walney channel – was ideally sited for the transporting of ore by sea, which rapidly replaced fishing as the town's main industry. The Furness Railway created the missing transport link, encouraging Schneider and Hannay to develop Barrow as a major port.

They sunk more mines and built blast furnaces. In 1864 they started a steel manufacturing company, which soon became one of the largest in the world, specialising in steel rails for the burgeoning railway network. For a few profitable years the

Ulverston Market Place, and the Sir John Barrow Monument, beneath a stormy sky.

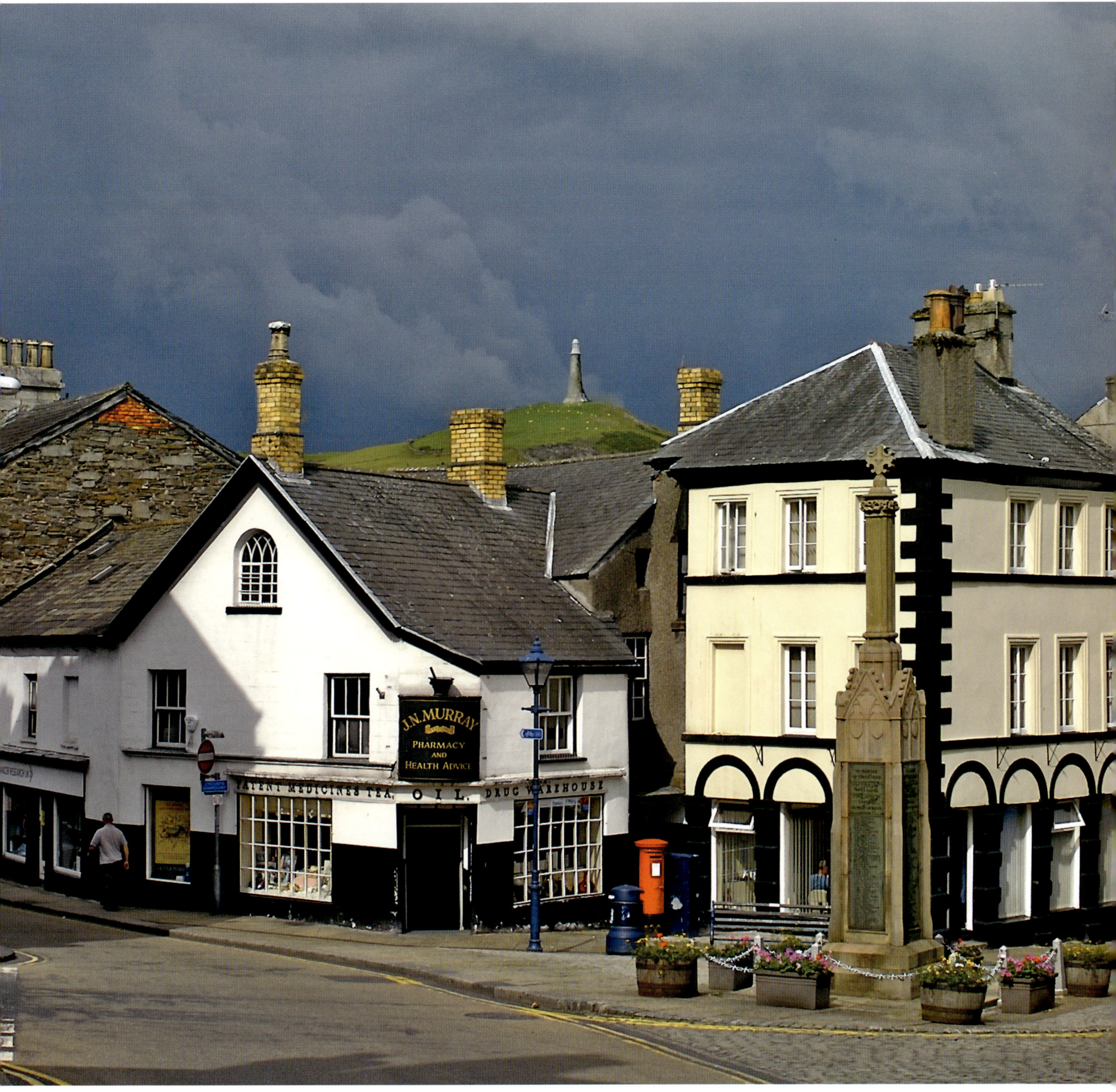
J.N.MURRAY
PHARMACY
AND
HEALTH ADVICE
PATENT MEDICINES TEA. O I L. DRUG WAREHOUSE

company had a virtual monopoly of the market, since Furness haematite was critical to the Bessemer steel-making process. It was boom time for Barrow which, like other towns that grew with Victorian energy and enterprise, was a planned community. The streets were laid out on a grid system, around the huge sandstone town hall.

As a man of wealth and influence, Schneider nurtured political ambitions. He entered parliament in 1857, only to be unseated by charges of corruption. He tried again in 1865, being returned unopposed as MP for nearby Ulverston. He won 2,000 votes: a strange result since only 1,000 people in the constituency were entitled to vote! He was unseated again, for bribing the electorate.

Undaunted, Schneider became Barrow's third mayor – serving out a three-year term without further mishap – and the driving force behind many other businesses that expanded around the town, of which the most successful was the Barrow Shipbuilding Company. Barrow Docks were built, on a massive scale, between the mainland and Old Barrow Island.

As befitting a captain of industry, Schneider lived far from the steel-rolling mills which lit up the night sky around Barrow. He settled in Belsfield, a large Italianate mansion on the eastern shore of Windermere, overlooking Bowness Bay.

Every working day started the same way. Preceded by his butler bearing breakfast on a silver tray, Schneider would stroll down to the lake, where the two-man crew of his steamboat, the *Esperance*, were ready to cruise down to Lakeside, at the southern tip of Windermere. Here he boarded his own private carriage on the Barrow train, where a secretary would hand him any important papers which required his signature (and, since Schneider was one of the directors of the Furness Railway, I doubt if the train ever left without him). The train delivered him to his office in Barrow. Now that is commuting . . .

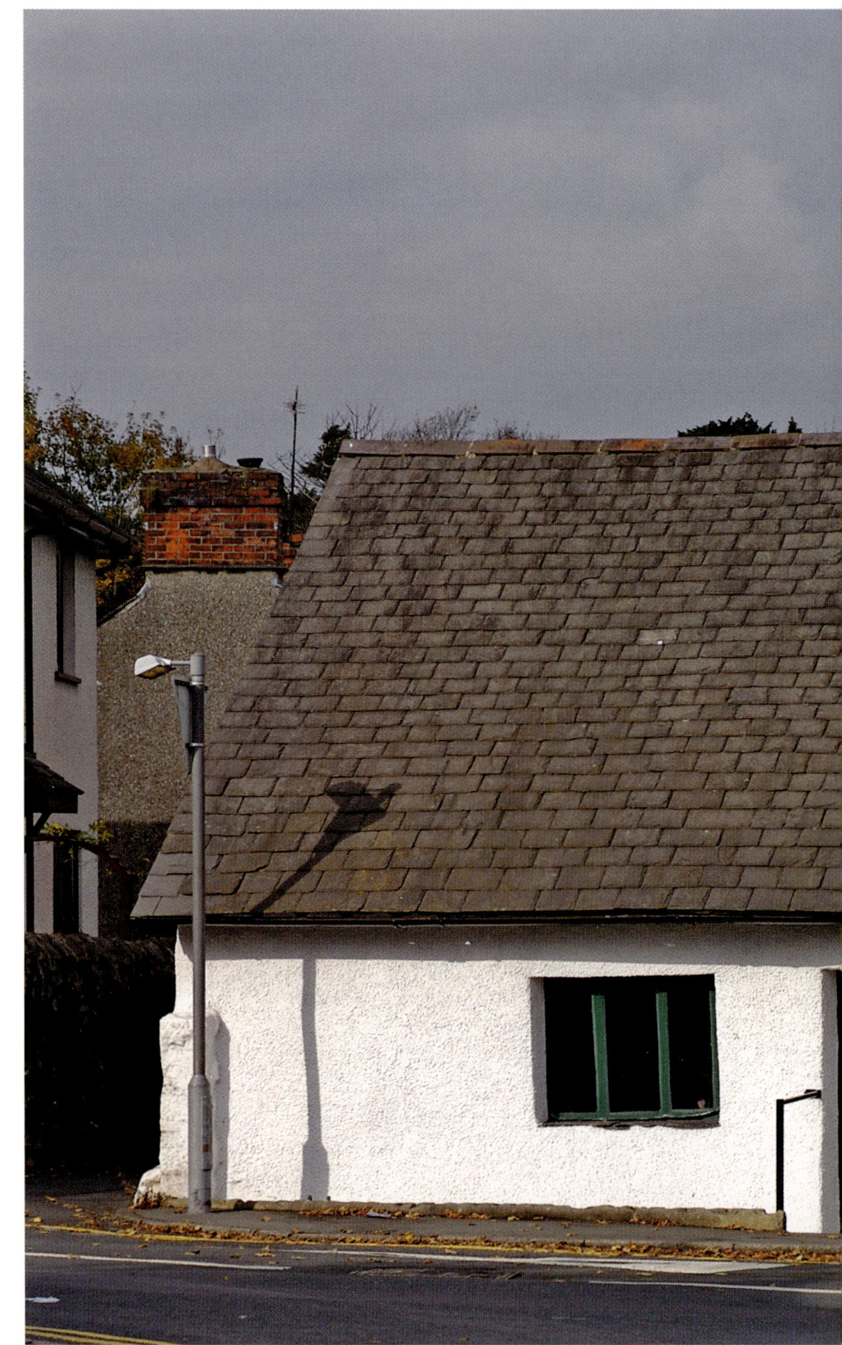

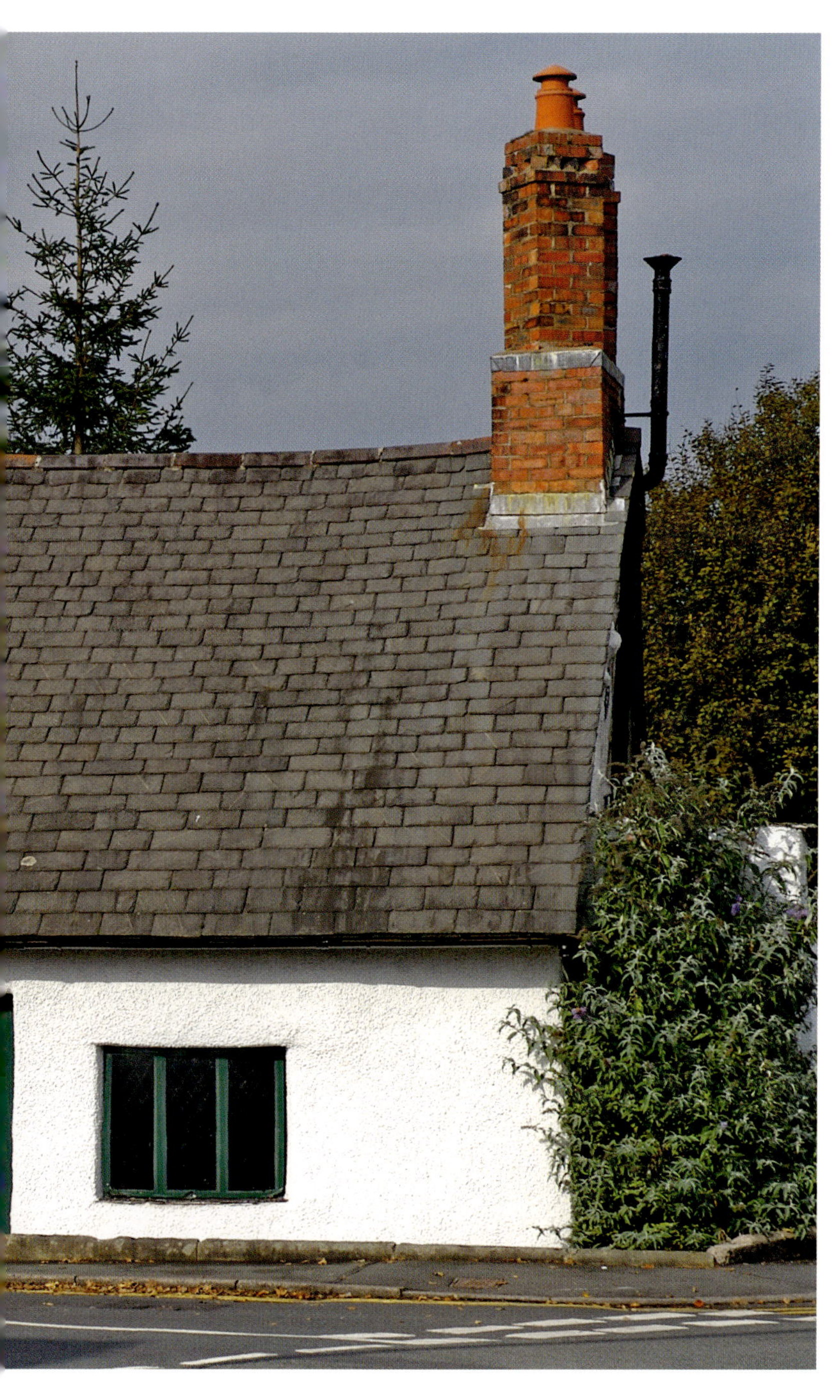

Henry William Schneider died peacefully at Belsfield in 1887, aged 72. Four years after his death, a statue of him, dressed in his mayorial robes, was unveiled in Barrow, in the square which bears his name.

The town continued to prosper; sepia-toned photographs show crowds cheering as another warship slid slowly down the slipway into Devonshire Dock. After the Royal Navy's first submarine was built here in 1901, the shipyard found its speciality. During World War II Barrow's population peaked at around 85,000.

Barrow has known lean times in recent years (even the town's own website describes it as 'one of the best-kept secrets in Britain', which sounds like a mild criticism of the tourism department). The number of men employed in the shipyard fell from over 20,000 at the start of the 1980s to just 3,000 by the end of the century. Nevertheless, Barrow remains the only deep-water port between the Mersey and the Clyde, and, if the Royal Navy orders more submarines, the work may yet go to Barrow. As a sign that more prosperous times may lie ahead, cruise ships now dock here – though passengers are whisked off to Windermere and Grasmere and anywhere associated with William Wordworth and Beatrix Potter, rather than being left to wander round the docks of Barrow.

I have a soft spot for Barrow, because I always root for the underdog. It's not easy for outlying Cumbrian towns to attract tourists when most of them head straight for the Lakeland honeypots. My parents took me to Barrow once; it must be half a century ago. My one abiding memory is of a street of unassuming terraced houses dwarfed by the flank of a huge ship that was being built in the dockyard.

If there are no such sights today, there are other reasons to visit Barrow. There's Furness Abbey, built in warm, red sandstone, between Barrow and Dalton. There's the Dock Museum, built across a nineteenth-century graving dock, which tells the story of Barrow's maritime history. And there's Walney Island: a narrow strip of land, 11 miles long, which shelters Barrow from high tides and stormy seas. Big waves break on the

pebble beach of Ernse Bay, leaving Walney channel largely
undisturbed. 'Ernse' is the old name for a sea eagle, a species that
hasn't been seen here for a couple of centuries.

Before Barrow expanded, Walney was a quiet backwater,
connected to the mainland by a ferryboat. After the building in
1908 of the Jubilee Bridge (one of only four bridges in the country
to use a rack-and-pinion system to open up for tall ships), Walney
was no longer strictly an island. The bridge was repainted – in its
original colours of black and gold – for its centenary celebrations.
When Vickers Shipyard needed more housing for their workers,
the company created Vickerstown – with streets named after
some of the ships that had been built here, such as Amphitrite,
Strathnaver and Naiad.

Roa Island is another 'not quite an island', having being joined
to the mainland at Rampside first by a railway on a raised causeway
then, in the 1940s, by a road. Henry Schneider built a holiday
home on Roa – a rather ugly brick affair – and, right on the tip, is
a lifeboat station on stilts to raise it beyond the highest tides.
Halfway along the causeway, Foulney Island, a spit of shingle,
branches off: the haunt of walkers and, each spring, huge numbers
of nesting seabirds.

A summer ferry service transfers people from the tip of Roa
Island to nearby Piel Island ('No need to pay now,' the ferryman
told me. 'Pay me on the way back.'). Piel has plenty of history,
including a fourteenth-century castle. From Roa Island it looks like
a romantic silhouetted ruin, but from close quarters you can see
how it dominates the topography of this tiny island. Not built for
show, Piel Castle was strategically important – guarding the
southern approach to the Walney channel. The only other
buildings on the island are a row of cottages and a pub, now sadly
and securely boarded up, whose landlord used to take the
honoury title, 'King of Piel.' The fact that there's a pub here at all

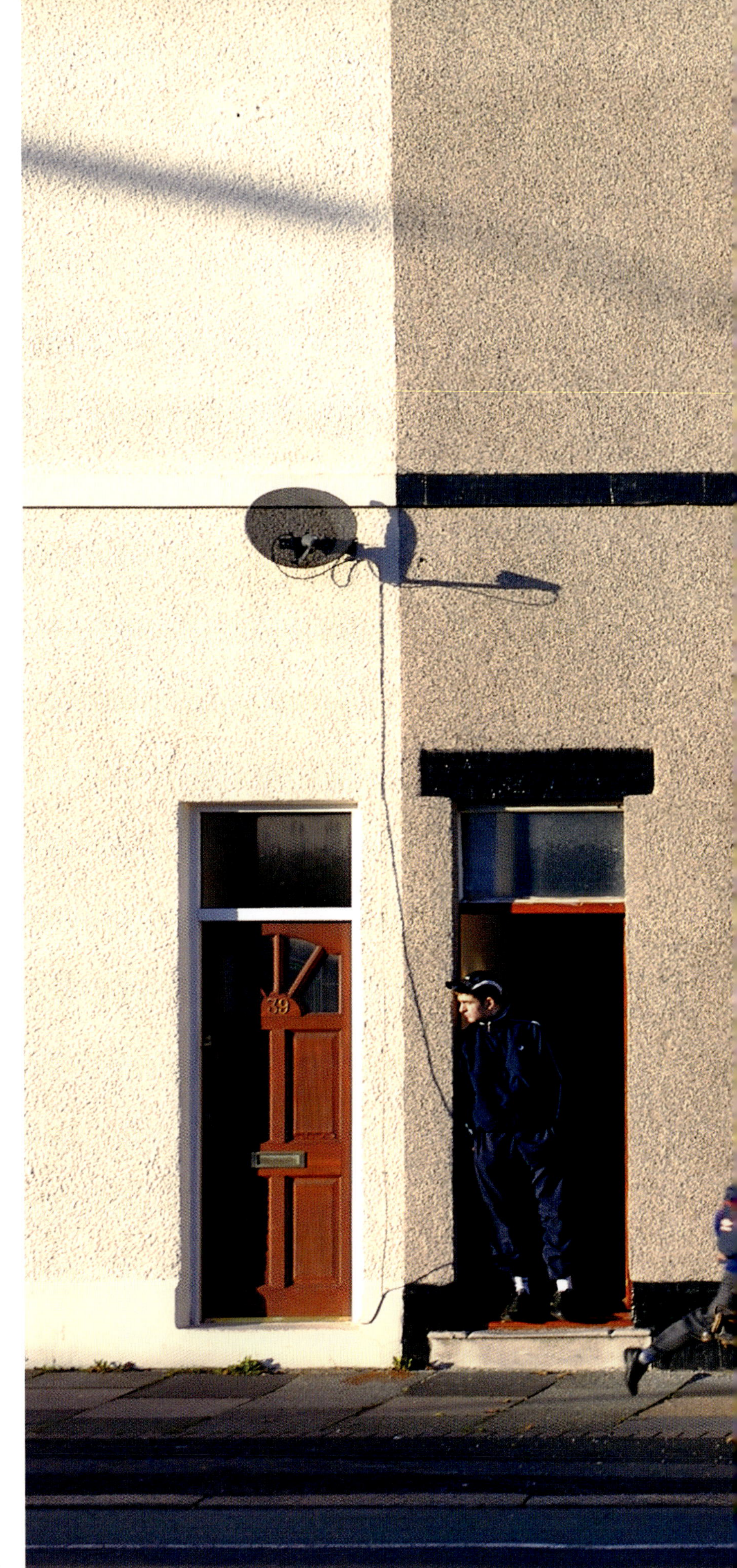

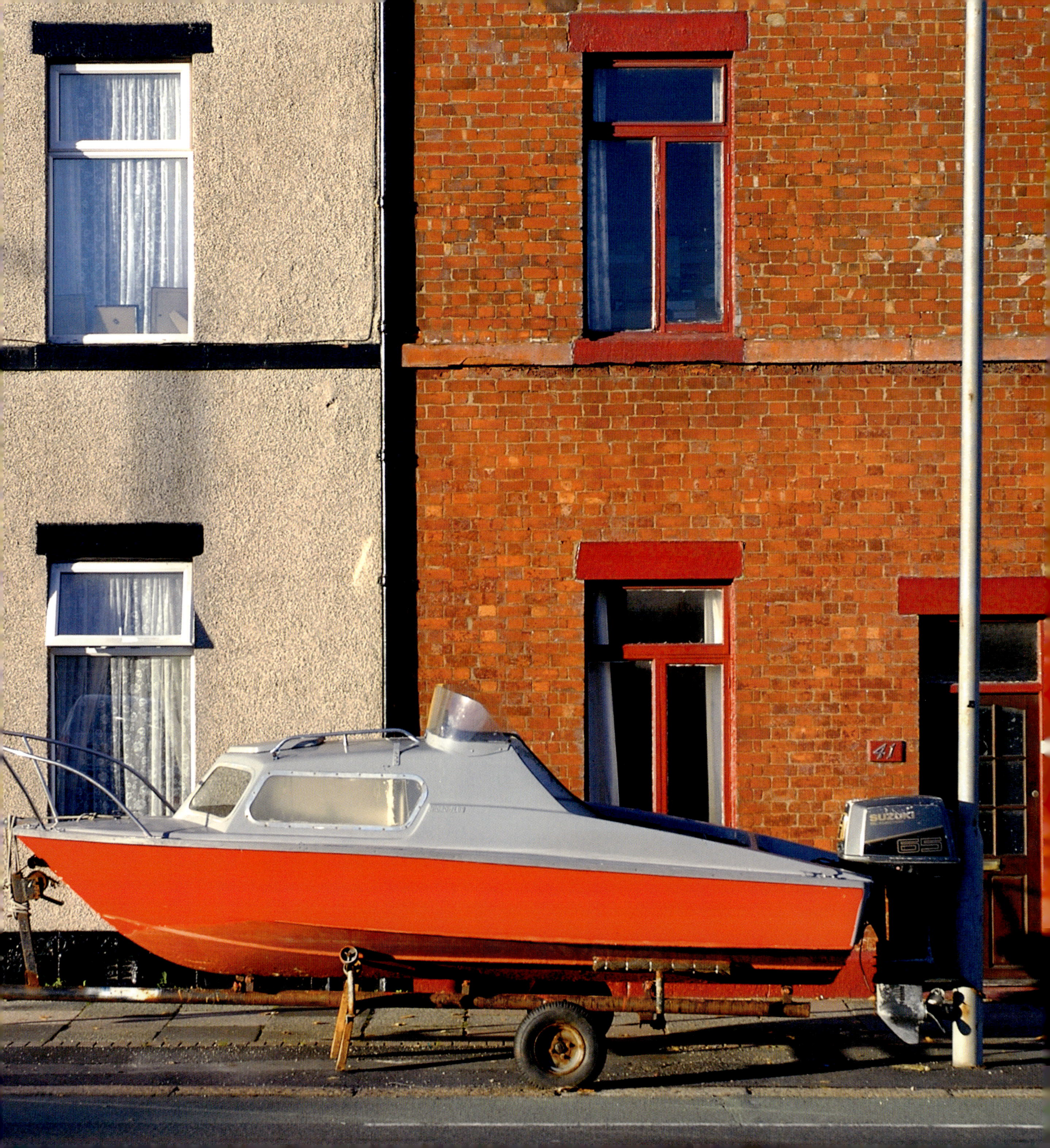

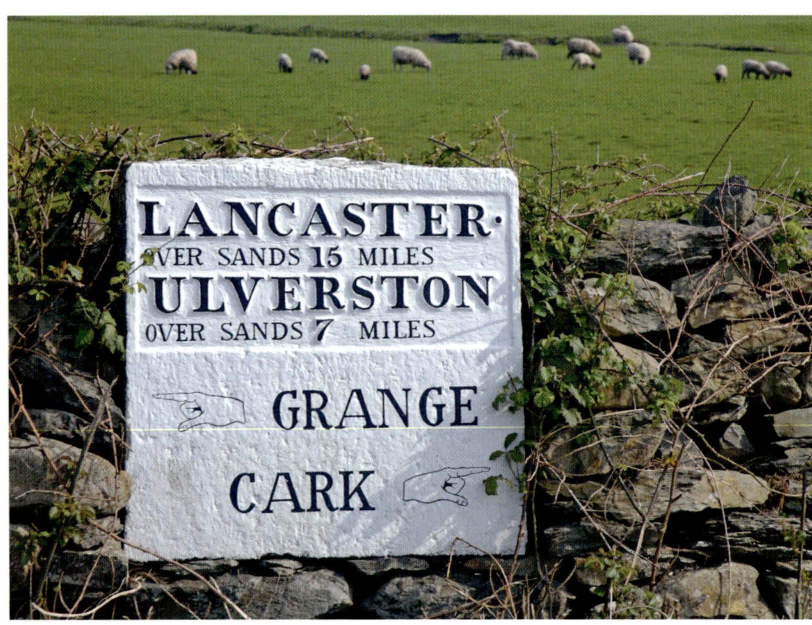

A sign for travellers in Cartmel, showing the distance to Lancaster across the Kent estuary, and Ulverston via the Leven sands.

is an indication that Piel Island hasn't always been so tranquil. It was known, for centuries, as a safe harbour and deep anchorage: safe from pirates, border raiders and stormy weather.

Though the A590 offers the quickest route from Barrow to Ulverston, anyone not in a tearing hurry should choose the Coast Road instead. It was constructed between the wars, by reduntant employees from local mines and munitions factories. The road hugs the coast; in places it is protected from high tides by a sea-wall. Traffic crosses Sea Wood and passes beneath the sheep-cropped pasture of Birkrigg Common until a much-loved landmark comes into view.

What visitors see on their approach to Ulverston is what appears to be a lighthouse on a hill. It's certainly shaped like a lighthouse – a faithful replica of the Eddystone Lighthouse, in fact – though no beam has ever swept across the sands of Morecambe Bay as a warning to sailors. It was built in 1855 out of locally-quarried limestone to celebrate the life and achievements of Sir John Barrow. Born in Ulverston, he went on to become Secretary to the Admiralty and was one of the founders of the Royal Geographic Society. The John Barrow Monument is its 'Sunday best' name; locals know it as The Hoad. On a clear day the view from Hoad Hill offers a splendid panorama, taking in the whole of Morecambe Bay.

Ulverston was another town that prospered with shipbuilding and the iron ore trade, after the opening in 1796 of the Ulverston Canal: the shortest, widest, deepest and straightest canal in the land. That's a lot of superlatives for a watercourse less than a mile in length. During the canal's busiest time, half a century later, a thousand ships docked at Ulverston in a single year. Trade declined with the coming of the Furness Railway and the expansion of Barrow; by the end of World War II, the canal was sealed up at the seaward end. When other towns declined, however, Ulverston adapted to changing times. The canal-side site was occupied by a vast pharmaceutical factory, now the town's main employer.

You could spend a couple of hours in the town (it's got some great little speciality shops) with little to remind you that the sea is so close. Having won its market charter in 1280, Ulverston has long been a place of trade, where market stalls spill out into the streets. The town's most famous son is Stan Laurel – the slim, gormless half of the famous Hollywood comedy duo – and a small museum celebrates their life and films. Ulverston promotes itself as a 'festival town'; no matter when you visit there's likely to be a festival underway. Be warned, though: a 'festival of flags' is still just . . . flags.

At Swarthmoor, just outside Ulverston, is Swarthmoor Hall, dating from 1586, which can claim with good reason to be called the birthplace of Quakerism. It was here that George Fox found a welcome from Margaret Fell, wife of a local judge. While attending a service at St Mary's Church in Ulverston, she witnessed Fox being ejected from the church and beaten up by parishioners, after he had challenged the minister on some matter of theology. For a man of peace, Fox got into a lot of fights . . .

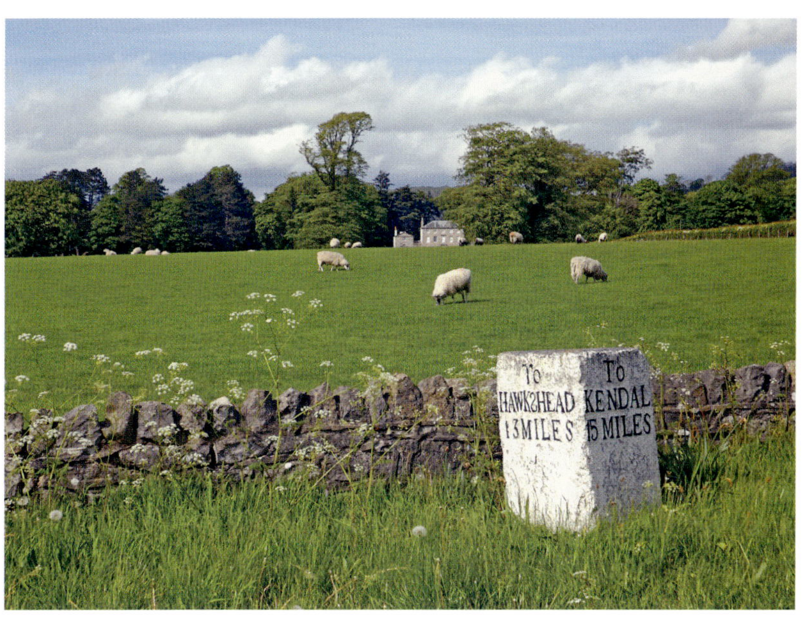

Another milestone, north of Cartmel, which would have been familiar to cross-bay traffic.



Though he never became a Quaker himself, Judge Fell's position in society offered some protection to Fox and his followers, whose religious non-conformity put them on the wrong side of the law. Margaret suffered for her faith, as did many of the early Quakers, by being sent to prison. Eleven years after the judge's death, George and Margaret were married, and Swarthmoor Hall became as close to a home as the tirelessly itinerant Fox would know. The meeting house near by, built in 1688, remains the only one that George Fox donated to the movement. Though he was buried in London, Margaret's resting place is in a small, and typically modest, Quaker burial ground on nearby Birkrigg Common.

Conishead Priory, built in 1160 on the Kent estuary near Bardsea, once vied with Furness Abbey for the administration of Furness. The monks employed a guide to escort them safely across the Leven estuary. When the priory met its end, a fine house was built on the site. But it wasn't half as grand as what came next: a gothic mansion, flanked by a pair of octagonal towers and set in an arboretum that extended over 70 acres (28 ha) down to the sands of the Leven. This Victorian extravaganza was created by Colonel Thomas Braddyll, the new owner of the estate, who also built a folly on diminutive Chapel Island out in the channel. He even employed a hermit to live in a grotto in the priory grounds, on condition that he remained 'in character' by not cutting his hair or fingernails!

Bradyll spent too much money on his mansion; when his mining interests failed, he went bankrupt. The building saw other uses (for a few years it was a convalescent home for Durham miners) until, in 1976, it was bought by the Manjushri Institute. Coming full-circle, and after a break of almost 500 years, monks once again live here in quiet contemplation on the shores of Morecambe Bay. Today though, they are Buddhist monks rather than the followers of St Augustine. As a stark contrast to the hall is the newly-built temple, in a traditional style. Of course, a style that's traditional to Buddhists is still somewhat incongruous on the edge of Morecambe Bay.

Greenodd, a few miles further up the Leven estuary, is where two rivers meet: the Crake and the Leven, draining the lakes of Coniston and Windermere respectively. Greenodd had a harbour on the creek, where ships were built – some as big as 200 tons. Then the railway came: the branch-line that used to take Henry Schneider from Bowness to Barrow. The line closed, though a four-mile section was reborn as the Lakeside-Haverthwaite Railway, a popular attraction for lovers of steam engines.

The building of the railway – and its subsequent replacement by a road – silted up the River Crake at Greenodd, leaving it unnavigable. The main street of Greenodd is now a cul-de-sac, ended, rather abruptly, by the dual carriageway of the A590. The only reminder of the days when goods were unloaded at the quayside of Greenodd is the sign on the village pub, the Ship Inn.

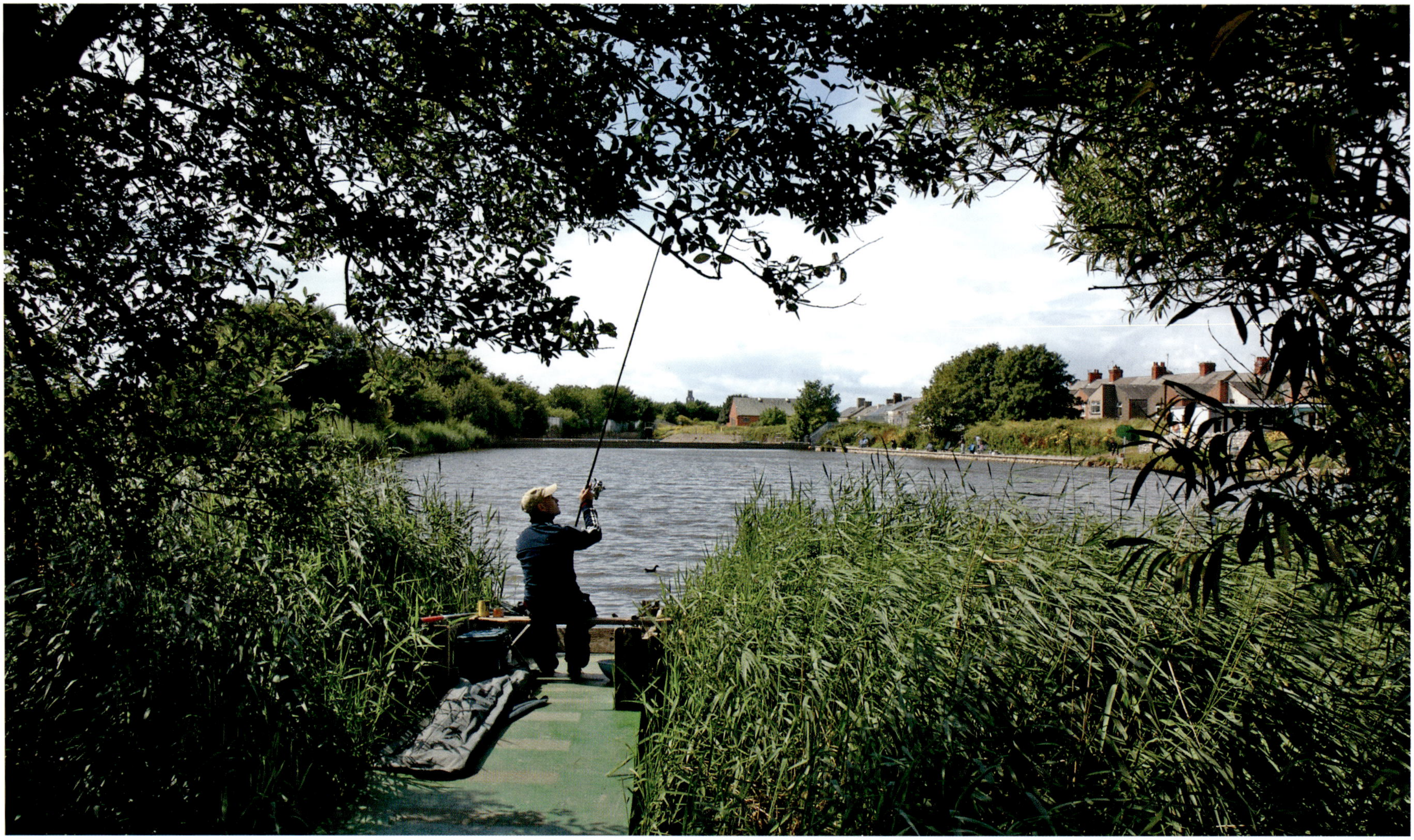

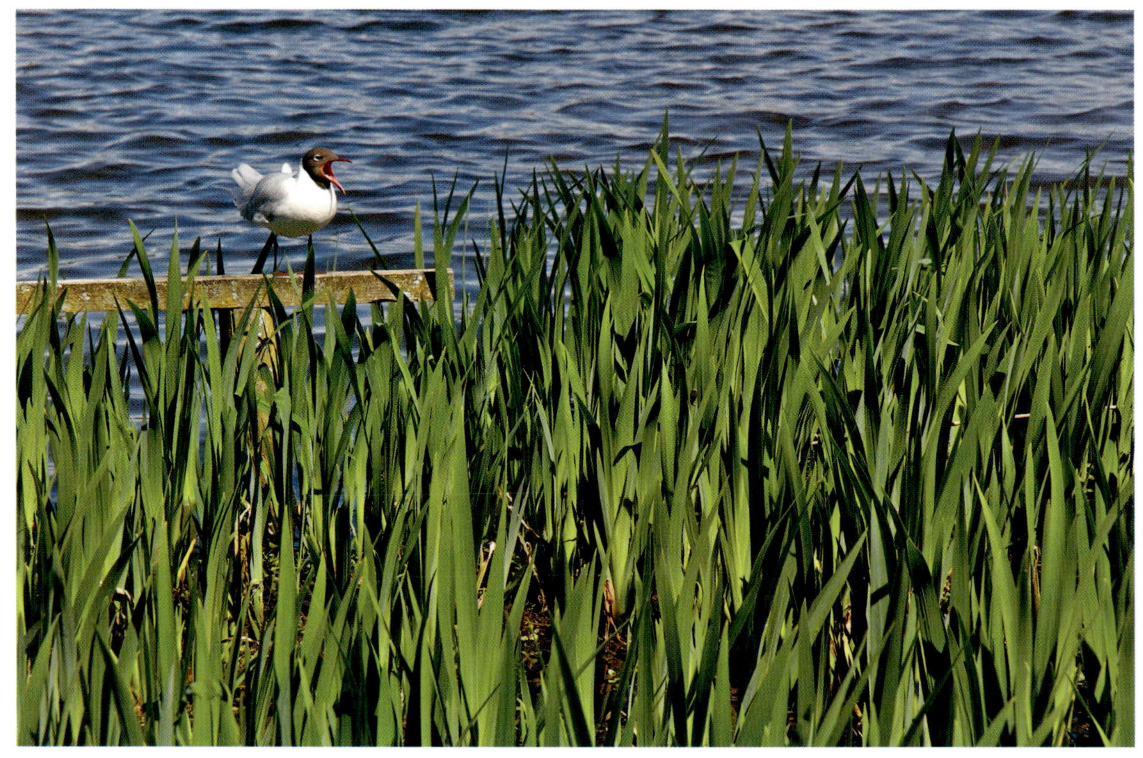

ABOVE
A peaceful day's angling on a fishing lake adjacent
to Cavendish Dock at Barrow-in-Furness.

RIGHT
A black headed gull in good voice – and full
breeding plumage – at Leighton Moss.

OPPOSITE
One of the lagoons at the RSPB reserve of
Leighton Moss, the largest remaining reed-bed
in north-west England.

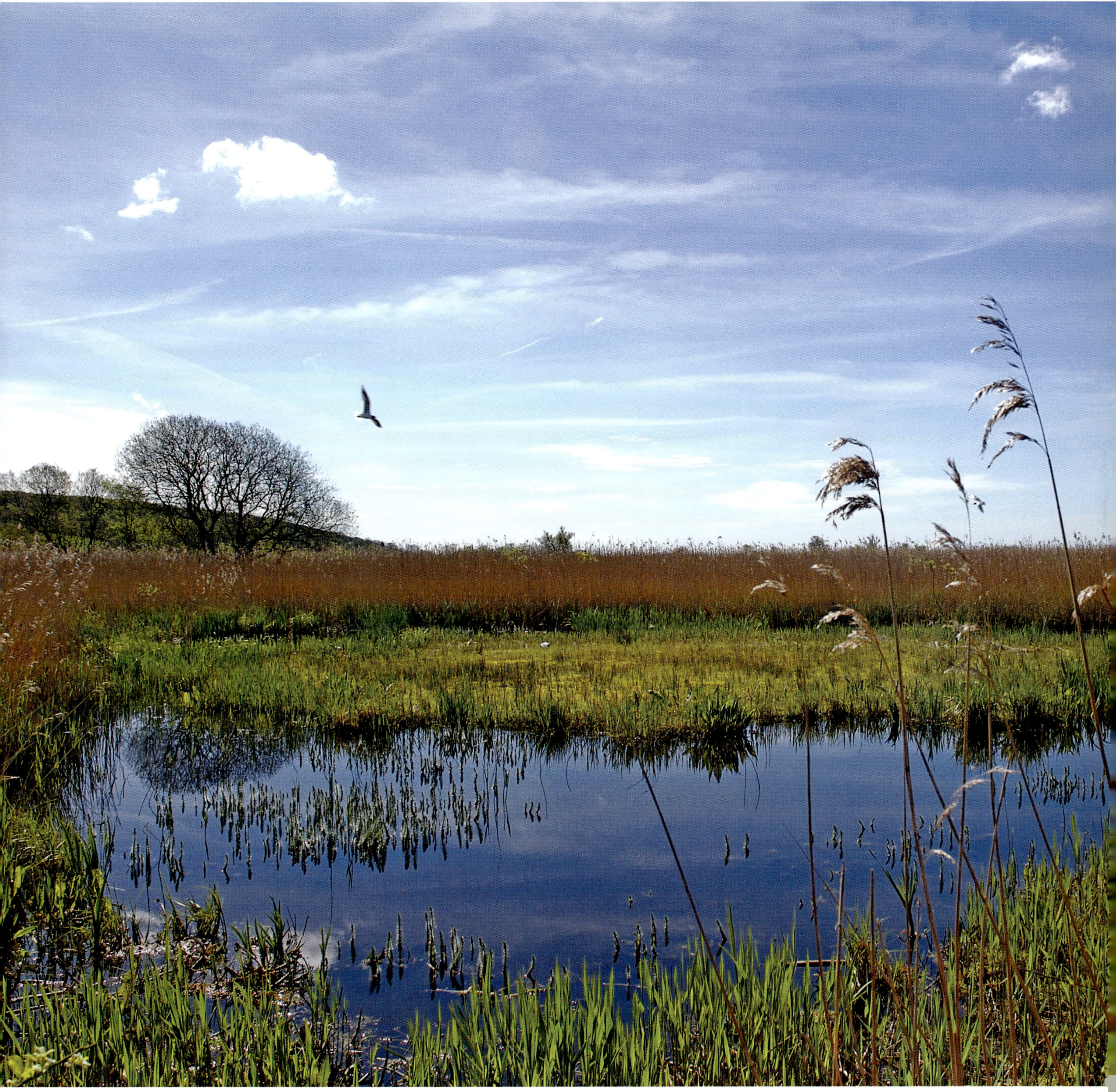

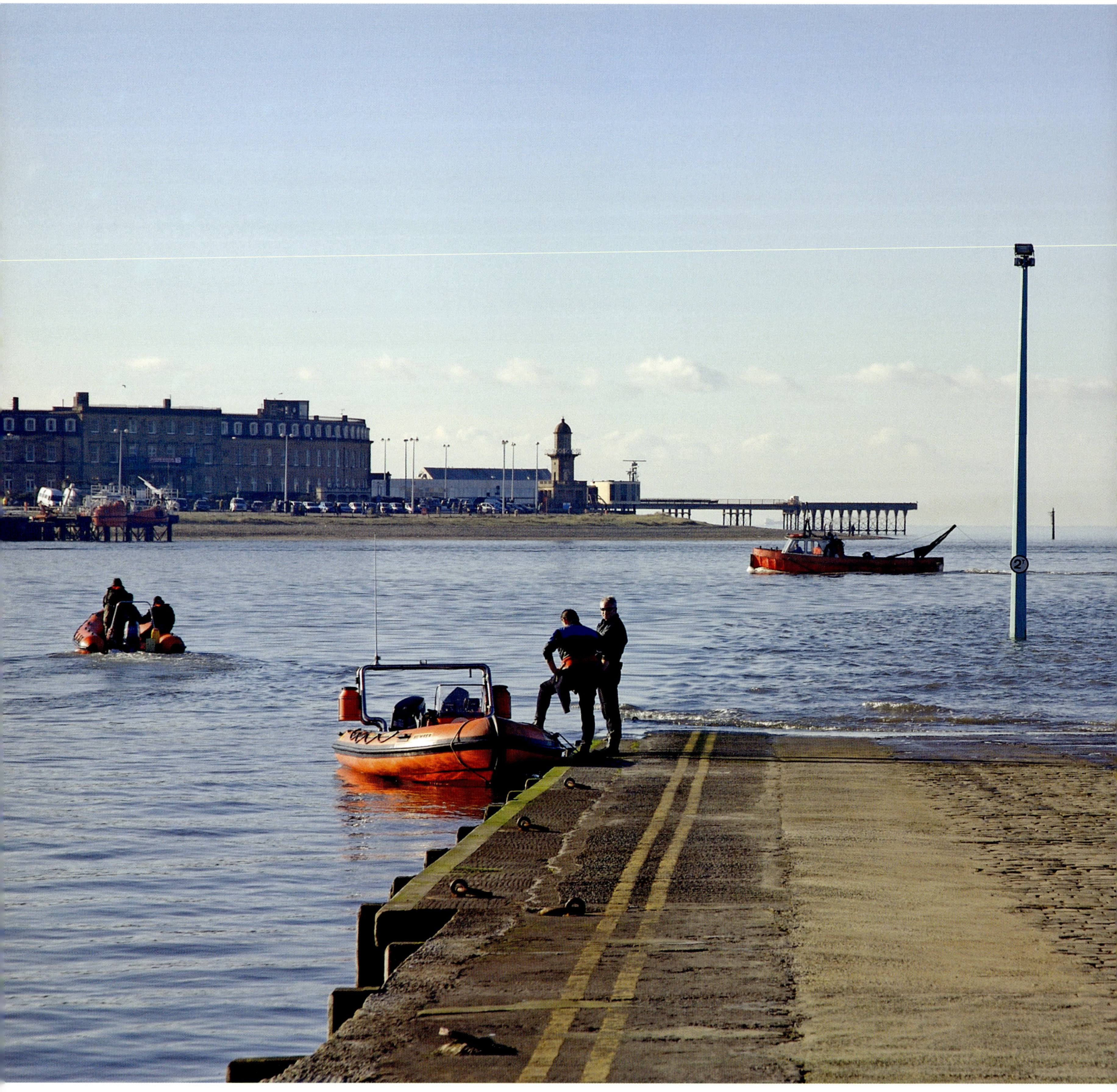

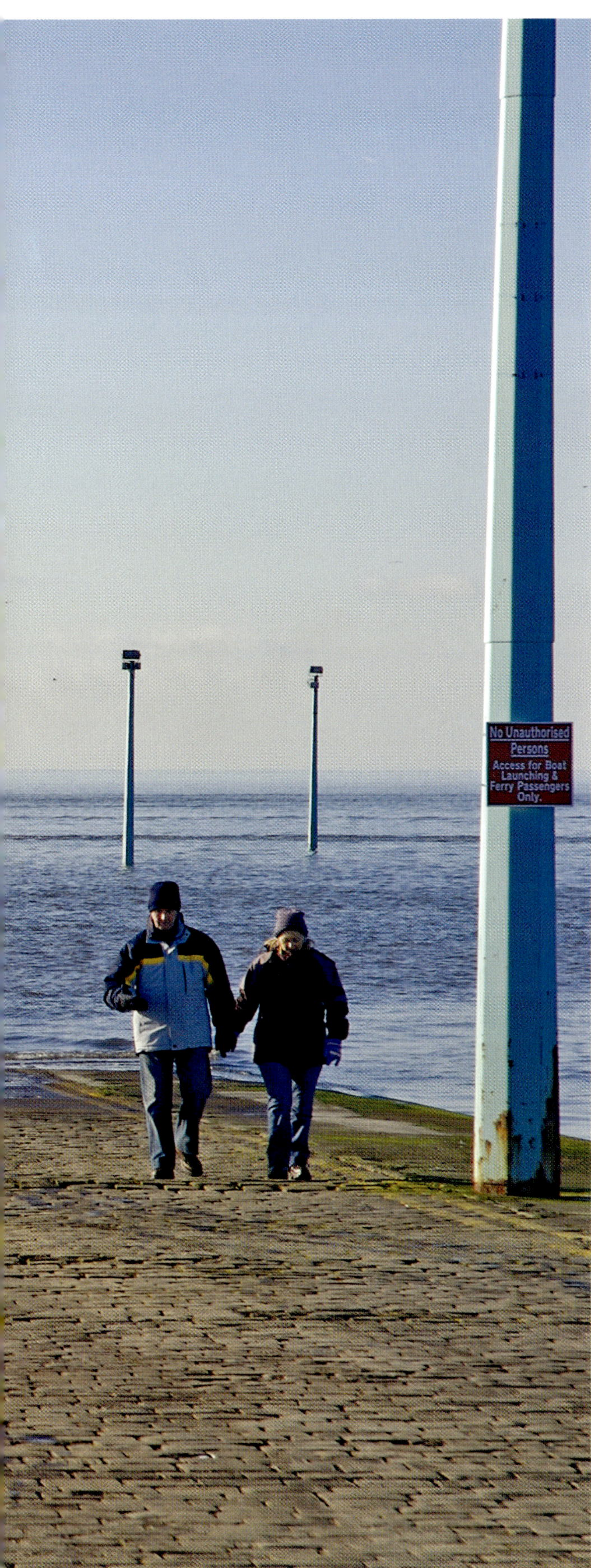

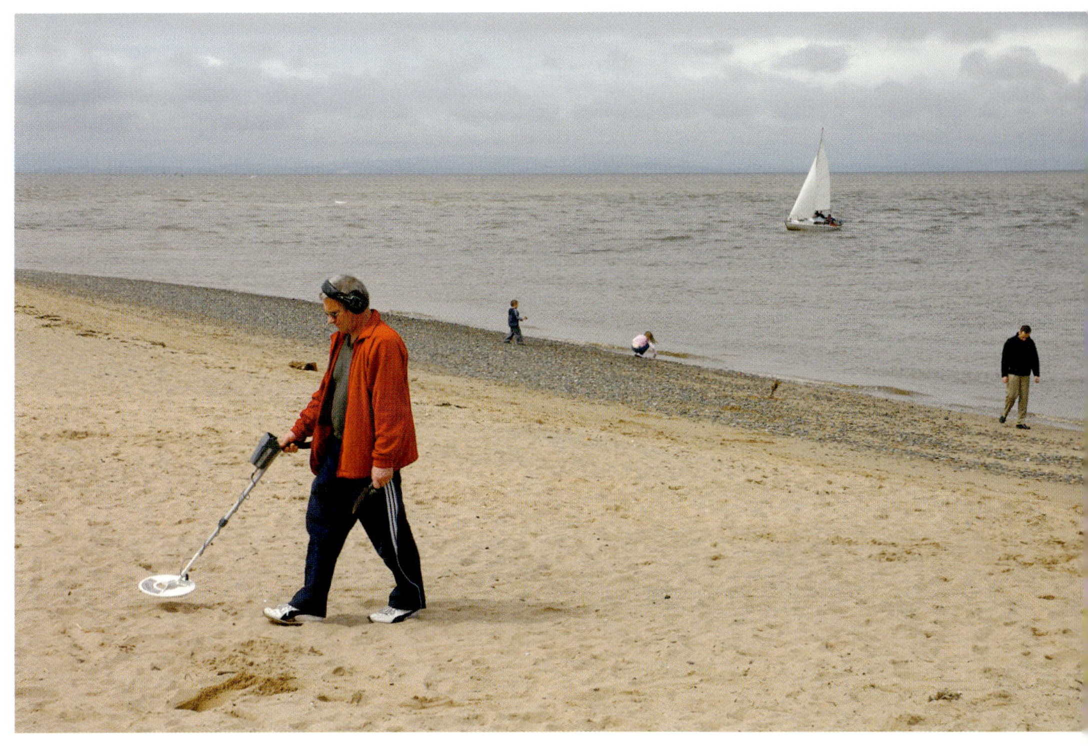



The slipway at Knott End, looking across the River Wyre to the port of
Fleetwood.


Fleetwood offers one of the few genuinely sandy beaches around
Morecambe Bay, ideal for metal detecting.

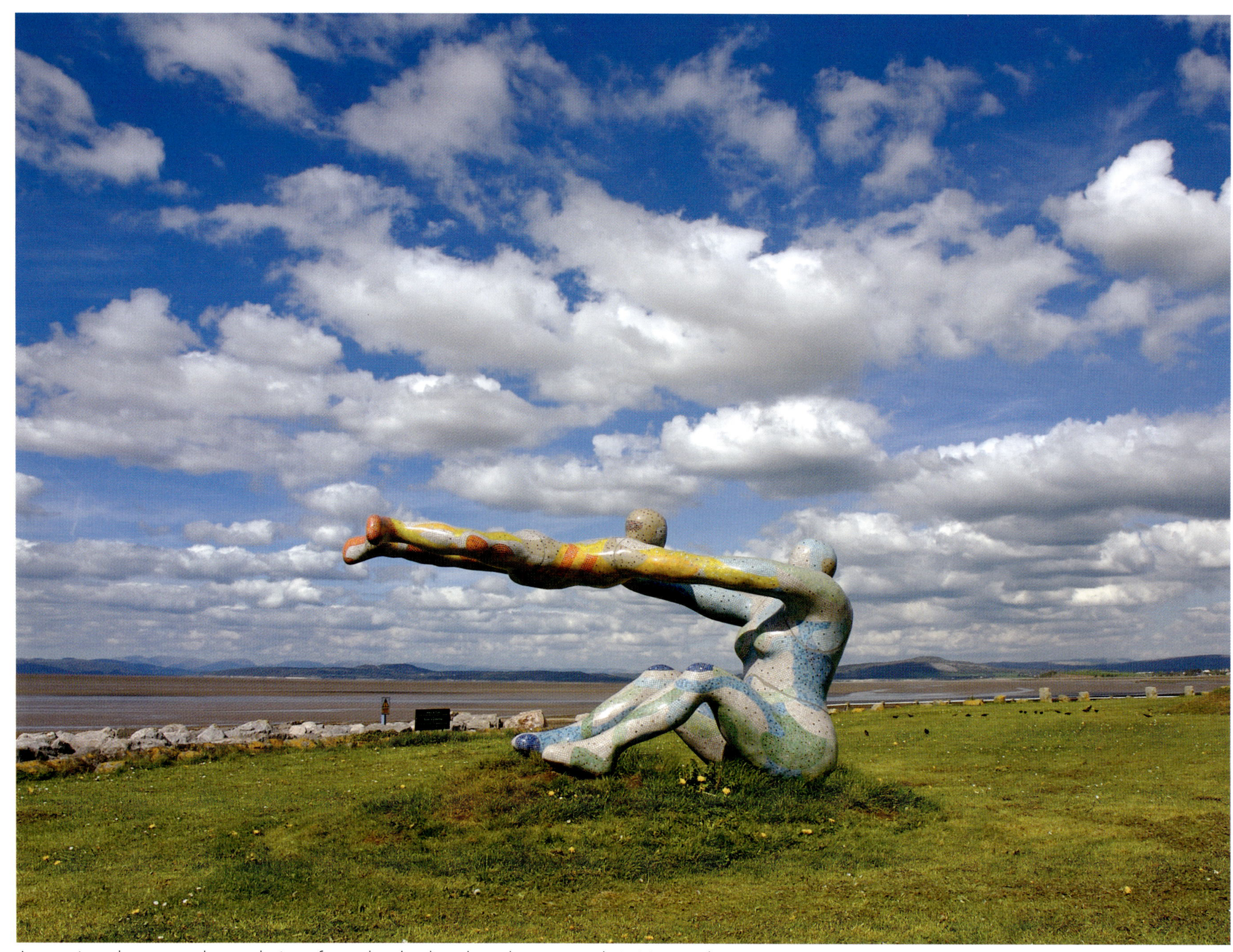

A ceramic sculpture – and an explosion of cumulus clouds – along the promenade in Morecambe.

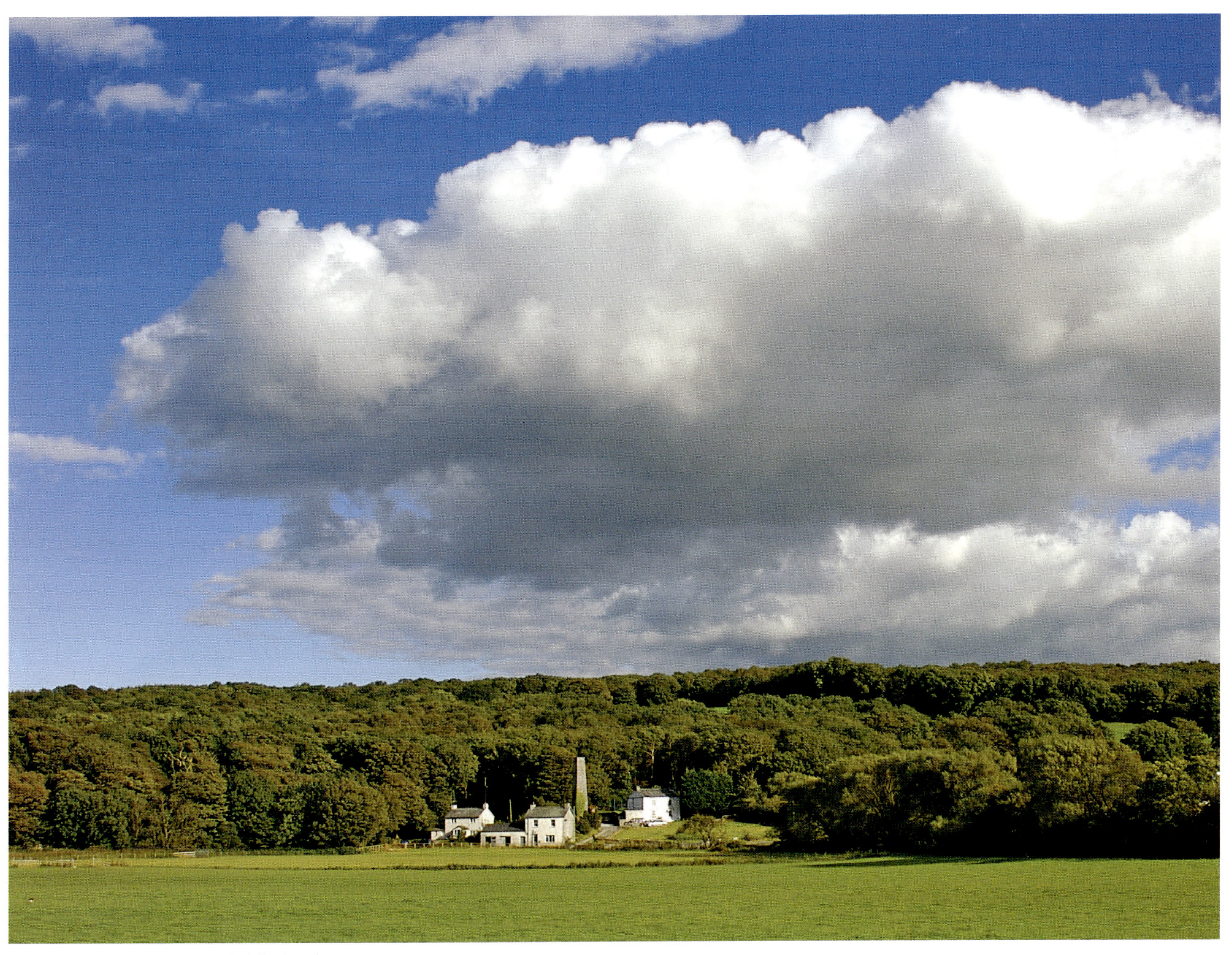

A cloud hovers over the wooded flanks of Warton Crag.

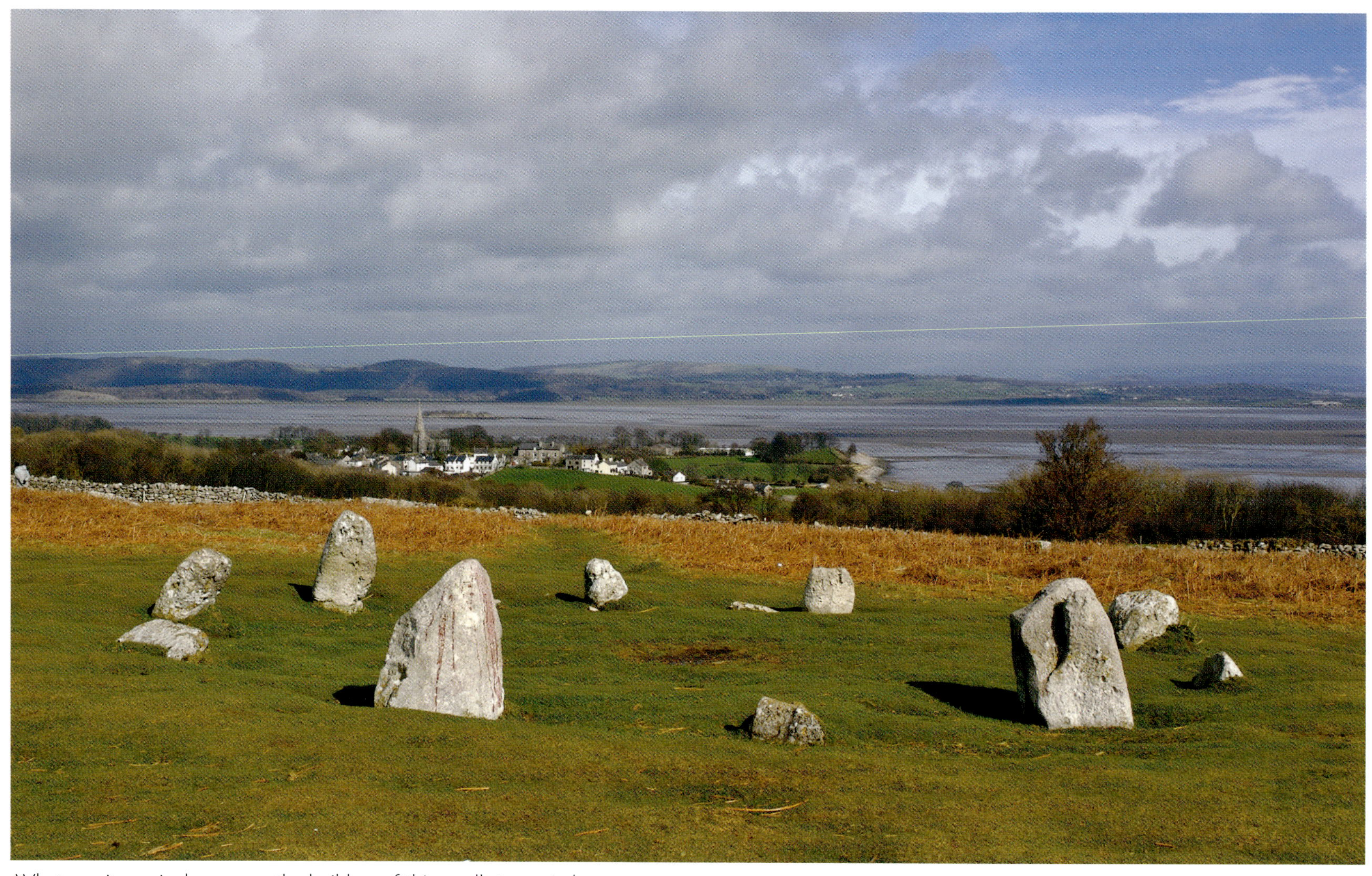

Whatever its orginal purpose, the builders of this small stone circle on
Birkrigg Common certainly picked an auspicious spot.


Waiting for the starter's signal to begin a circuit of the River Wyre near
Skippool Creek.

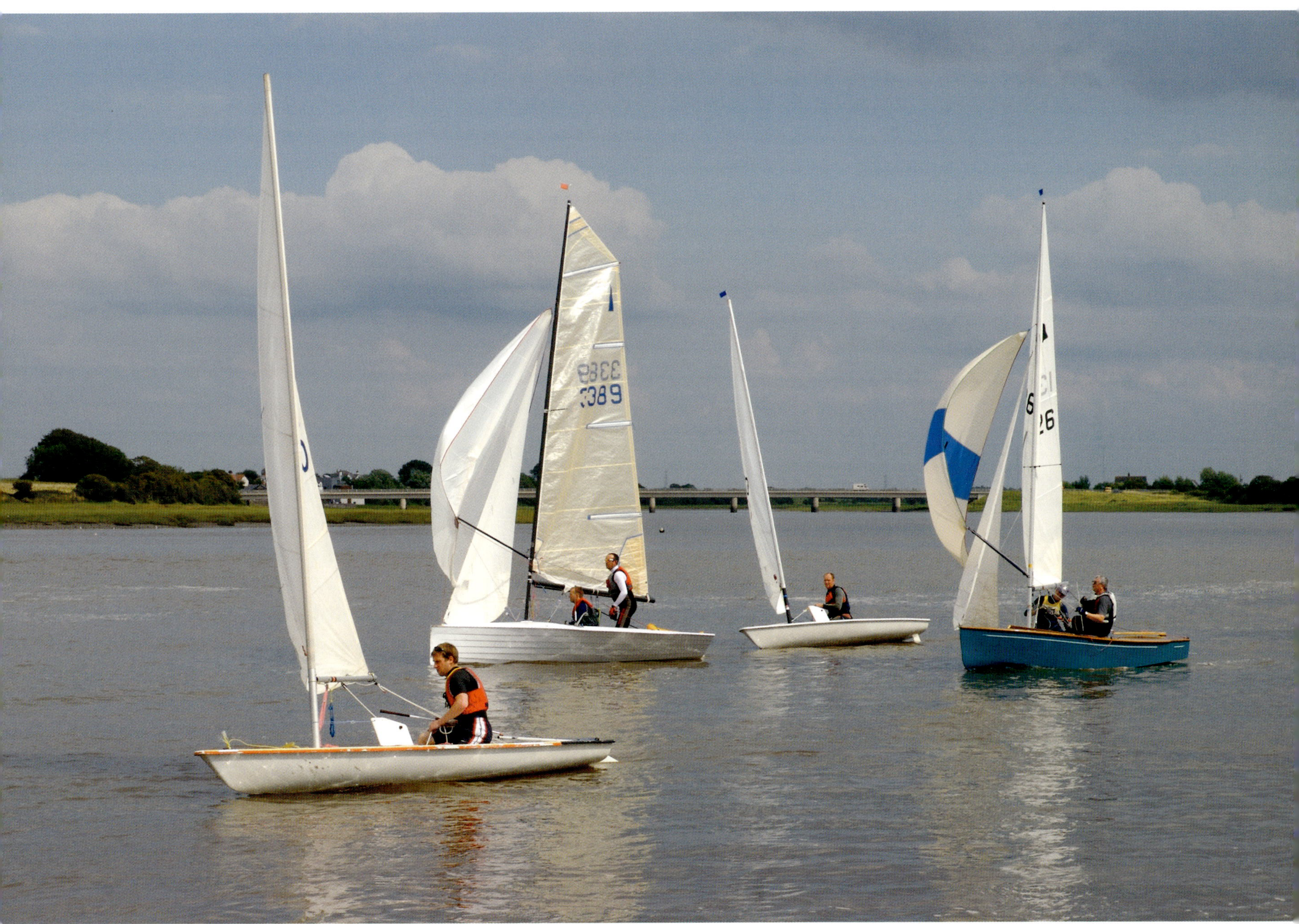

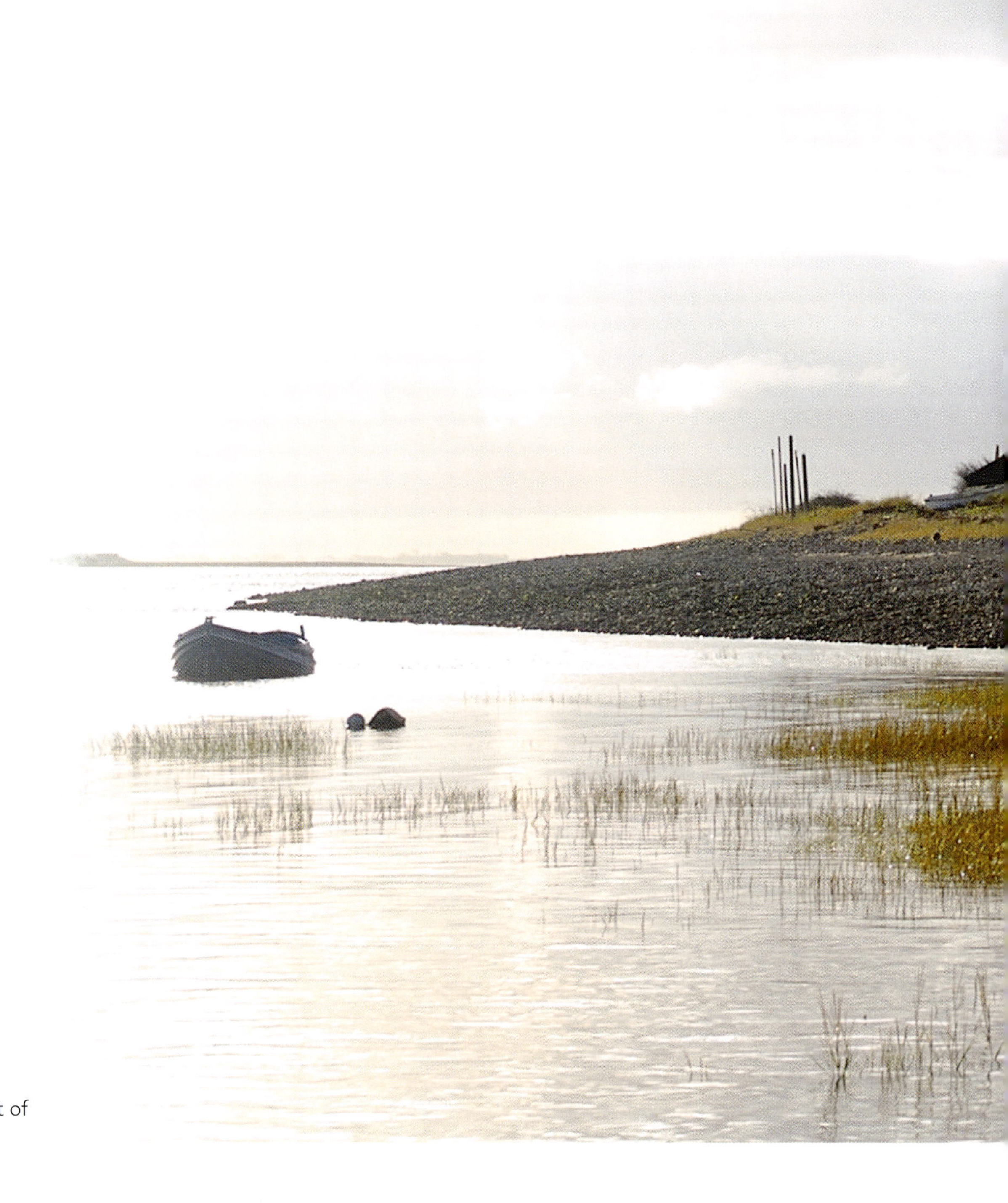

Muted colours, and a pale wash of a sky, give this shot of
Sunderland Point the look of a watercolour painting.

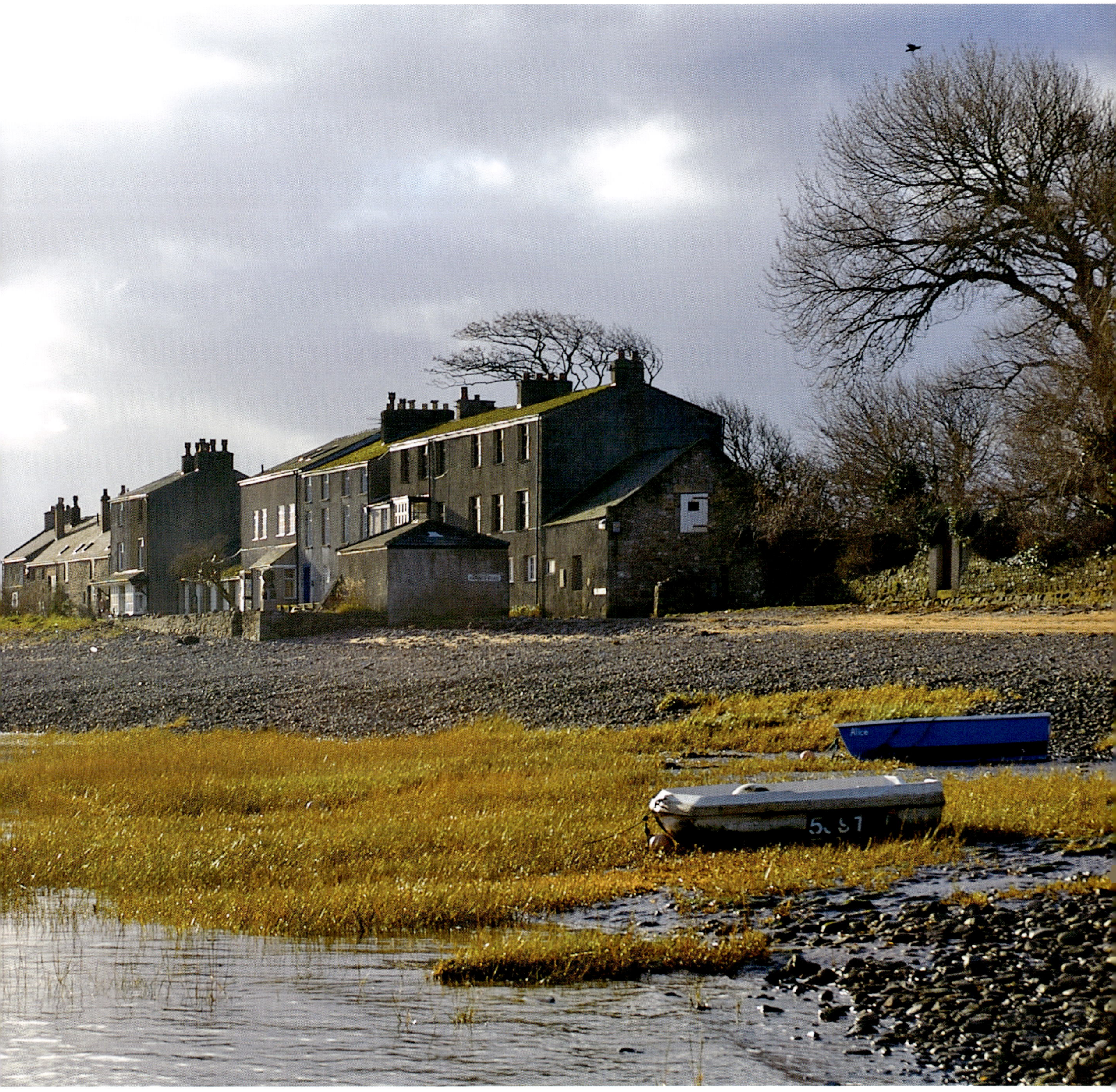

# THE CARTMEL PENINSULA

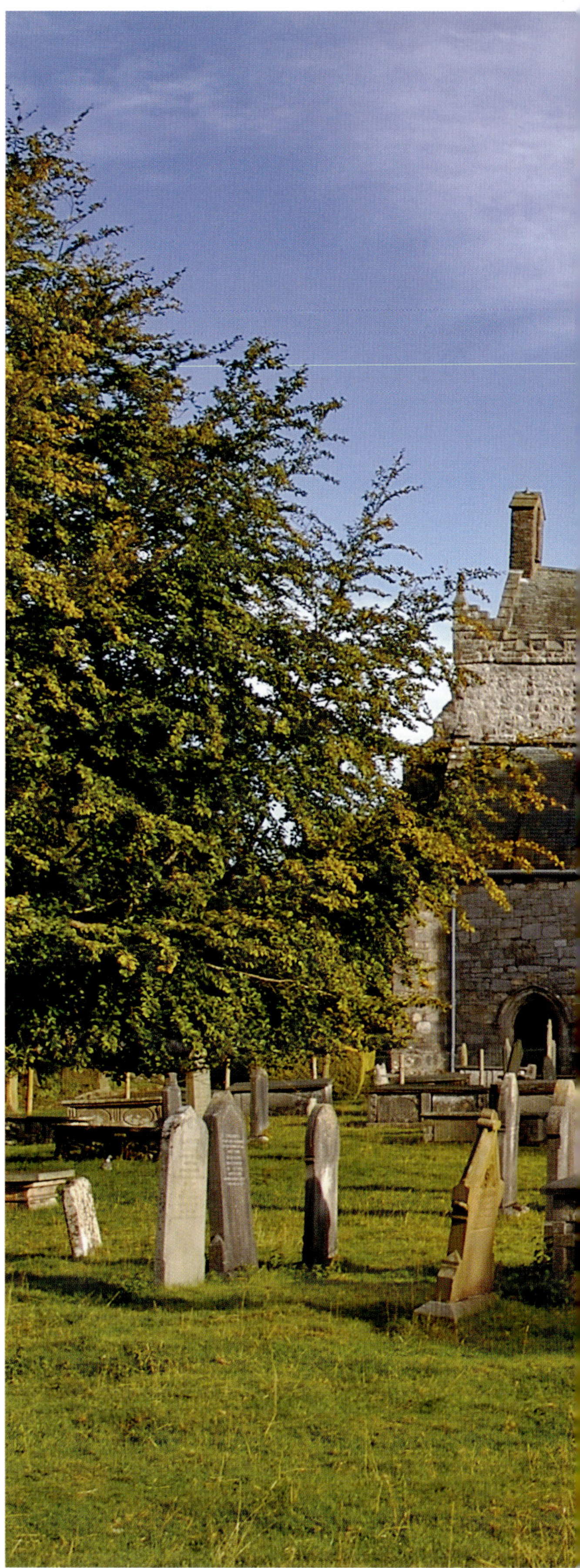

The Cartmel peninsula is bordered to the west by the estuary of the River Leven, and to the east by the sands of the Kent. Surrounded on three sides by water, this was, until the eighteenth century, one of the most isolated parts of the country. Today though, motorists can turn off the A590 at Haverthwaite (the southern terminus of the Lakeside–Haverthwaite railway), cross the River Leven and approach the extensive Holker estate.

Holker Hall, the seat of the Cavendish family for more than 200 years, dates back to the end of the sixteenth century. The hall that visitors come to see, however, is a Victorian rebuild in red sandstone. The formal gardens merge into parkland – grazed by fallow deer – which extend down to the sandy shores of the Leven estuary.

The long main street of Flookburgh used to be washed twice daily by the tides. It would have seen a lot of traffic too; wedged between the estuaries of the Kent and Leven, the community lay on the cross-sands route between Ulverston and Lancaster. Flookburgh was twice lost to the flames – fanned by Robert the Bruce and his men in the fourteenth century then in 1686, by accident. Between these events, Flookburgh was visited – twice – by the plague. Then, because of the silting up of Morecambe Bay, the village was marooned more than a mile from the sea.

Flookburgh people made their living from fishing the bay (and during the eighteenth century from smuggling). Nearby Cark – with a beck running through the middle, marked, tellingly, on the Ordnance Survey map as 'Mill Race' – relied instead on industry. There was a ship-building yard here and a large, water-powered cotton mill. The village pub, the Engine Inn, was named after the pumping engine, invented by James Watt, which once serviced the mill. Today Flookburgh and Cark are so close together that they're almost conjoined.

When visitors come this way today, it's usually to the village of Cartmel, though 'village' seems an inadequate term for a place that boasts a racecourse

Cartmel Priory, topped by its curiously offset tower.

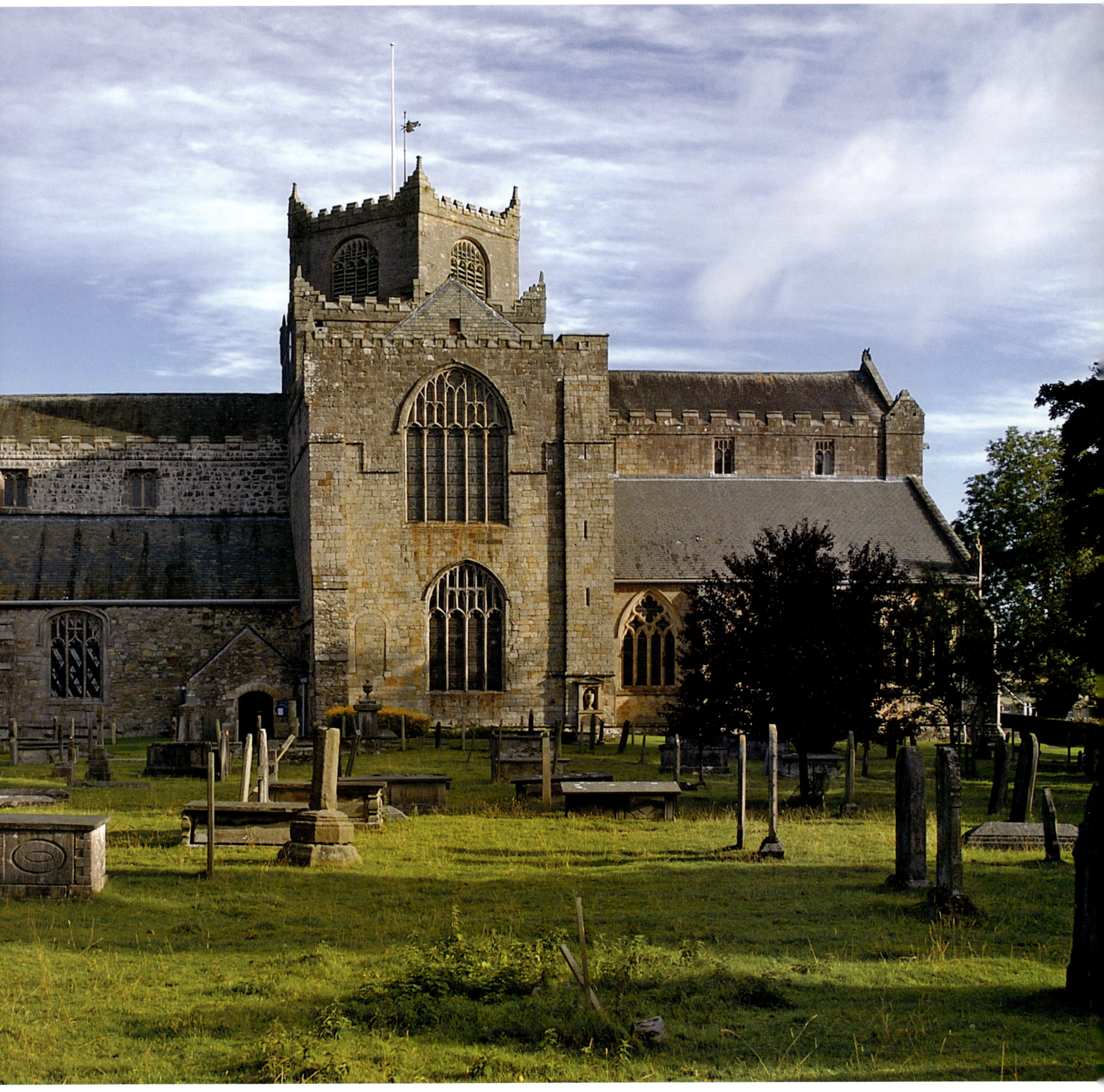

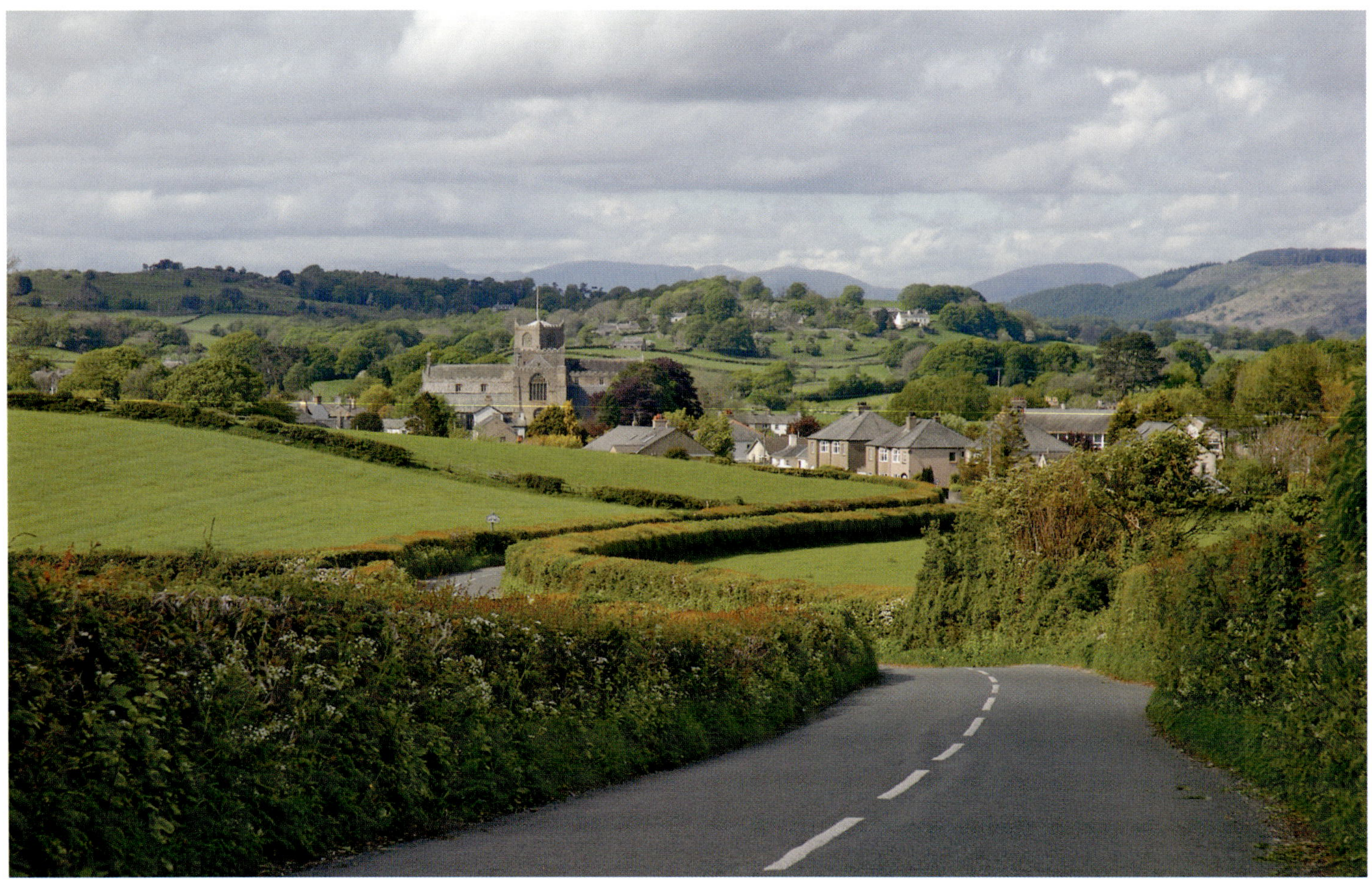

The priory rises head and shoulders above the village of Cartmel.

and one of our great churches. The church dominates the village square; even from a distance it stands head and shoulders above the houses of Cartmel. If it seems disproportiately large it's because the building is actually the chapel of Cartmel Priory, founded in 1190 by William Marshall. Life for the black-robed Augustinian monks of Cartmel continued in quiet contemplation until 1536, when, during the dissolution of the monasteries, ten of the monks were hanged. While most monasteries were destroyed, locals petitioned for the chapel of Cartmel Priory to be saved, pleading that this was their only place of worship. They got their way, though for many years the building was roofless and open to the elements.

A lot of cross-bay travellers made the short detour to pass through Cartmel – perhaps to give thanks for one safe crossing and to pray for the next. When the priory tower was extended, it was orientated at an angle of 45 degrees to its base: a design that's unique in England. The chapel saw use as a prison and grammar school before being restored to the way it looks today.

The chapel, and the gatehouse in the village square, are all that now remain of the original priory.

At the southern tip of the Cartmel peninsula is Humphrey Head, a windblown limestone promontory which sticks out into the bay. Years ago, people came here to 'take the waters' from a holy well, which was reckoned to be good for whatever ailed them. The lead miners of Alston in the North Pennines were so convinced by the water's curative powers that they made an annual pilgrimage, on horseback. On a coast almost bereft of cliffs, Humphrey Head, at a mere 160 feet, is a prominent landmark. This is where, according to legend, the last wolf in England was killed.

Old photographs reveal that ships used to dock at the pier of the Edwardian resort of Grange-over-Sands; until an ambitious sea-wall was built, high tides used to flood the main street too. These days, though, the sea keeps its distance, and where the boats used to dock is now a prairie of sheep-cropped spartina grass. Grange grew rapidly with the coming

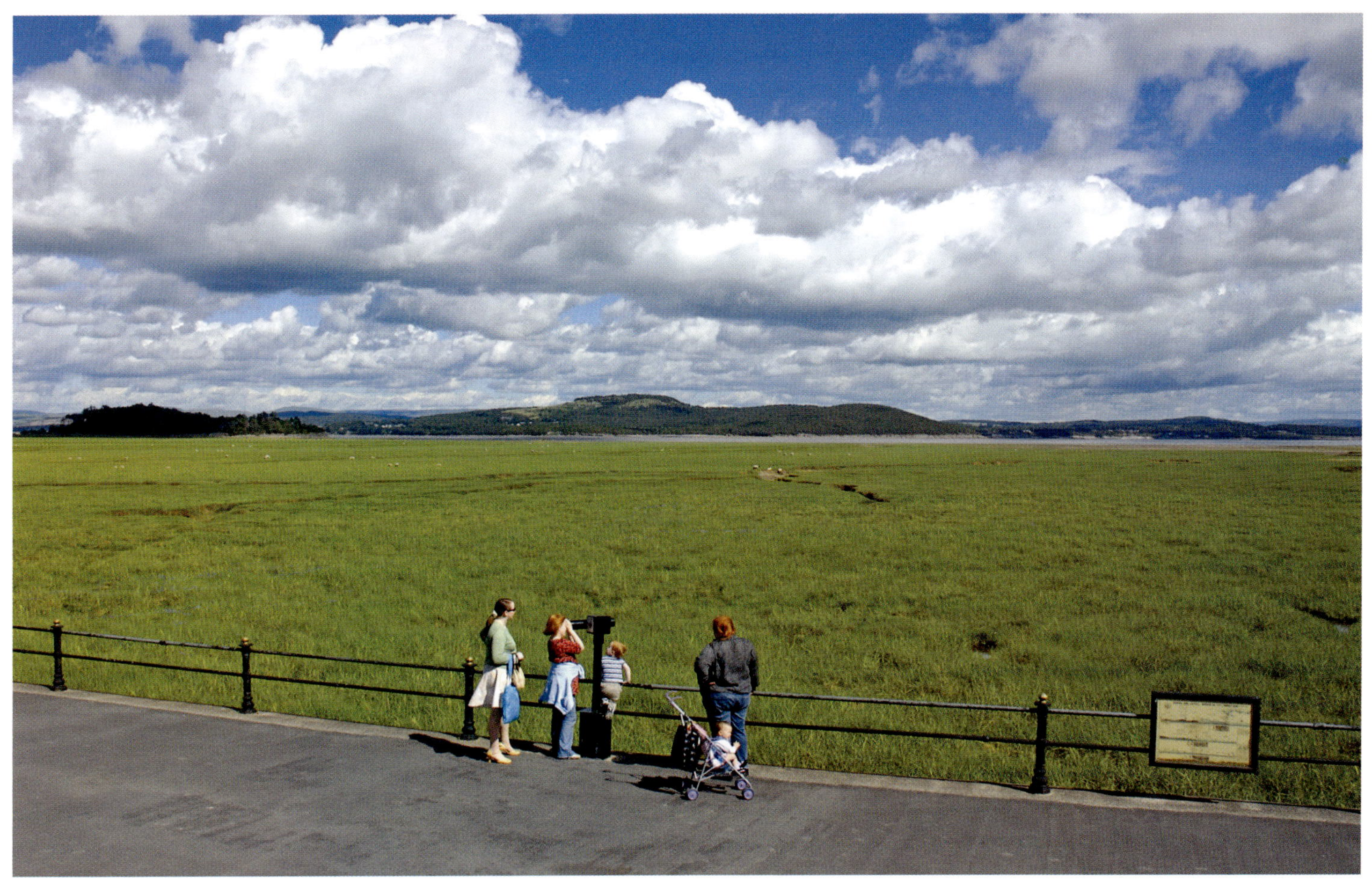

Hard to believe now, but boats used to dock at Grange-over-Sands. Then the river changed its course and the grass took over.

of the railway, and added the suffix 'over-Sands', to give this compact resort a more upmarket image. Unusually for Morecambe Bay, Grange is built on a hill, which forced the railway engineers to run the line between the town and the sea. A long promenade was built on the seaward side of the tracks to provide sea views, and a park created around a small lake and stocked with exotic wildfowl.

Grange is Cumbria's only south-facing resort and, thanks to the Gulf Stream, the climate is generally mild. The town grew as a prosperous and genteel resort, with hotels, hydros and sanatoriums being built to cater for holidaymakers and well-heeled hypochondriacs (some of these buildings, with views of the bay, have now been converted into old people's homes). One hotel was advertised as being 'on the South coast of Northern England', which neatly sums up the town's aspirations. When their working days were over, a lot of visitors decided to spend their retirement years here. A writer in the *Westmorland Gazette* summed up Grange's attractions in 1867:

'It is not fast nor boisterous nor overcrowded,' a description which still holds good today.

Overlooking the town is Hampsfell, a hill topped by an area of limestone pavement. At the highest point is a small square tower of a style that can be seen on many a hillside around the bay, known as Hampsfell Hospice. It was built in 1846 by the vicar of Cartmel, to provide shelter for travellers, and – for those who climb the stone steps – a viewing platform offering panoramic views across Morecambe Bay and beyond. On the top is an ingenious indicator which, when turned, identifies landmarks as distant as Snowdon and the Isle of Man.

FOLLOWING PAGE
Having made his fortune from oil-cloth and linoleum, Lancaster-born Lord Ashton wanted to honour his late wife. Inspired by the Taj Mahal, he created this grandiose limestone folly, which is such a landmark when seen from the M6 motorway.

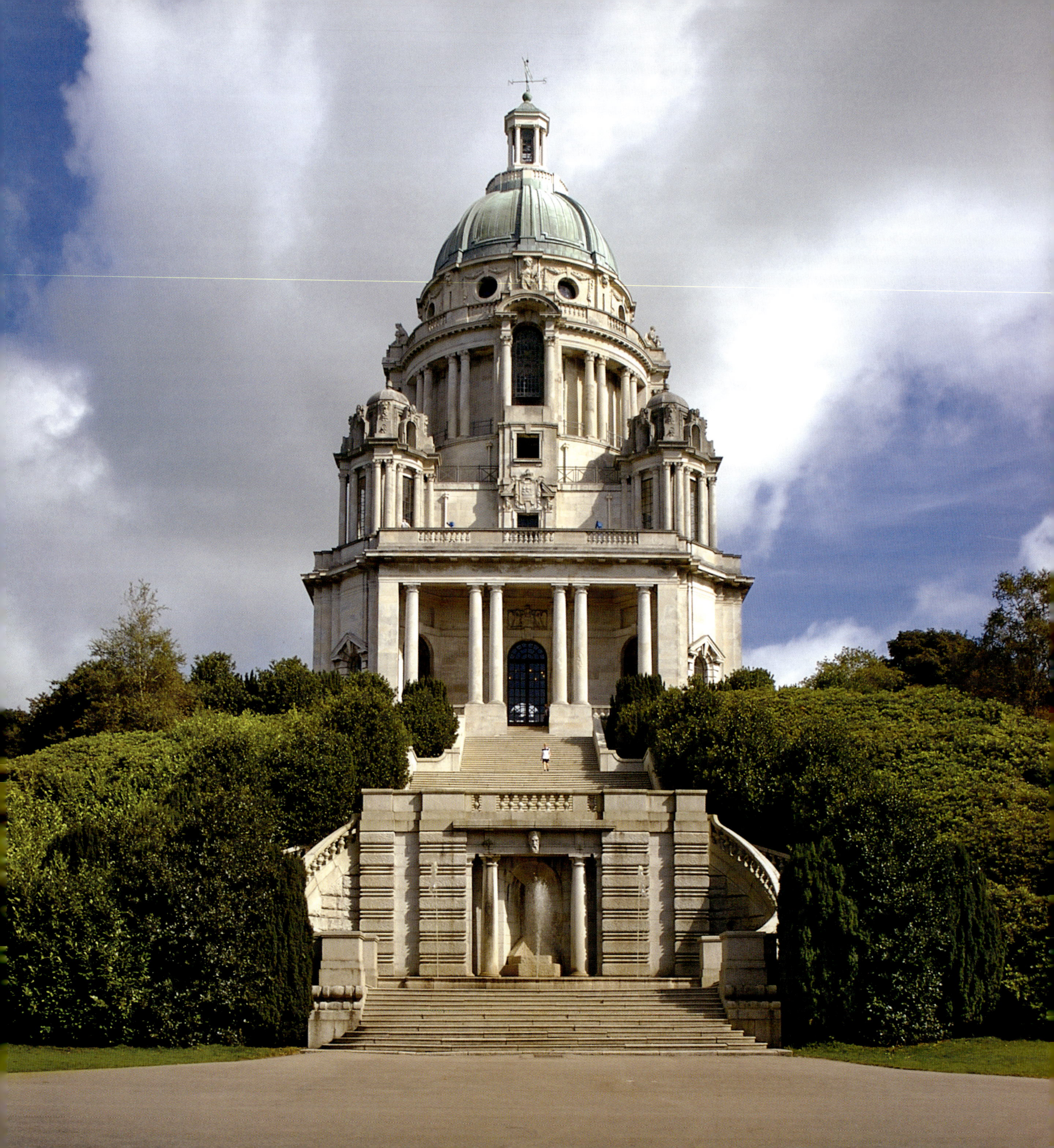

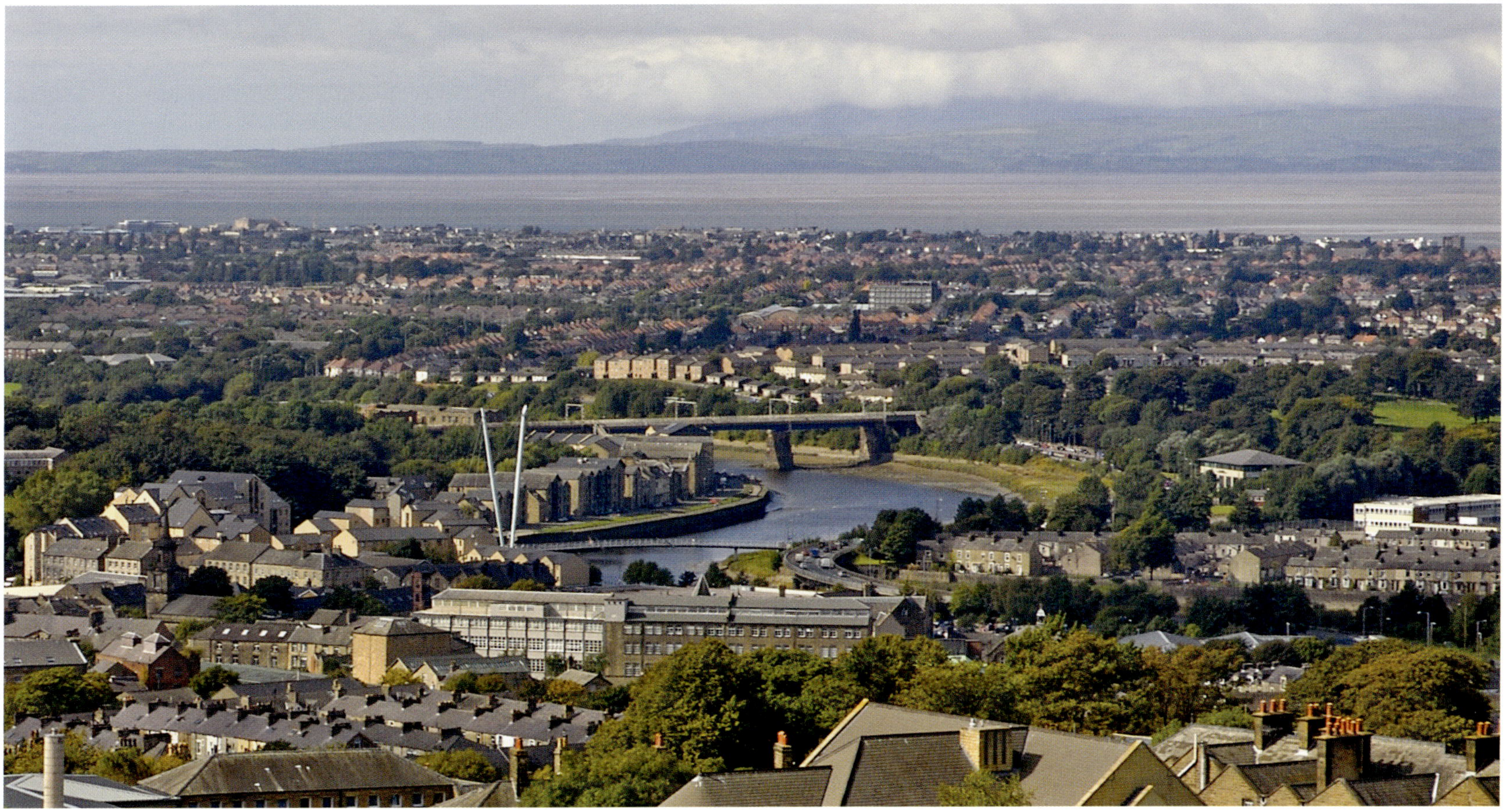

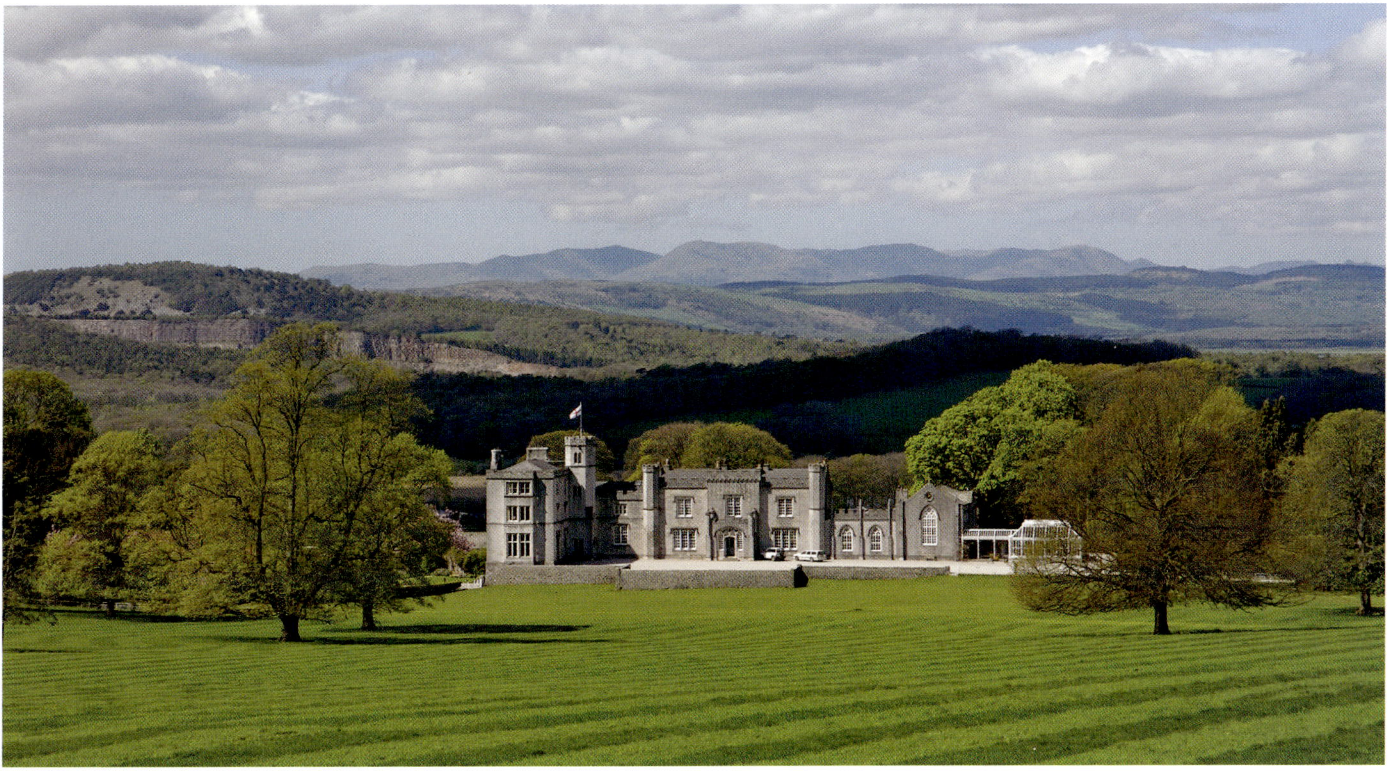

This view from the Ashton Memorial makes the climb worthwhile: the city of Lancaster, a bend in the River Lune and the sands of Morecambe Bay.

Leighton Hall, another confection of pale limestone – set in grassy parkland against the Lakeland hills.

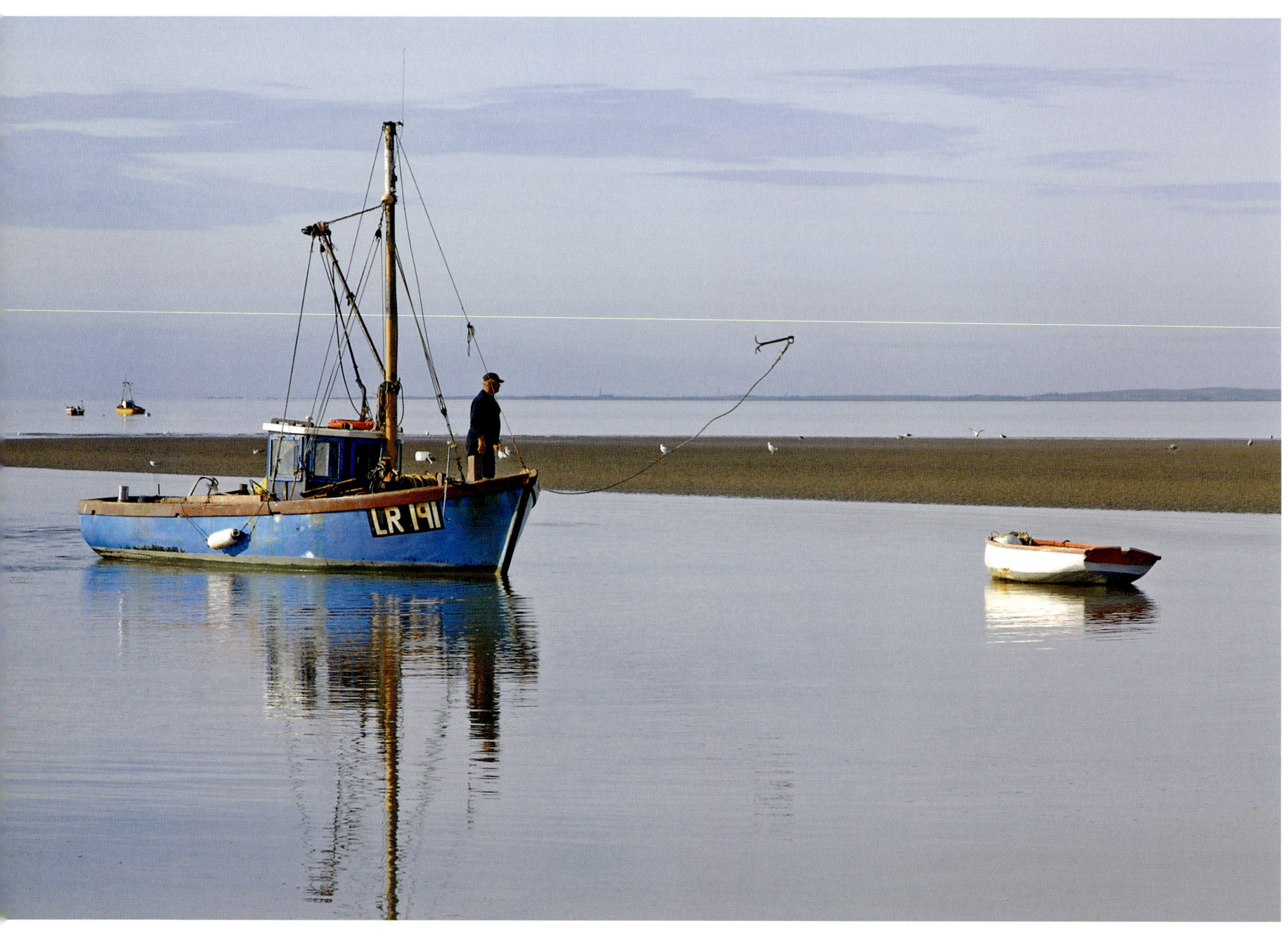

With no harbour to moor in, the fishermen of Morecambe have to use a
tender to get ashore.

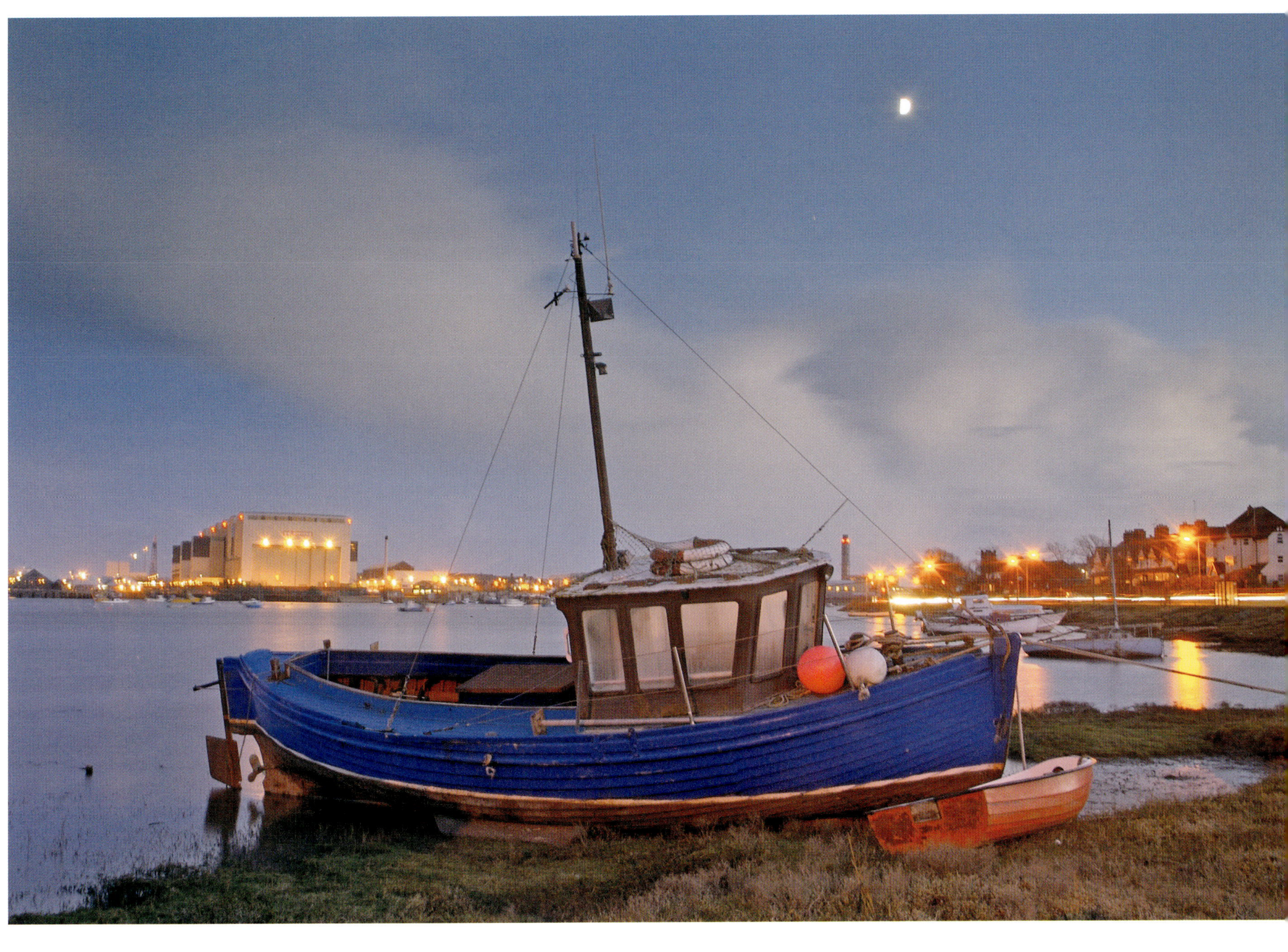

Barrow-in-Furness by moonlight – with the town to the left and Walney
Island to the right.

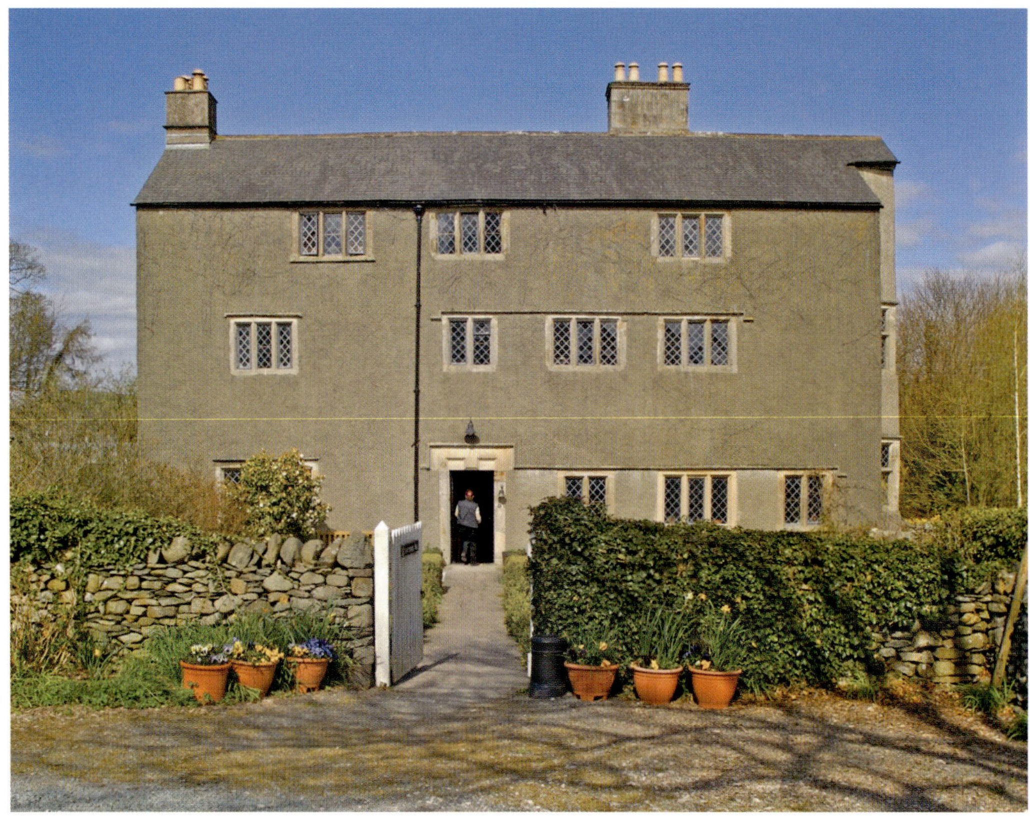

Swarthmoor Hall, near Ulverston: wilfully asymmetrical and far from beautiful.

RIGHT
For the last few years of his life, Swarthmoor Hall was the home of George Fox, founder of the Society of Friends, better known as the Quakers.

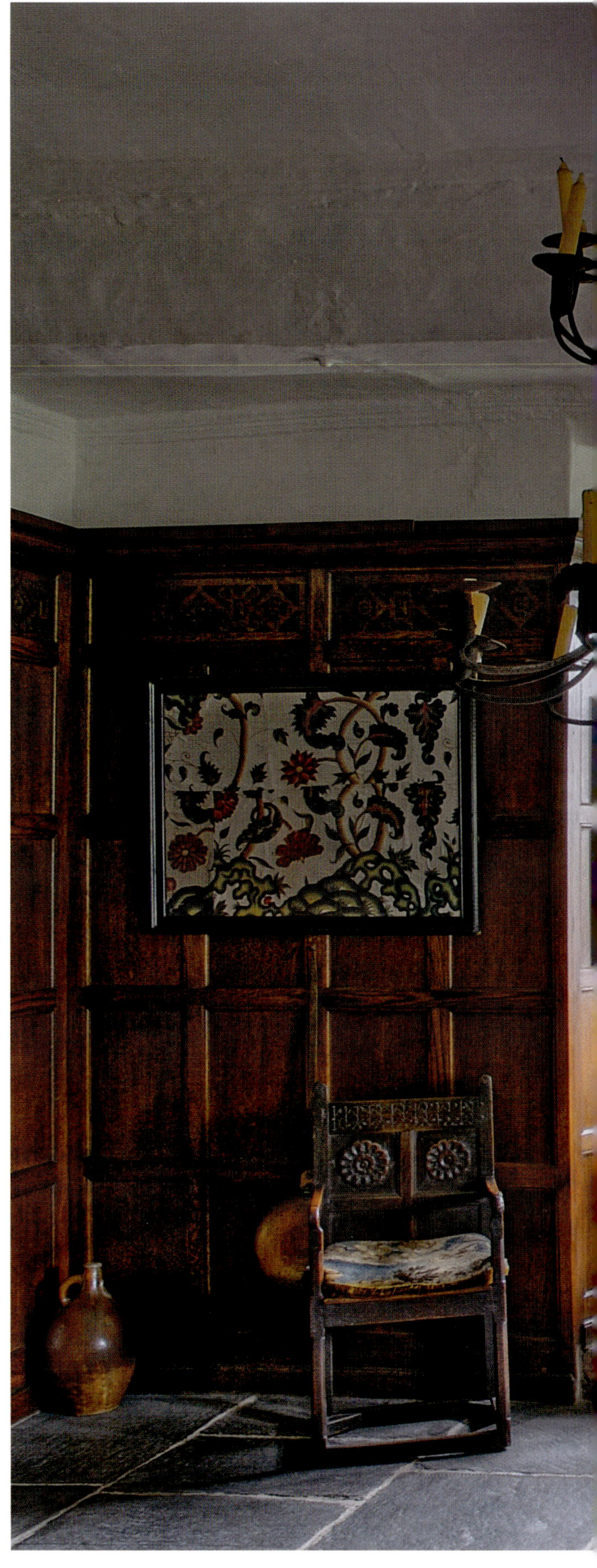

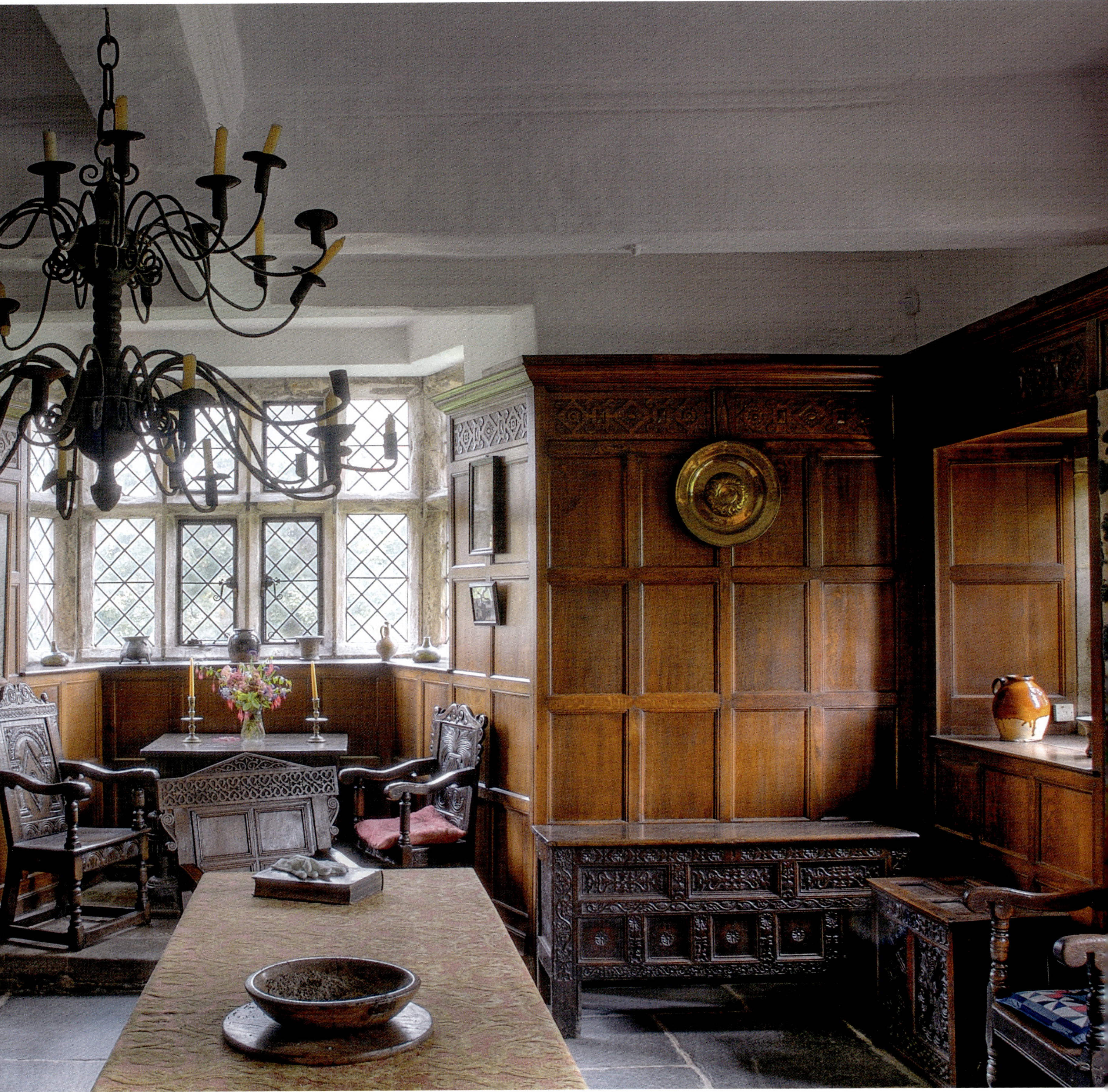

BELOW
Sea fishing from the rocky shore at Heysham,
next to the port's emasculated lighthouse.

RIGHT
Anglers trying their luck in the Kent estuary
near Arnside.

FOLLOWING PAGES
The light plays across Piel Channel, from the
vantage point of Roa Island.

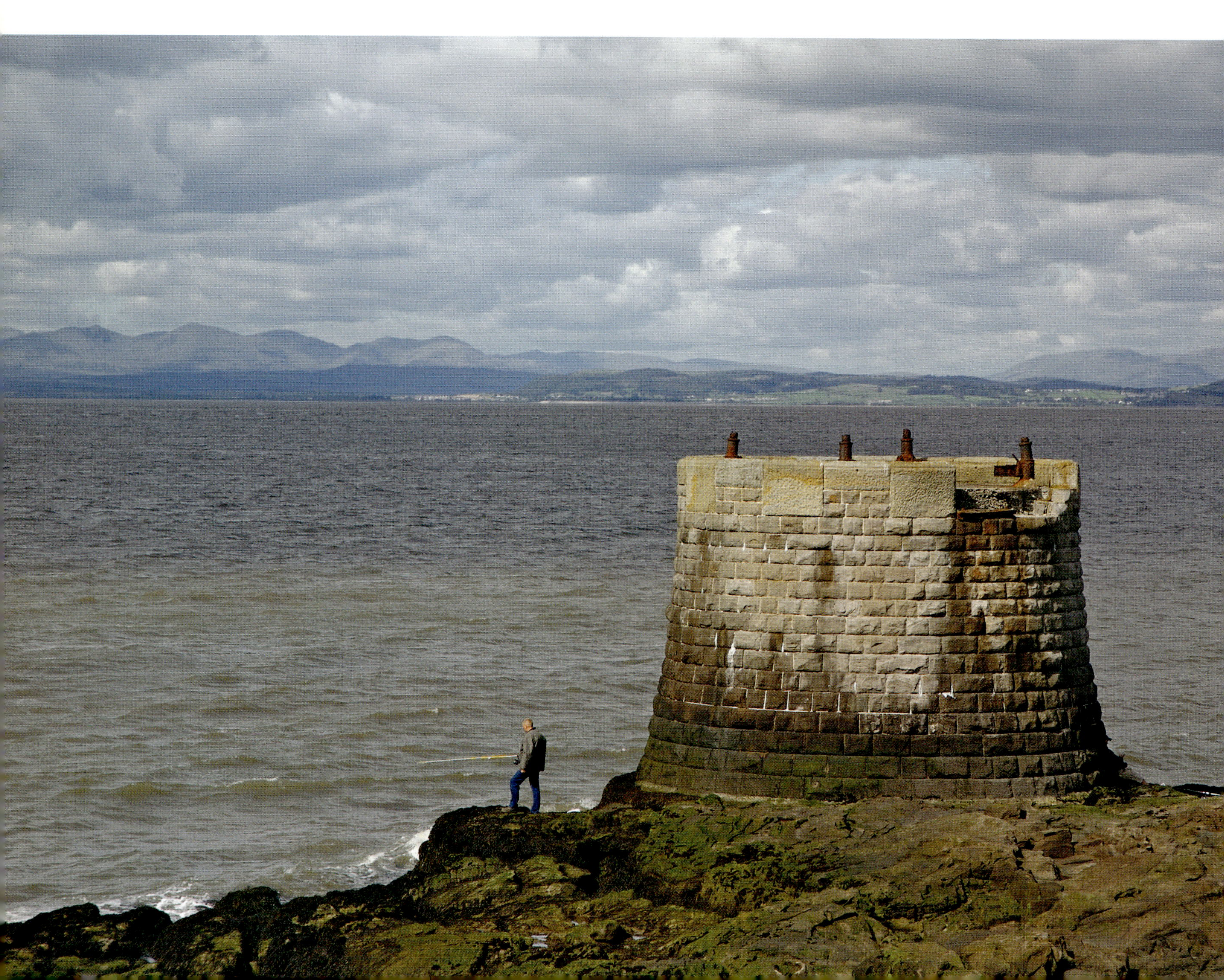

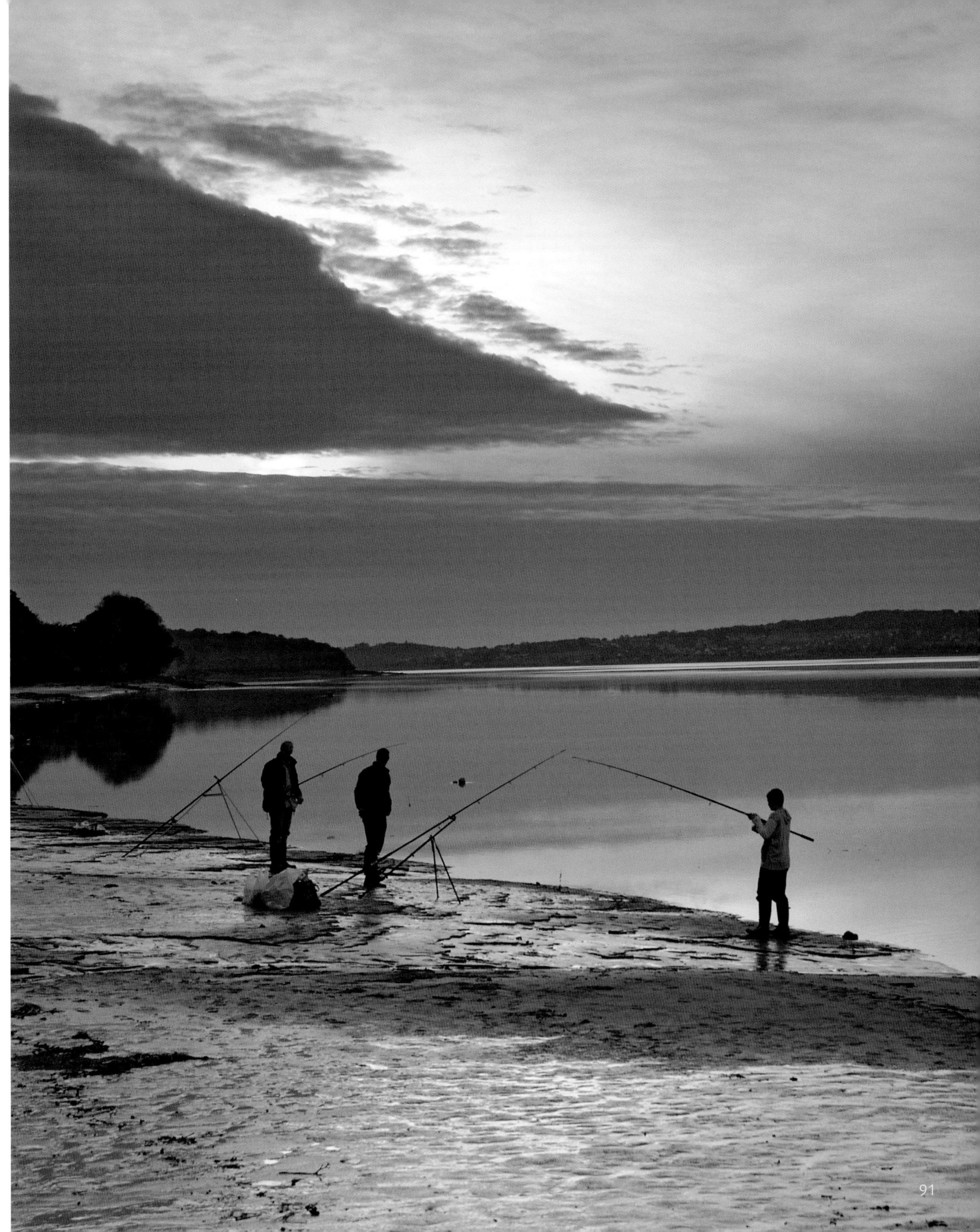

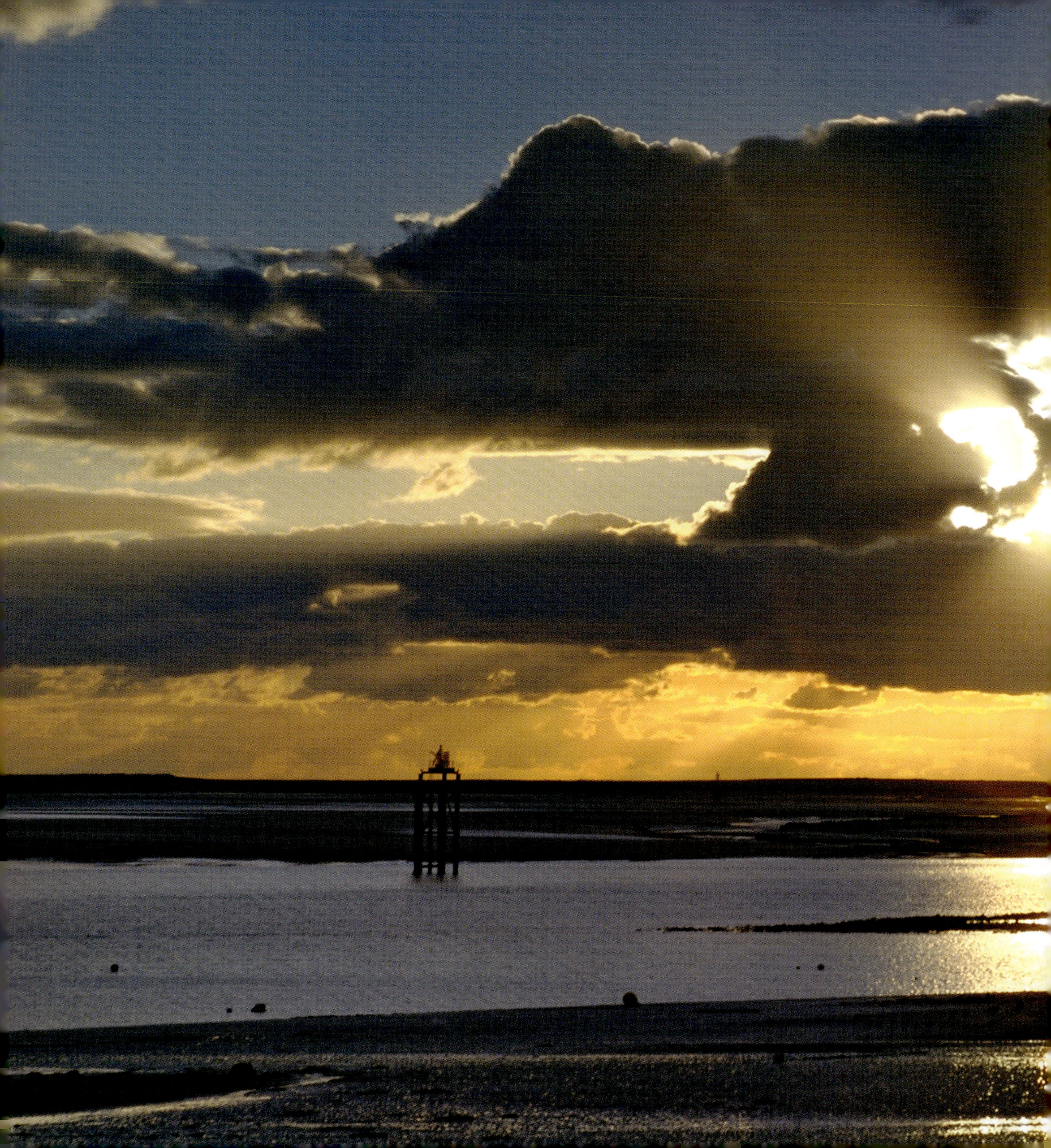

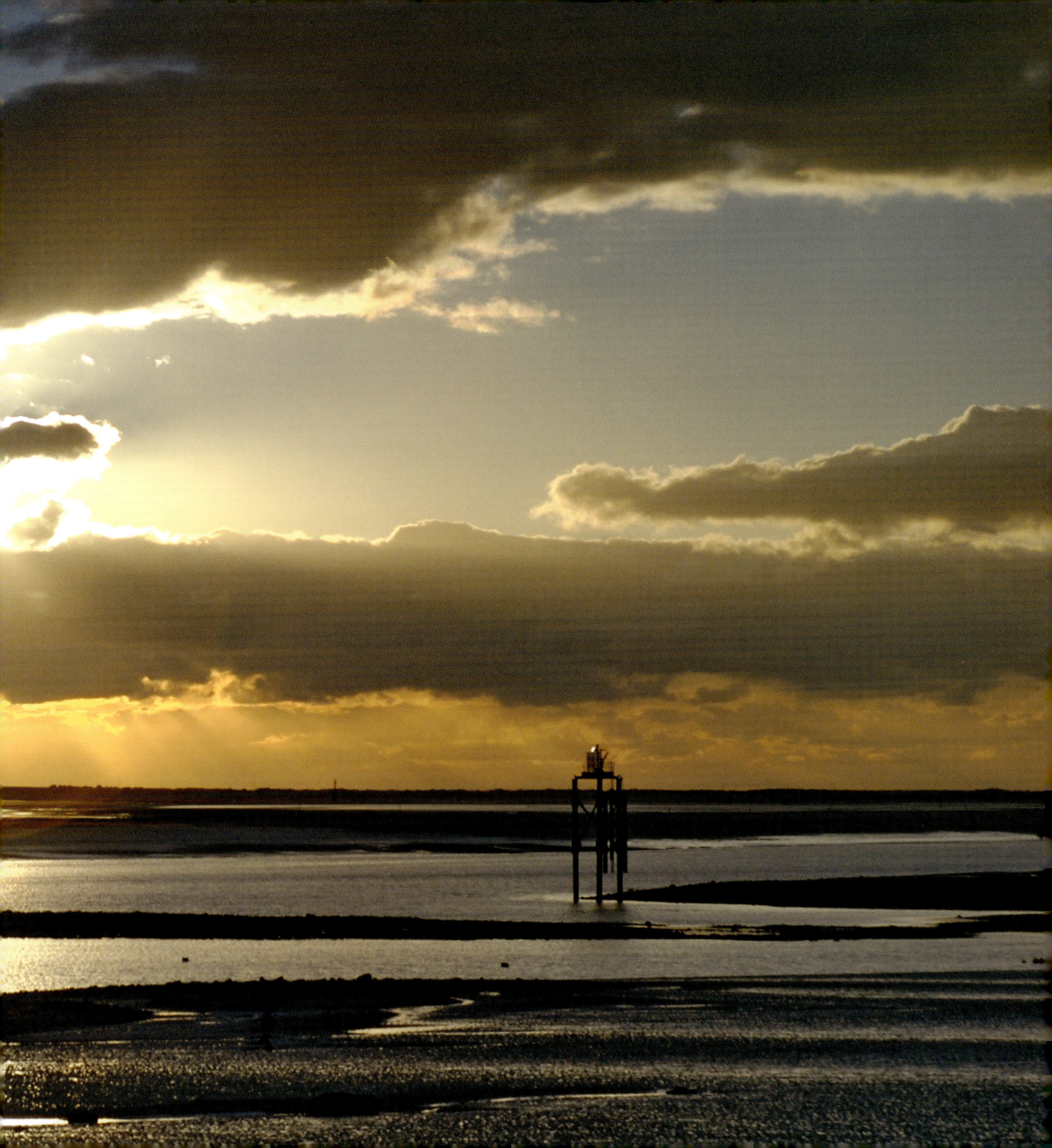

# KENT AND KEER

The Kent is one of the fastest-flowing rivers in England. Whenever it has changed course – as it has done at regular intervals, by carving a new channel through the sands – it has had a dramatic effect on the towns and villages clustered around its estuary.

The A6 crosses the River Kent at Levens Hall, a fine Elizabethan house which incorporates a fourteenth-century pele tower. As fine as the hall is, it's the formal garden that draws the crowds. The topiary in the Grade 1 listed garden is some of the oldest in the world, with yew trees primped and preened into a variety of remarkable shapes. The garden was designed (and tended for the last forty years of his life, until he died in 1730), by Guillaume Beaumont, who was responsible for designing a number of other gardens.

East of the Kent estuary, and west of the A6, are some of the most varied landscapes around the bay, and some of the best walking country too. Turn right at Milnthorpe and cross the River Bela to discover the countryside around the villages of Arnside and Silverdale – designated as an Area of Outstanding Natural Beauty. This is limestone country, with knuckles of rock pushing through sheep-cropped grass to form, in places, extensive limestone 'pavements'. Taking millions of years to form, these landscape features are literally irreplacable, which makes it all the more lamentable that they have been quarried for years to provide gardeners with decorative rocks. The limestone pavements which remain – mostly in the northern counties – are now thankfully protected.

The arrival of the railway transformed Arnside from a small village into a holiday resort, and effectively ended the need to cross the bay on foot. The railway company built a stone pier at Arnside to replace a previous wooden jetty, and the sand guides were compensated for their loss of business. A storm in the winter of 1977 changed the course of the River Kent, so it now runs closer to Arnside than to Grange. On some other stormy night, a few years hence, the course of the river will no doubt change again.

South of Silverdale is Jenny Brown's Point. Why Jenny Brown? Well, it was 1898 that Jenny Brown – just eighteen and 'fair of face' – fell in love with Adam Billings, a handsome lad and the son of a local fisherman. Jenny's father disapproved of the relationship; he decided his daughter could do better, and forbade the lovers to meet. Though Jenny and Adam planned to elope together, fate intervened.

Adam set sail one August day, in the hope of a good catch . . . but his boat never returned to harbour. Jenny was unconsolable. Every afternoon she kept a lonely vigil on the headland, gazing out to sea, hoping in vain to see her sweetheart again. Her lifeless body was found one winter's day on the point which now bears her name. Did she die of cold, or a broken heart? We'll never know . . .

Arnside Knott and Warton Crag rise out of the flat landscape, offering extensive views of the bay. To the south of Warton is one of the most-populated areas of Morecambe Bay. Carnforth means, simply, the 'ford of the Kerne,' an old name for the River Keer. Carnforth is followed by Bolton-le-Sands and Hest Bank (where passengers used to board horse-drawn coaches for the cross-sands trip) to form a ribbon development along the coast. At Hest Bank the Lancaster Canal is a mere stone's throw from

A train crosses the Kent estuary, seen from the viewpoint of Arnside Knott.

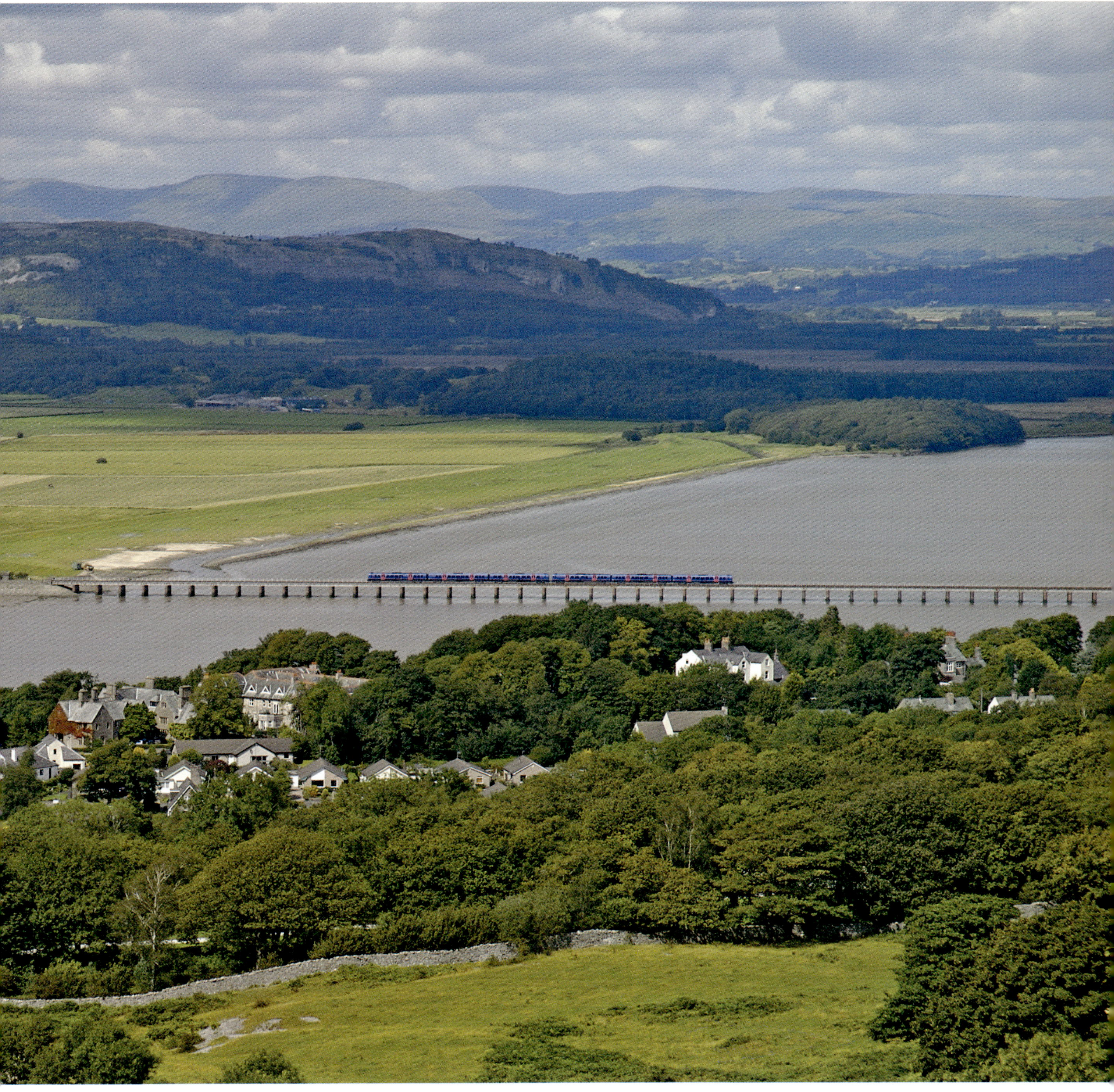

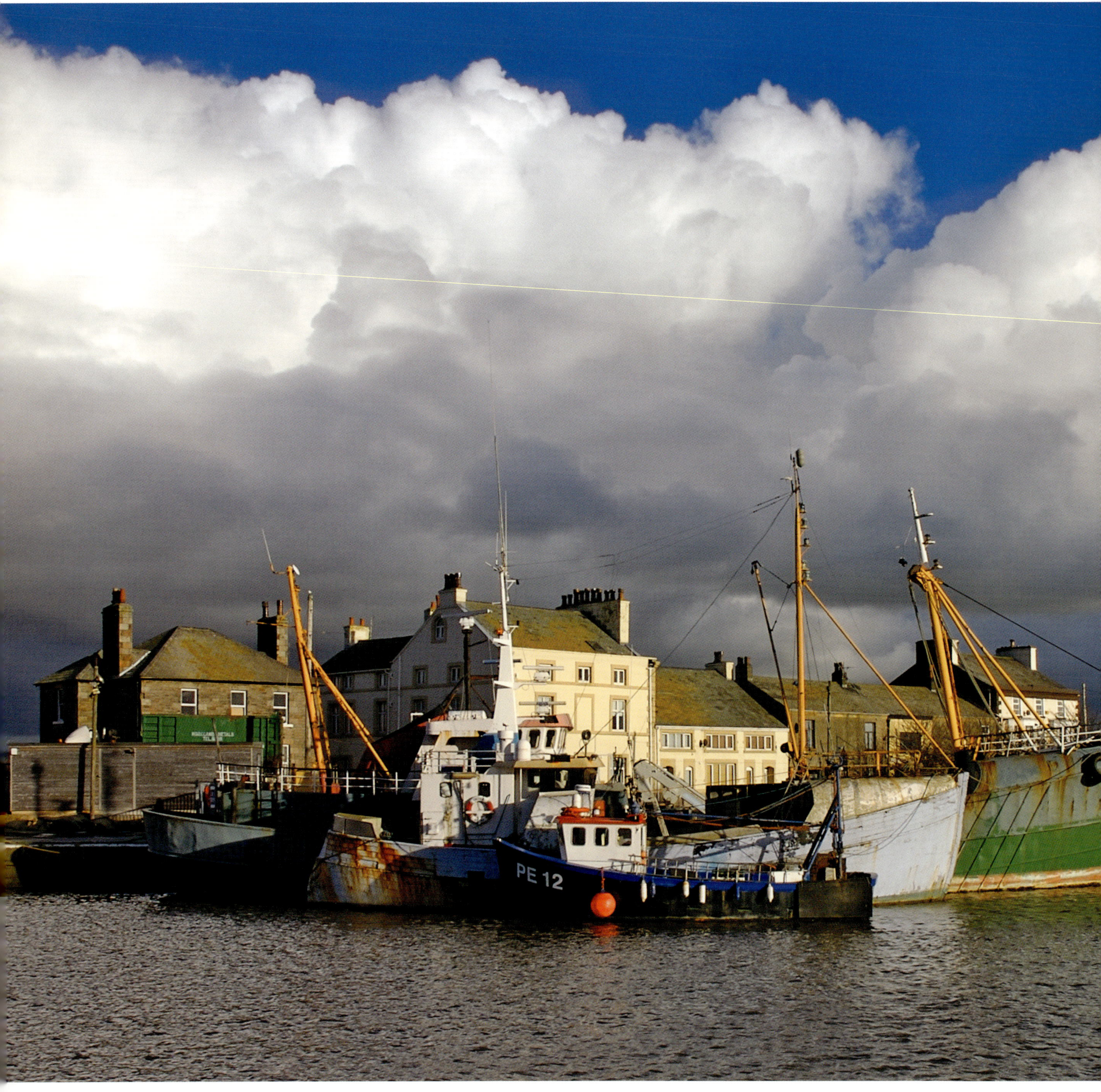
PE 12

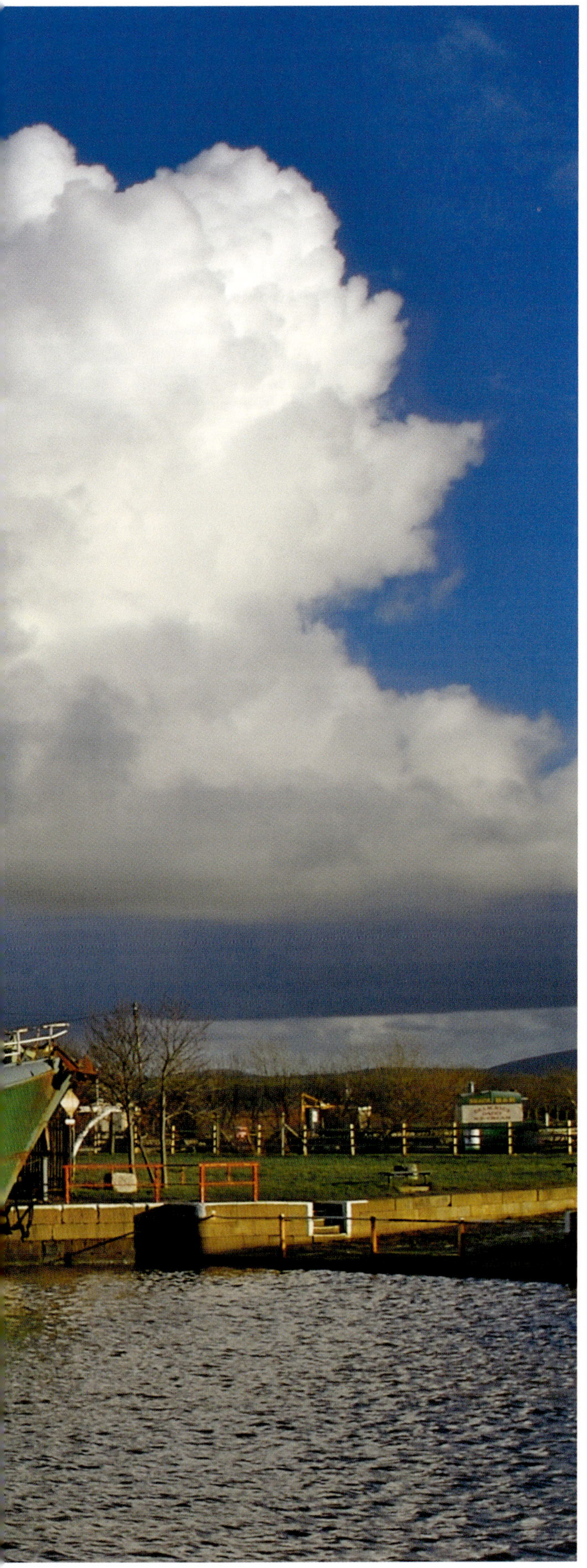

the sea, before it crosses the River Lune on an aquaduct and continues into the city of Lancaster.

The Lune has long been vital to Lancaster's prosperity. The Romans built a garrison here – where the Lune was navigable when the tide was in, and fordable when it was out. By the eighteenth century, Lancaster was a busy port whose riches were won from trade with the West Indies. It was the notorious three-way trade. Ships arrived at St George's Quay laden down with tobacco, sugar and rum; slaves brought from Africa filled the holds for the return voyage. It was a profitable trade too, attested by the fine buildings which line the quay and give the city a sense of prosperity and style. One of the city's mayors was a former slave captain. The Napoleonic War interrupted Lancaster's trade; when links were re-established after the war, it was the port of Liverpool which profited the most. Lancaster's story is told at the Maritime Museum, housed in the Custom House on the quay.

Despite the boom years, when Lancaster was reckoned to be the fourth-largest port in the country, the River Lune created as many problems as opportunities. With rocks in the Lune estuary limiting the size of the ships that could dock at the quay, other options were sought. The solution was found five miles down-river, with the construction of Glasson Dock: the first dock in England with retaining gates to ensure a constant water level, even at low tide. A ruler-straight spur of the Lancaster Canal was dug in 1826, widening to form a basin; and a railway link was established, hugging the River Lune between Glasson Dock and Lancaster.

After a few profitable years, Glasson Dock declined in importance. Trains stopped running, too, and barges no longer plied the canal. The Glasson Dock of today is a place of recreation: one of the many places around Morecambe Bay where people can enjoy messing about in boats.

Lancaster and Morecambe are the odd couple of West Lancashire towns: so close together that they've almost merged into one, yet separated by the River Lune and their contrasting tourism strategies. Morecambe tells a 'rags to riches and back to rags' tale.

The name of the bay came first: 'mwr', meaning 'great' and 'cwm' meaning a bow-shaped valley, both words from the Celtic. Morecambe's origins were as the

Glasson Dock, built to take bigger ships than were able to dock at Lancaster Quays.

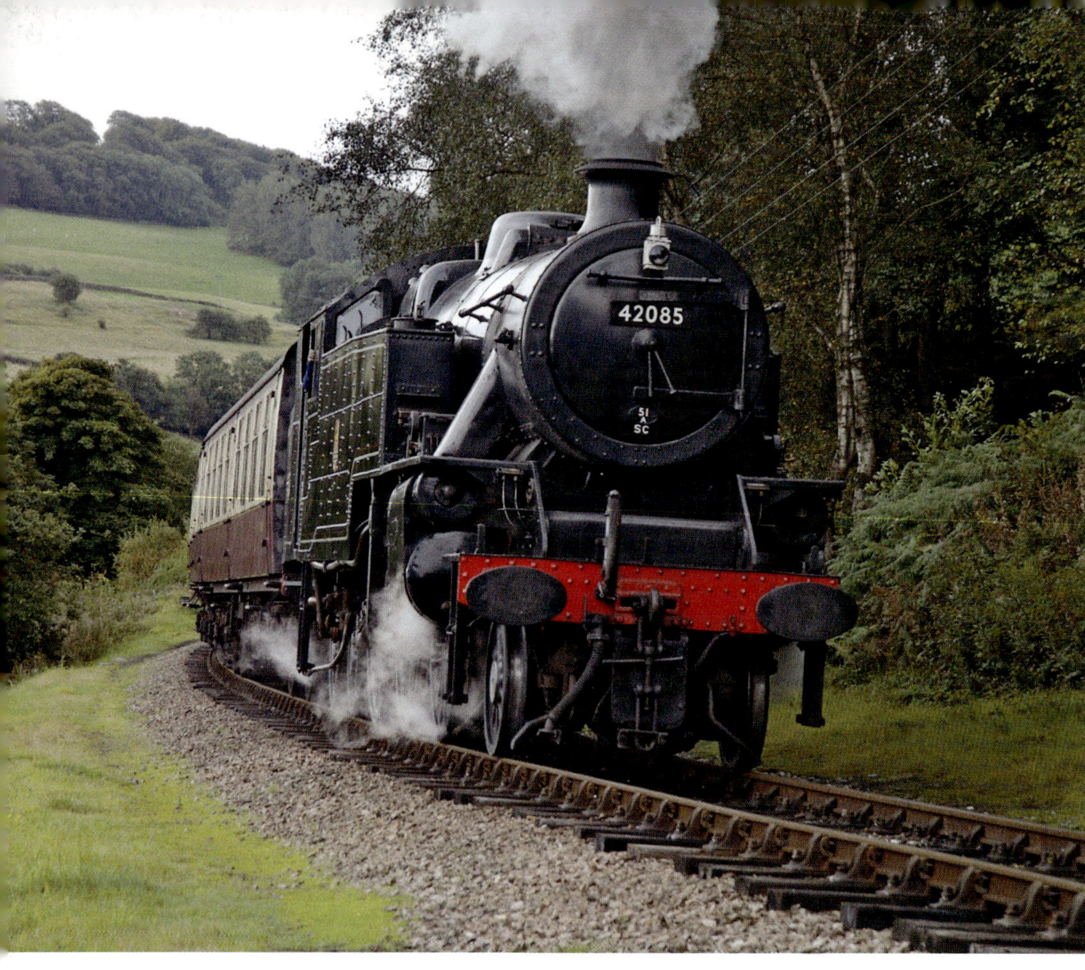



LEFT

A steam-hauled train rounds a bend on the Lakeside-Haverthwaite Railway.

RIGHT

Big skies over the ubiquitous, box-like shape of Heysham power station.

village of Poulton, which became Poulton-le-Sands to differentiate it from Poulton-le-Fylde, a few miles down the coast near Blackpool. People farmed both land and sea, though fishermen had to be particularly aware of the tides, since there has never been a harbour here. Richard Ayton, making a visit in 1813, was unimpressed by the locals. 'Their manners to strangers, whether their equals or their betters, are of the same rude, untempered kind that they indulge in amongst themselves.'

The coming of the railway changed Poulton-le-Sands for ever, with the town's link with West Yorkshire being completed by 1850. The new resort – an amalgamation of Poulton-le-Sands, Bare and Torrisholme – had adopted the name of Morecambe a few years earlier. And, only half in joke, the town was known as 'Bradford-by-the-Sea' when the millhands of West Yorkshire escaped to the chilly Lancashire coast during Wakes Week for a few days of fresh air and fun away from their claustrophobic workplaces.

Morecambe's claim to fame has always been the bay itself, with its distant blue background of Lakeland peaks. A steamship,

*Windermere*, took tourists across the bay, to Grange-over-Sands, where they could investigate the Lakeland fells at closer quarters. Morecambe had three piers. Central Pier opened to visitors in 1869; West End Pier – a more elaborate structure with a rather grand pavilion at the end that the locals dubbed 'the Taj Mahal' – was completed in 1896. The Pavilion was destroyed by fire in 1915; West End Pier itself was washed away by a storm in 1977. The remains of Central Pier were demolished in the 1990s, leaving just the clocktower to remind people where it once stood.

The third pier was the Stone Jetty, built in 1833 – not for promenading but as a railway terminus serving ferries bound for Ireland and Scotland. This is the one pier that has survived, as the best place in town to watch seabirds wheeling and the sun going down over the bay.

Morecambe was the last town in England to have horse-drawn trams, but the first to have full-scale illuminations. If the numbers game that opened in the fairground wasn't new, the name certainly was: bingo. In the resort's heyday the entertainment ranged from the highbrow – Edward Elgar – to the lowbrow – pretty much everybody else. Harry Lauder trod

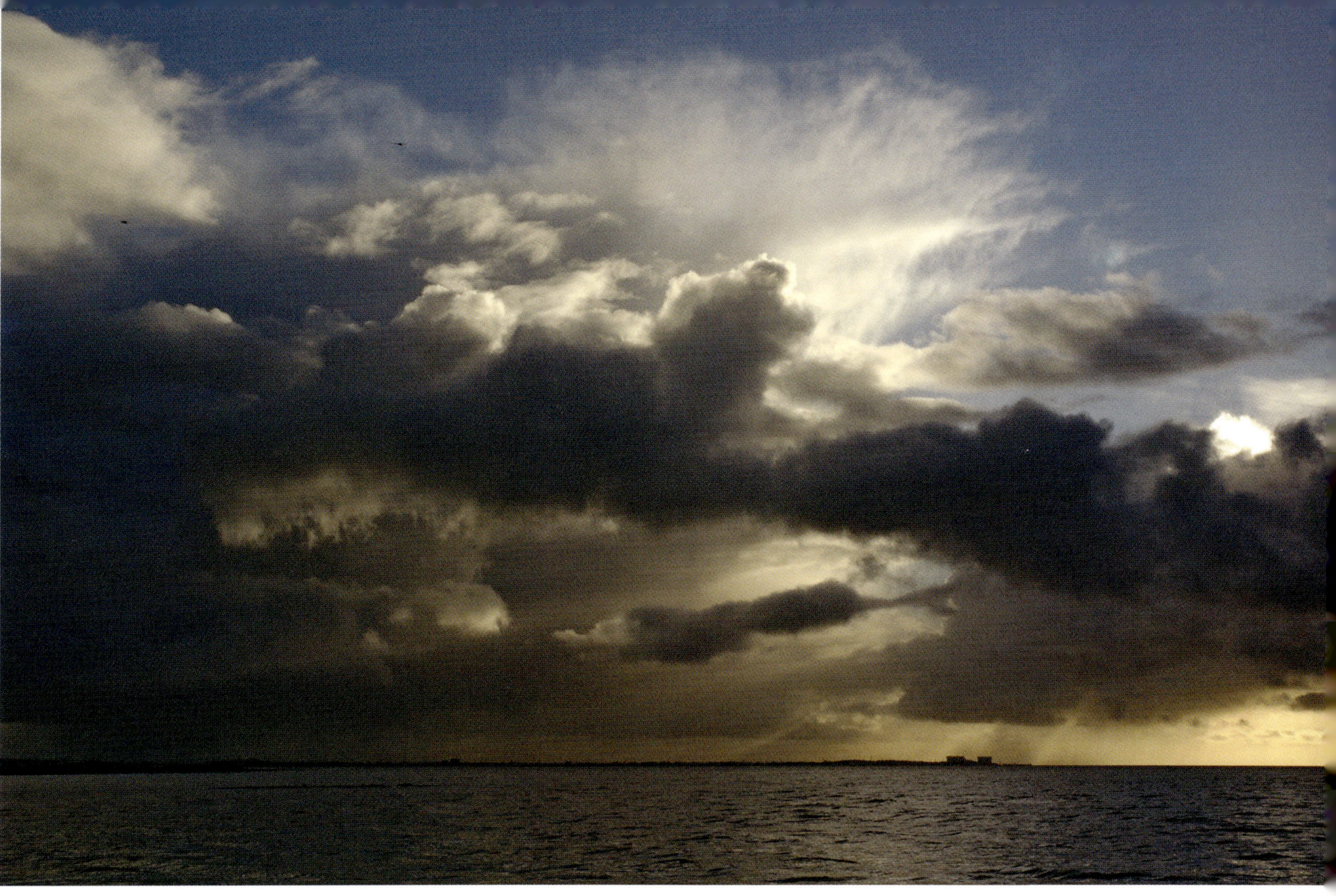

the boards, Gracie Fields too. George Formby played his little ukelele and began a tradition for adopting Lancashire towns as stage names which Eric Morecambe and Jimmy Clitheroe would continue.

Morecambe had a few successful years, though it has always come off second-best to Blackpool, its bigger, brasher brother a few miles down the coast. The mayor of Morecambe revealed a degree of realism, when organising a beach event for children, by calling it a 'sand and mud castle competition.' Photographers like me may enjoy the way the light is reflected off the mud-flats, but holidaymakers prefer golden sands to the sand/mud/silt mixture which Morecambe Bay has to offer.

The advent of cheap package tours in the 1960s hit Morecambe hard, as holidaymakers plumped for sun, sand and sangria instead of a breezy stroll along Morecambe's promenade. The town is trying manfully to revive its fortunes – the promenade is peppered with newly-commissioned artworks – though it looks to be an uphill struggle. One sculpture recreates the contours of the Lakeland hills which can be seen across the bay, and puts names to them. But, ironically, the sculpture merely reminds visitors that they're in Morecambe, rather than enjoying the freedom of the Lakeland fells.

Heysham offers an intriguing mixture of history and modernity. On a clear day the ugly landmark of Heysham power station can be seen from almost anywhere around Morecambe Bay. It rubs shoulders with Heysham harbour, where passenger ferries and container ships set sail for Belfast and the Isle of Man. The village of Heysham, though hemmed in by suburbia, has managed to keep its own identity. The squat shape of St Peter's Church gazes out – across the sands of Morecambe Bay and more than a thousand years of Christian faith and fellowship. With the church being built so close to the shore, exceptional tides have washed graves out to sea.

Heysham Head is a rocky headland: like Humphrey Head, a rarity in Morecambe Bay. Here can be found the scant ruins of St Patrick's Chapel – actually more of a cell than a chapel. Close by is a remarkable collection of graves cut out of a huge, flat rock. And Heysham Head is yet another of the places (there are dozens of other candidates) where the last wolf in England was killed.

Sunderland Point, at the mouth of the Lune, is one of Morecambe Bay's more eccentric places. Reached from Overton across a tide-washed causeway, the community is cut off to traffic twice a day, though a path to Middleton is always available to pedestrians. Wandering round the Sunderland of today – a peaceful backwater, a handful of houses, boats perched at angles on the mudflats waiting for high tide – it's difficult to imagine the place in its eighteenth-century heyday as a major port. It was involved in what was euphemistically called the 'West Indian Trade,' which meant rum, sugar – and slaves. A story goes that the very first consignment of cotton was unloaded at Sunderland Point, but remained on the quayside for more than a year because nobody knew what to do with it!

A slave boy was brought ashore in 1736. When his master was called away on business, the boy pined to death. Not knowing his name, the locals called him 'Sambo;' not knowing his religion they buried him in unconsecrated ground. Sambo's grave can still be seen, sited incongruously in a field and decorated with colourful offerings from local schoolchildren.

The Sunderland of today is a place of echoes and memories, the silence broken only by the melancholy cries of the seabirds. It's easy to lose yourself in reverie: not a good idea when the tide is coming in. A substantial lady interrupted my picture taking. 'When are you planning to leave?' she asked, matter-of-factly. 'Oh, soon,' I said. 'No . . . now,' she bellowed. And she was right. By the time I had driven to the Overton end of the causeway, the water was lapping around the wheel-arches of my car. I like Sunderland Point a lot, though it's not a place you necessarily want to be stuck in, because the pub closed more than a century ago.

Between the Lune and the Wyre the landscape is mostly low-lying farmland. Ironically, stone from Cockerham Abbey was used to create the sea-wall which now protects the scant ruins from the waves. The coastal footpath, pleasant rather than dramatic, comes to a halt in Knott End, at the mouth of the River Wyre. Pedestrians can take the ferry across the Wyre to Fleetwood, home of those fiendishly-strong cough lozenges known as Fisherman's Friends.

Fleetwood marks the southern extent of Morecambe Bay . . . well my Morecambe Bay, at least. Echoing Barrow-in-Furness, at the top of the bay, Fleetwood is a planned town which dates from the reign of Queen Victoria. Sir Peter Hesketh had grandiose plans for the Rossall Estate he inherited in 1824: a resort and a port where rail passengers could board steamers bound for Scotland. The building of the west-coast railway line ended this role as a travel terminus, while Blackpool, a few miles down the coast, took most of the tourists.

Fleetwood reinvented itself as a fishing port; by the 1920s there were 9,000 people employed in the fishing industry. The good times didn't last, though, and Fleetwood – along with many other fishing ports – went into decline. The 'cod wars' of the 1970s almost finished it off; today, most jobs are in processing fish rather than catching them.

Fleetwood is the only town to have three lighthouses (all built during the 1840s). Wyre Light rests on piles sunk into the seabed, the Lower Lighthouse is still a characterful landmark on the sea-front, while the Upper Lighthouse is sited, surreally, in the middle of a street where it now doubles as a traffic roundabout. On a clear day you can stand on the sea front at Fleetwood and gaze across the full extent of Morecambe Bay to the Lakeland hills beyond.

A blue sky, and a sailing boat, reflected in the River Wyre near Fleetwood.

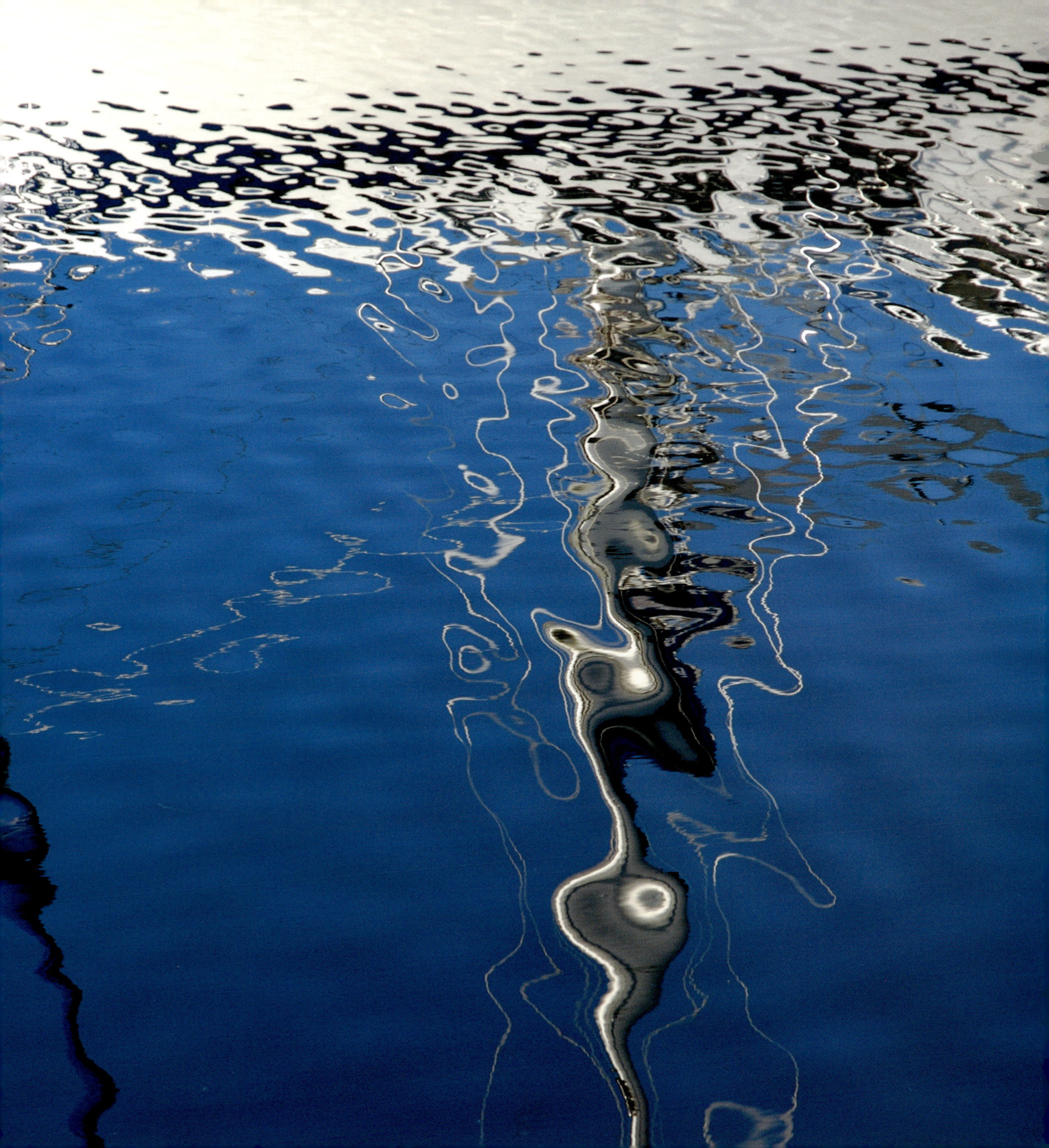

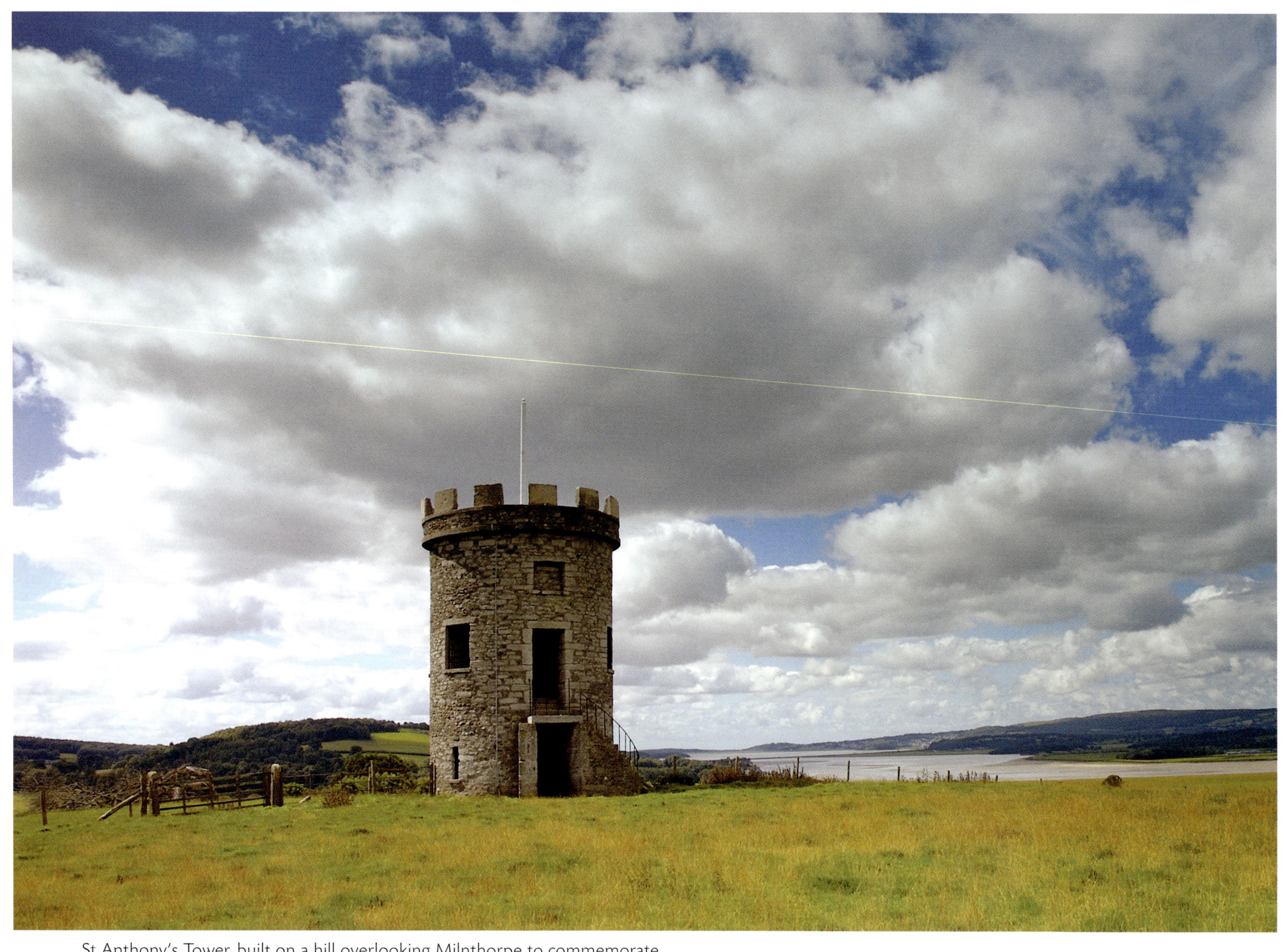

St Anthony's Tower, built on a hill overlooking Milnthorpe to commemorate
the Reform Bill of 1832.

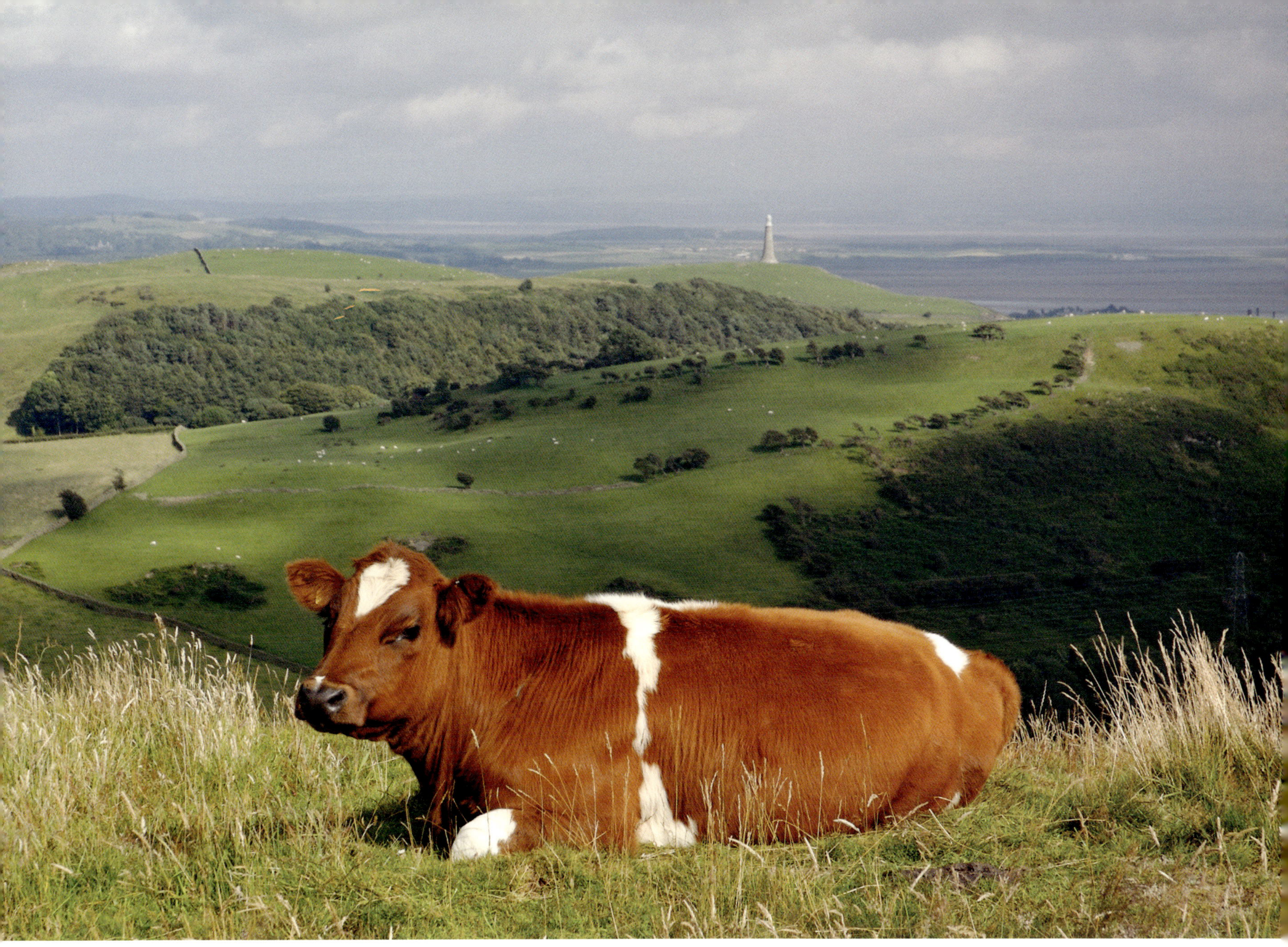

The Hoad, celebrating the life and achievements of Sir John Barrow, is a familiar landmark in Furness.

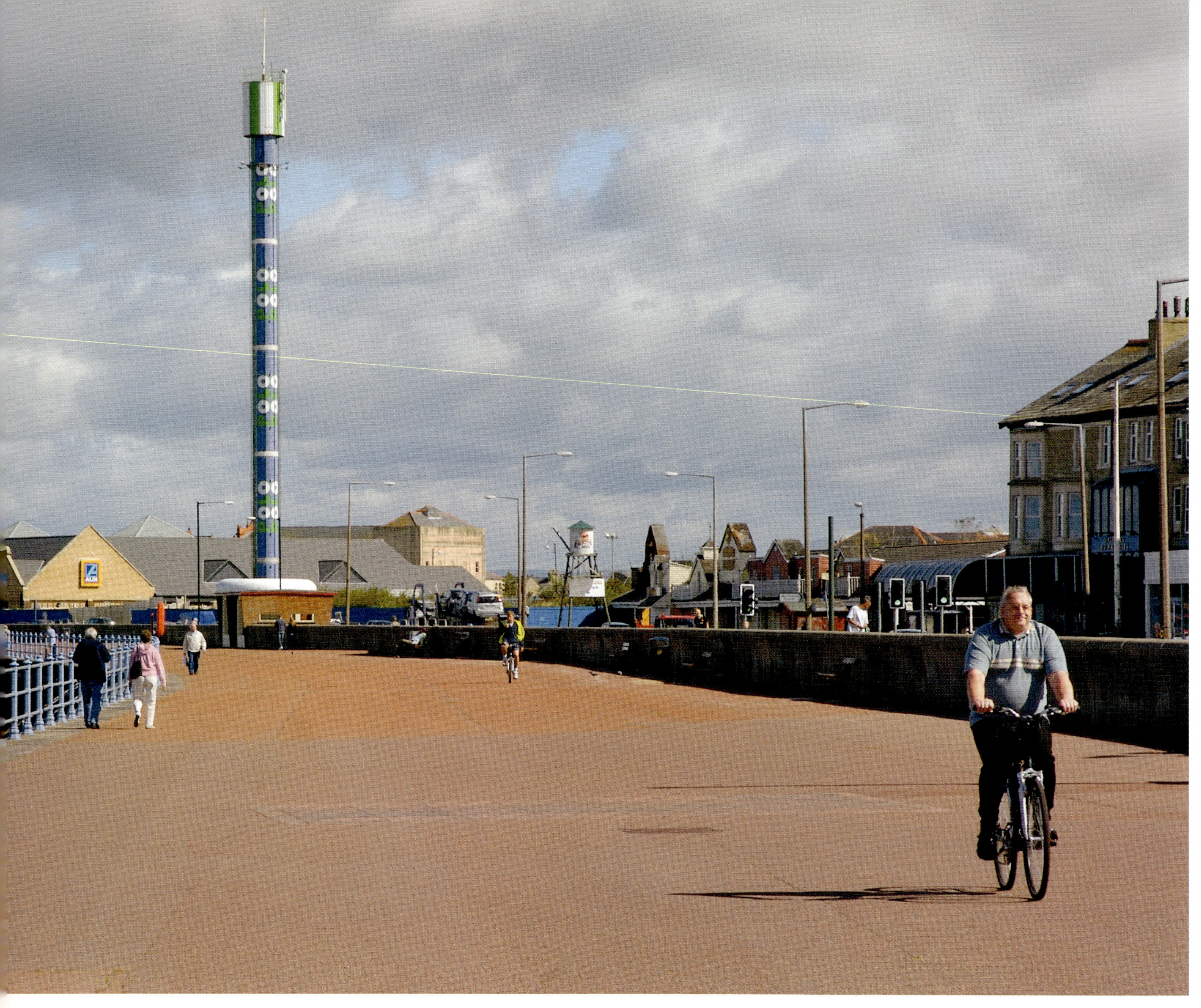

Blackpool, down the coast, has its iconic tower; Morecambe, in contrast,
has a giant tube of Polo mints.

The view across the beach at Morecambe, past the big wheel to the
Stone Pier.

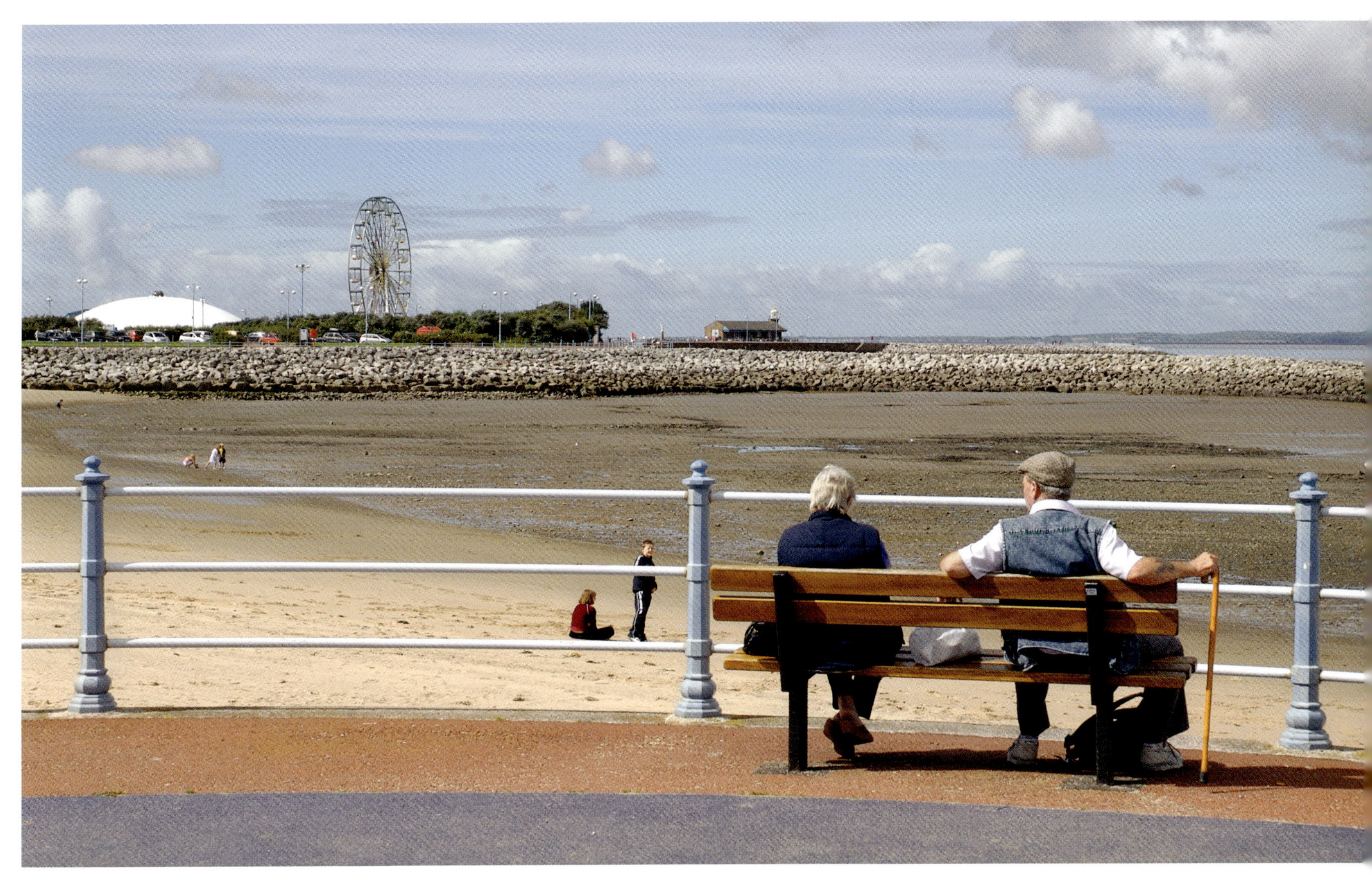

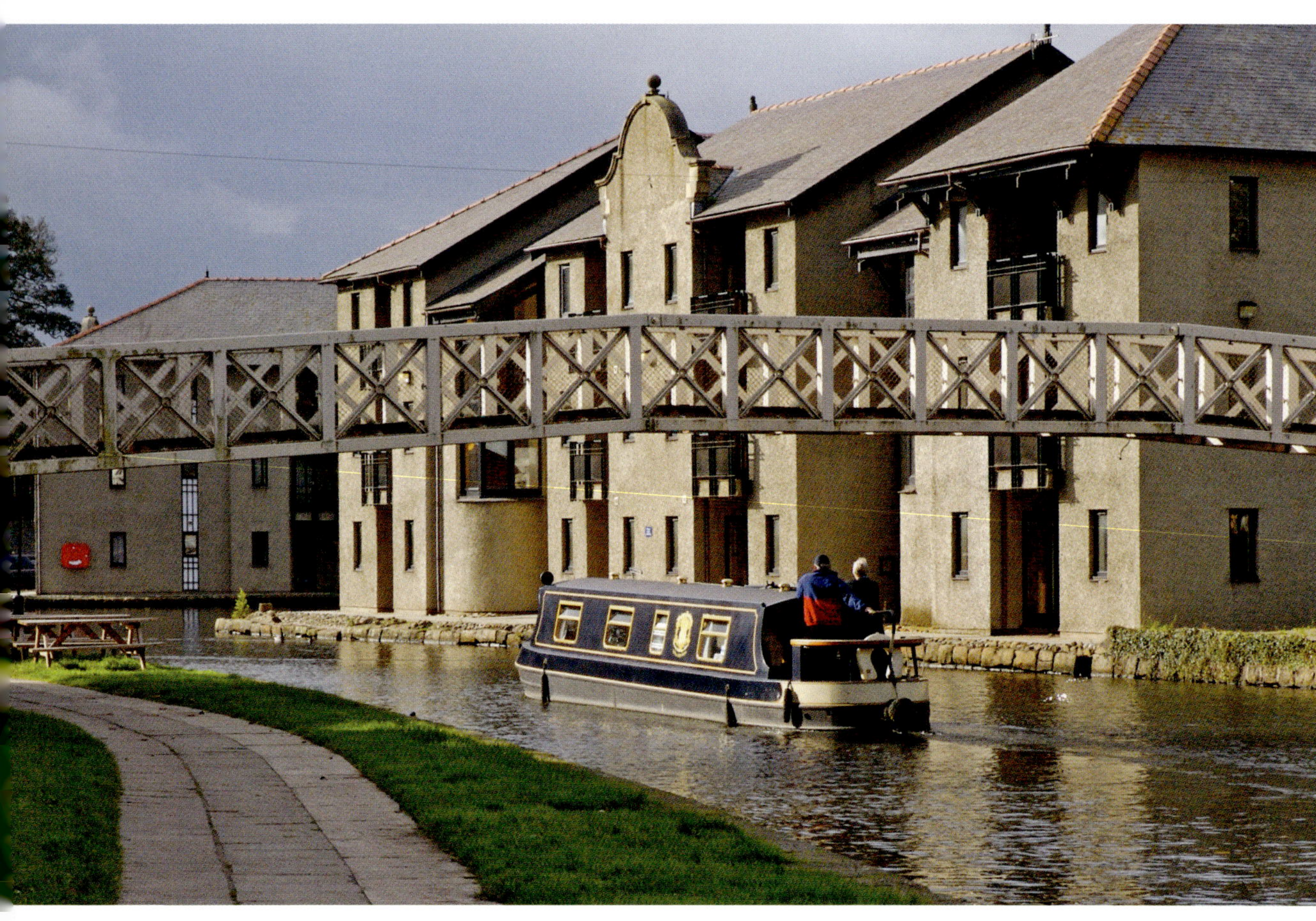


LEFT
The Lancaster Canal was driven straight through the heart of the city.

BELOW
Evening comes to Barrow-in-Furness.

RIGHT
When the 10 mph speed limit made Windermere off-limits for speedboat racing, the event moved to Cavendish Dock in Barrow.


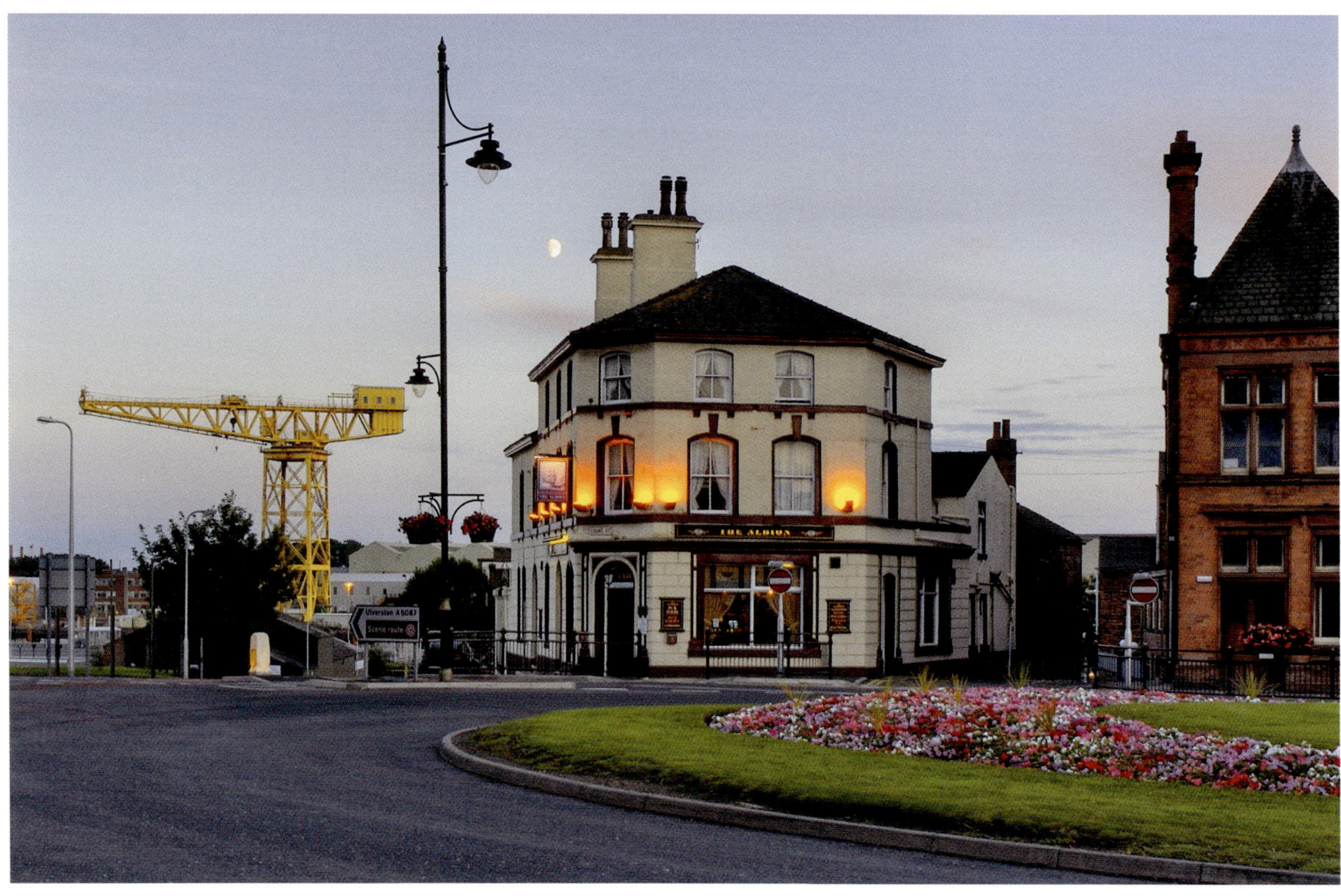

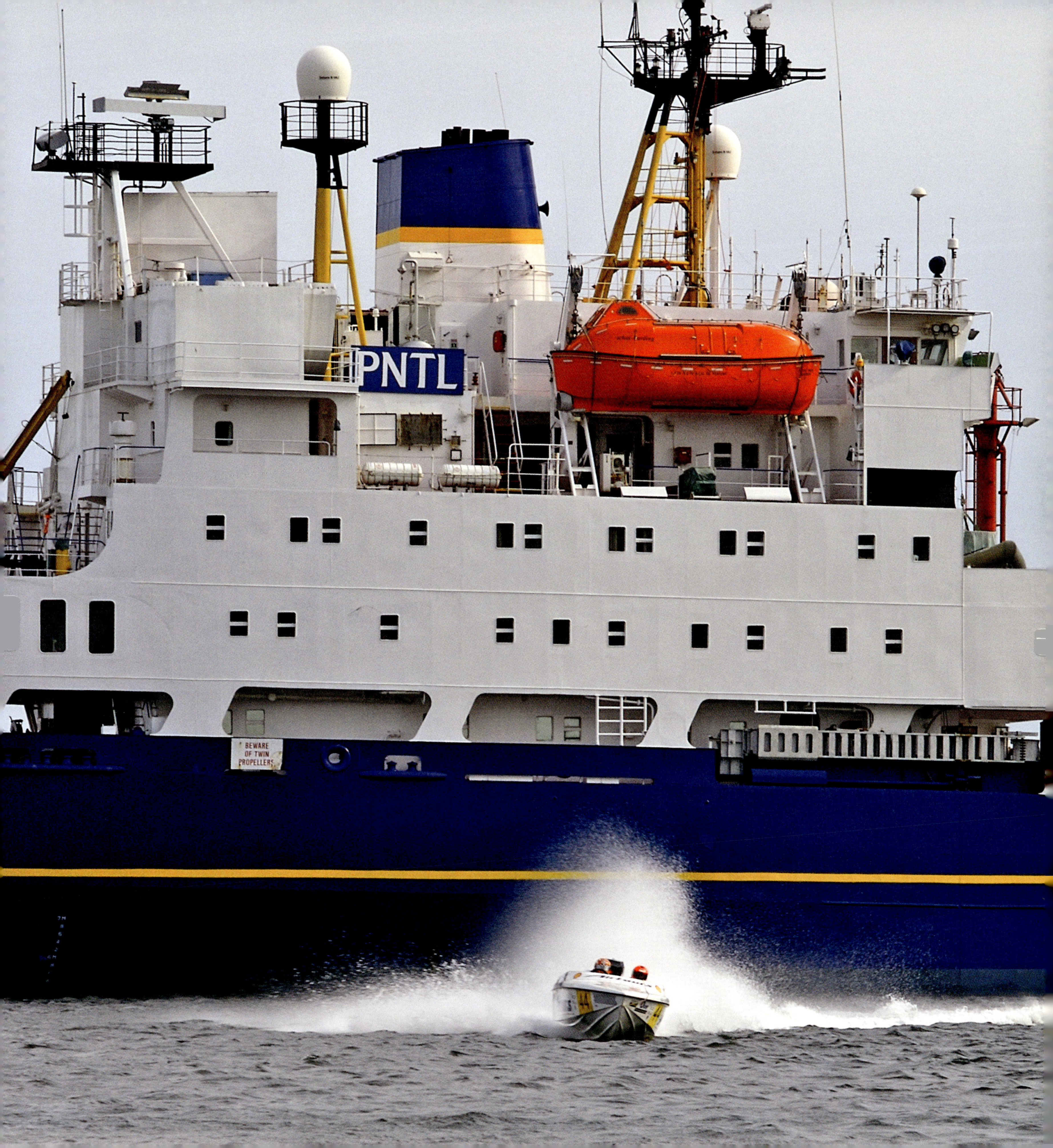

PNTL
BEWARE OF TWIN
PROPELLERS

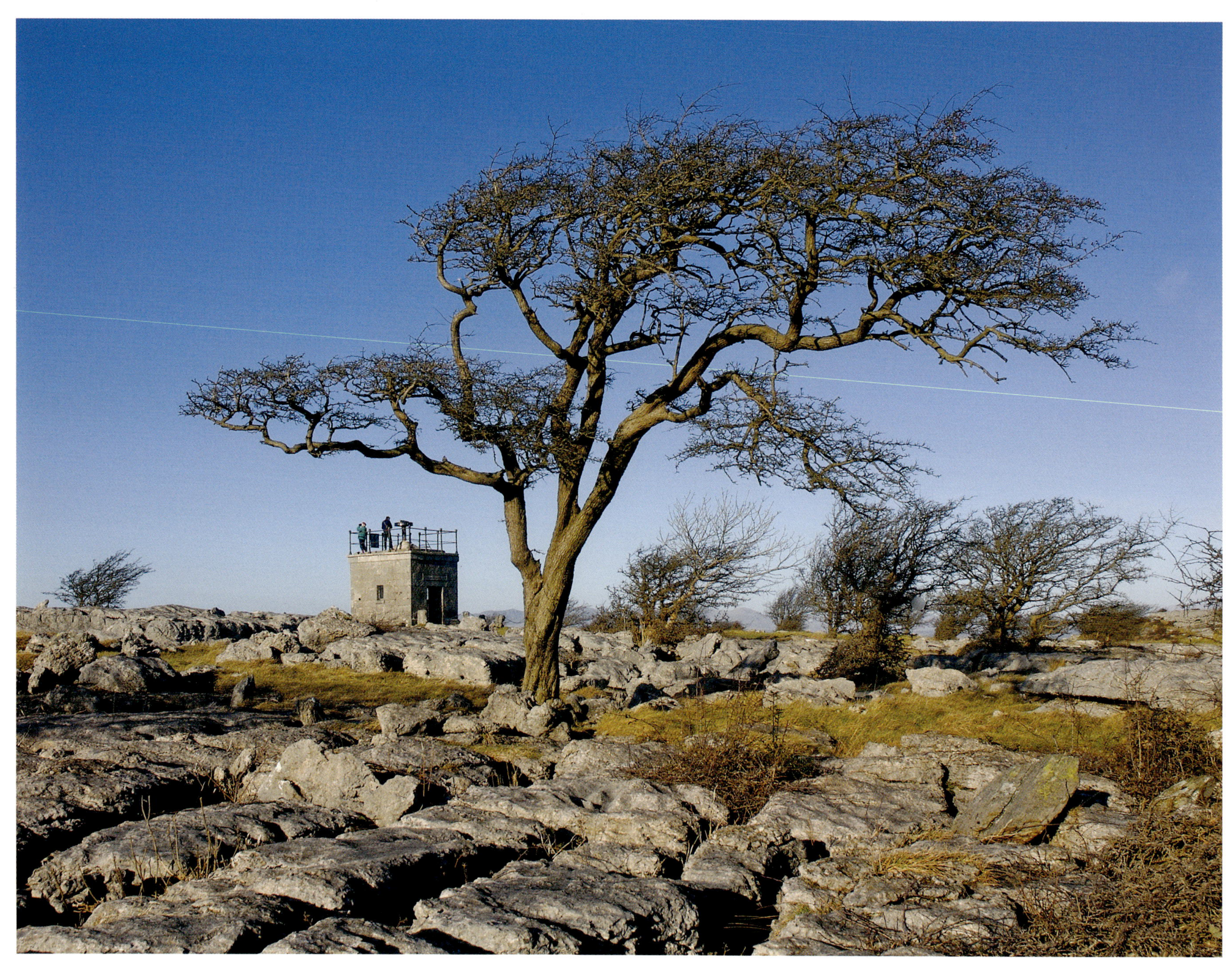

The hospice on Hampsfell, surrounded by an area of limestone pavement.

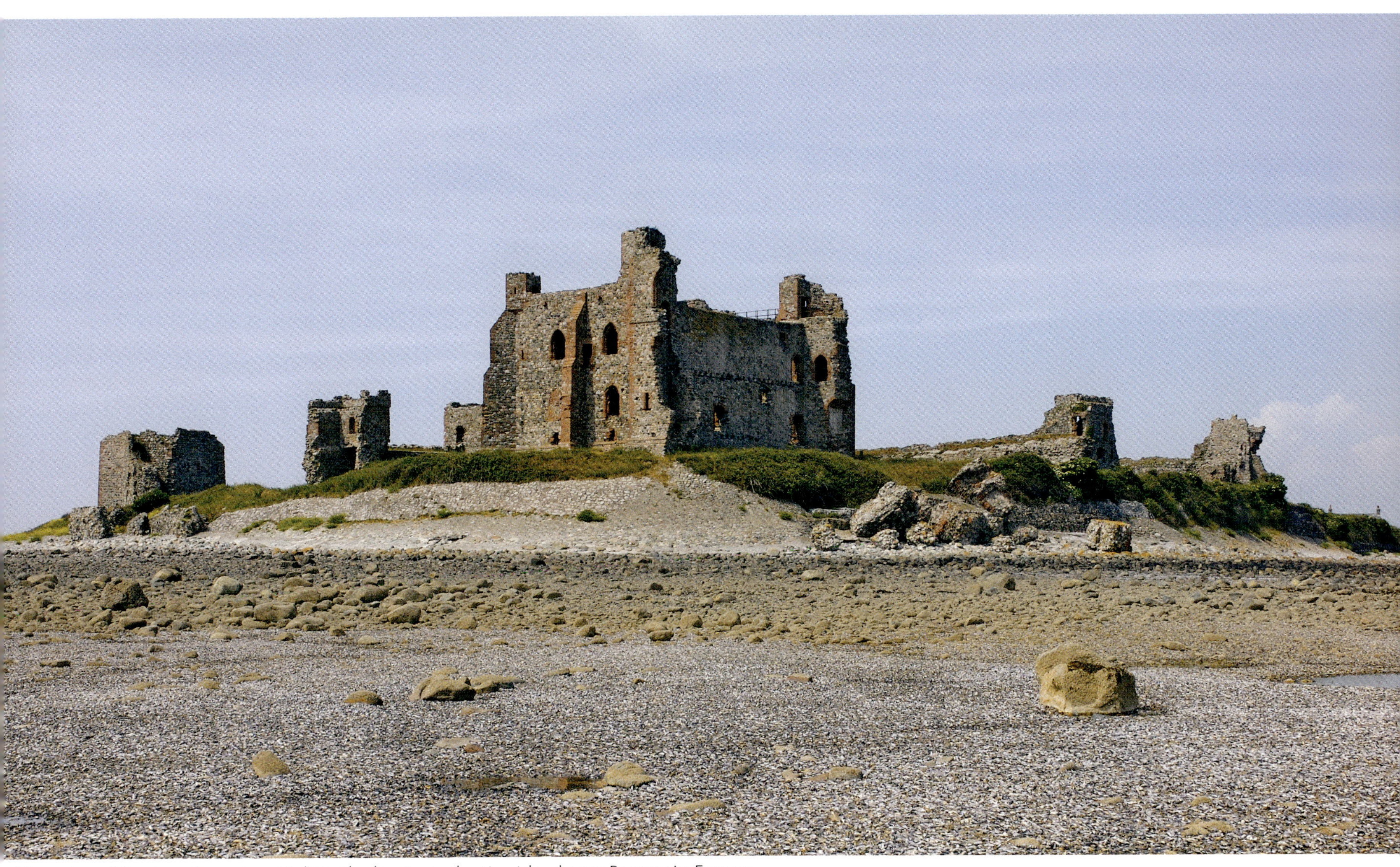
The ruins of fourteenth-century Piel Castle dominate the tiny island near Barrow-in-Furness.

FOLLOWING PAGES
Winter at Sunderland Point, when the skies are filled with huge flocks of wildfowl.

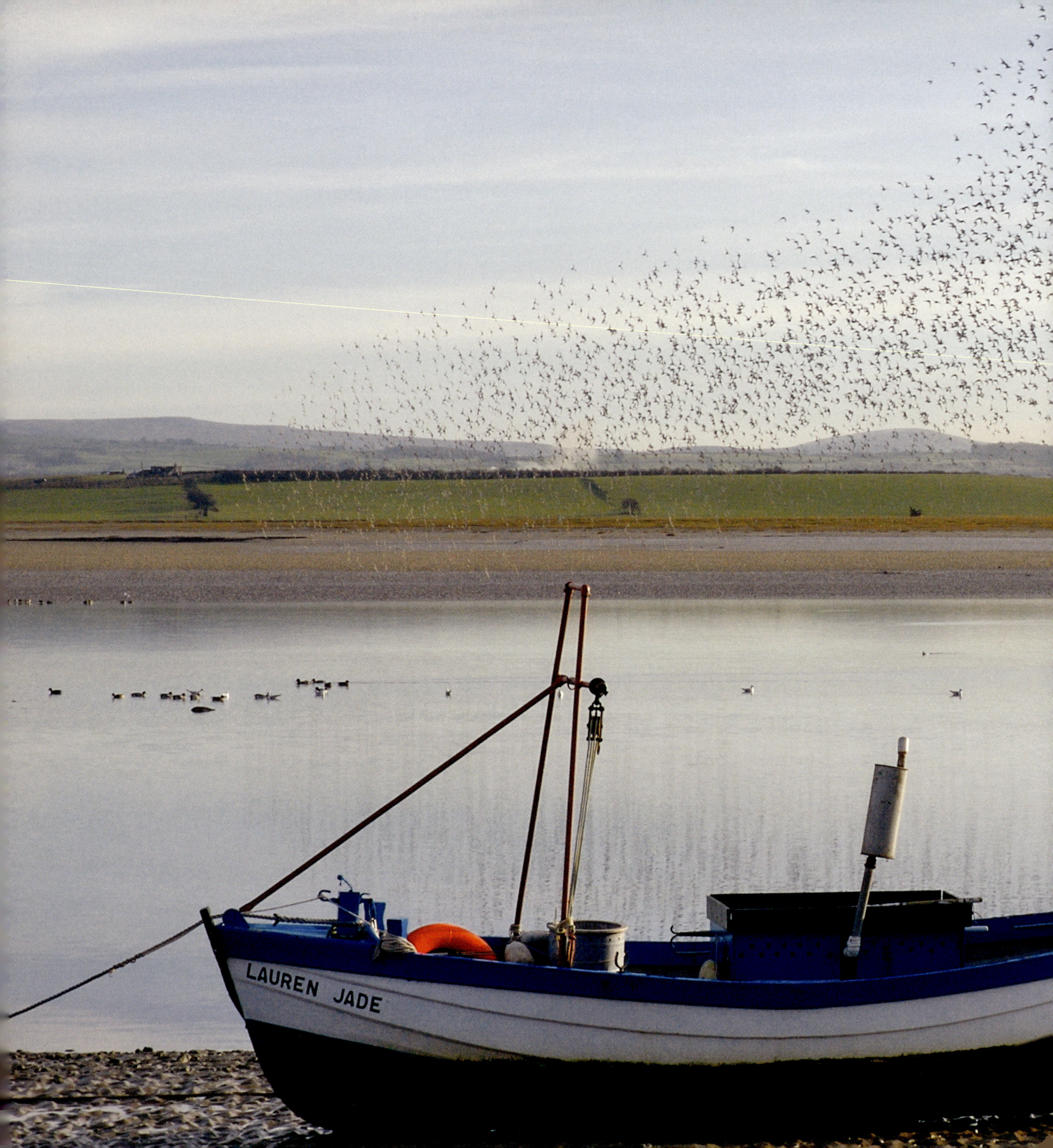
LAUREN JADE

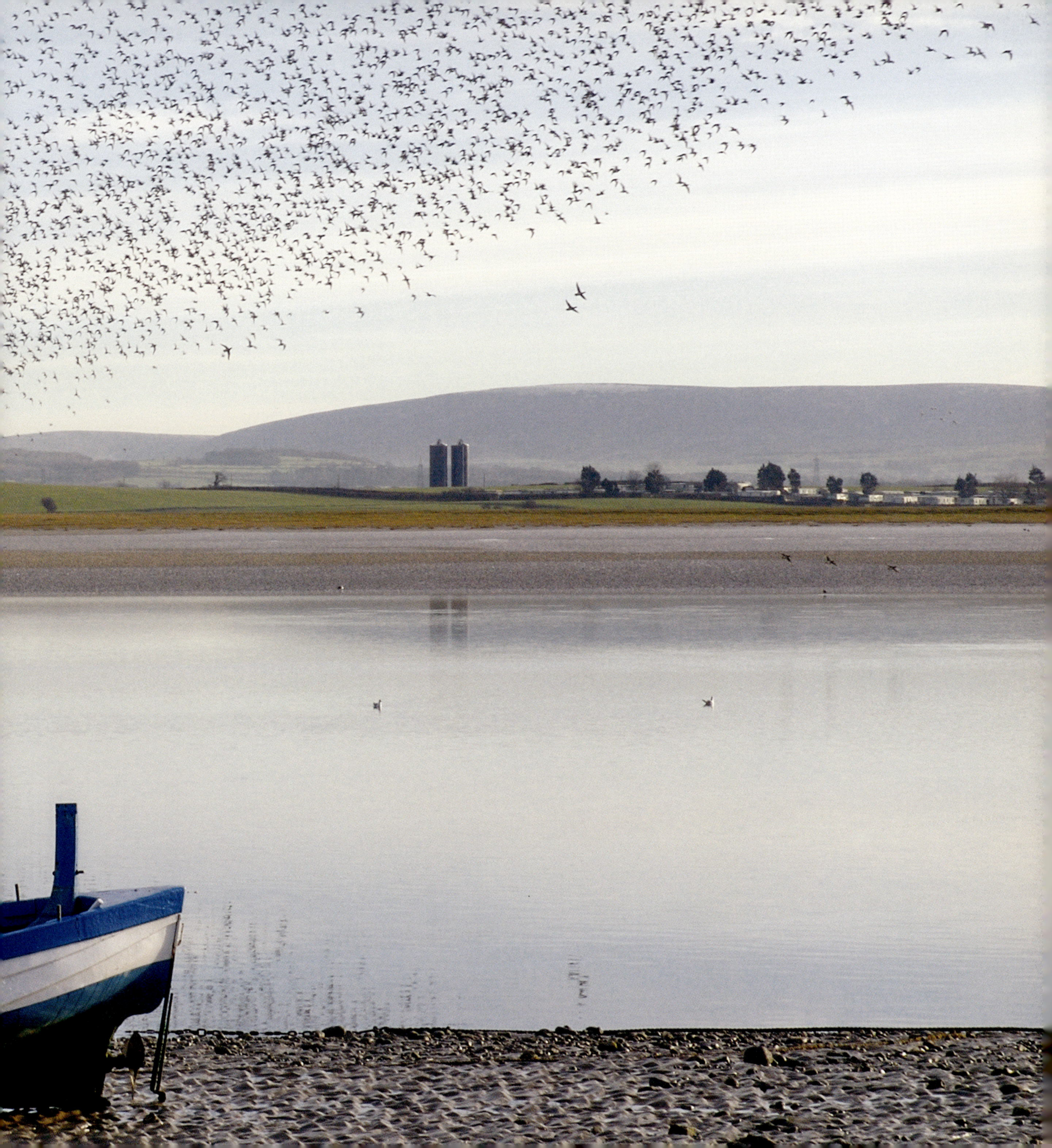

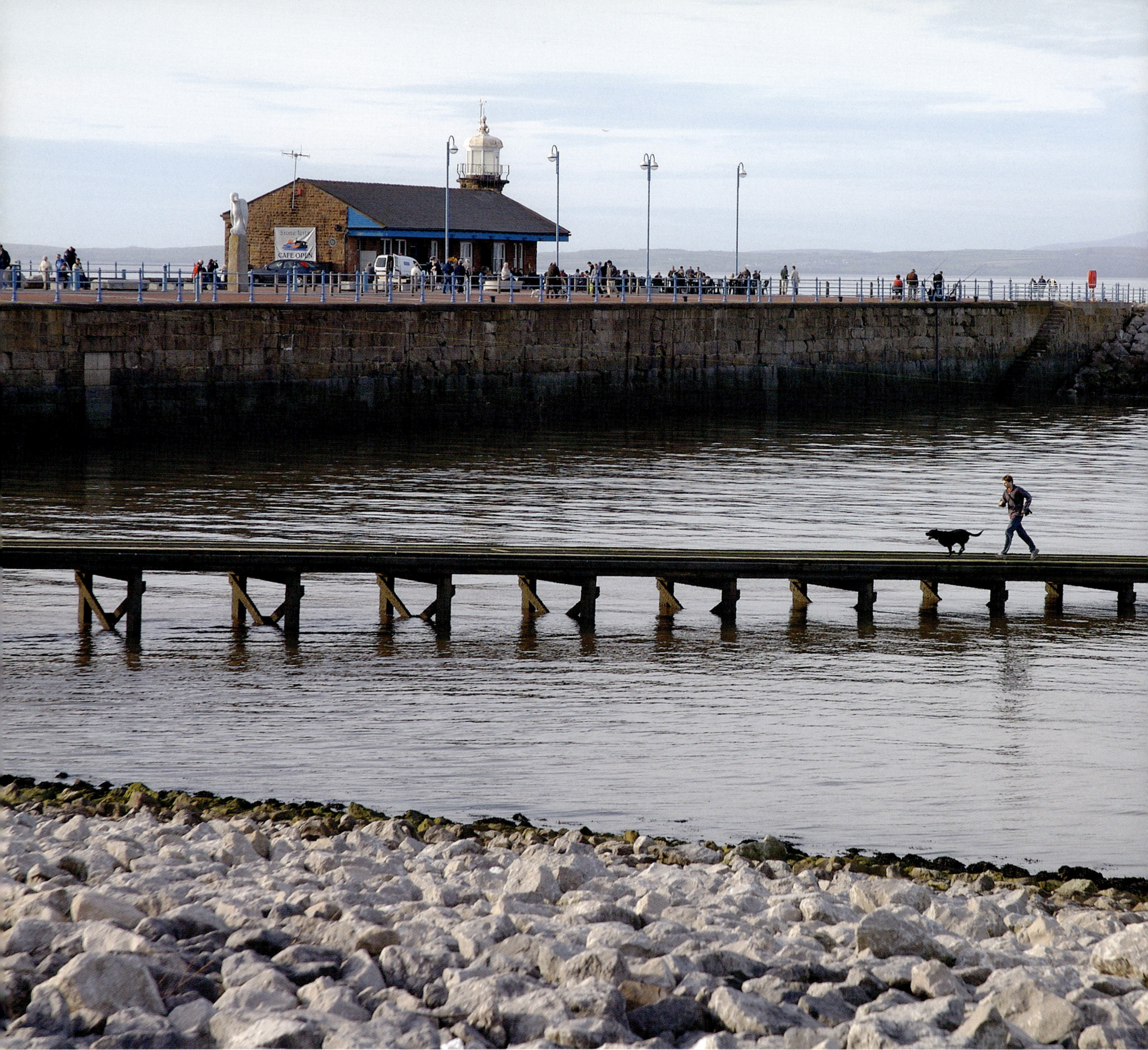

The Stone Pier at Morecambe: good for a stroll, though
originally built as a railway terminus.

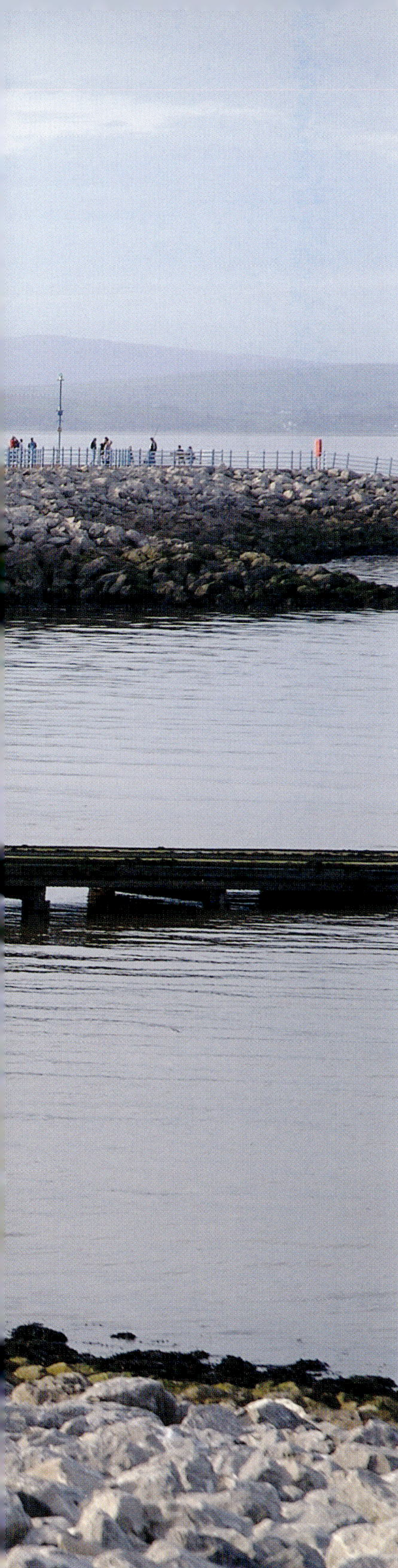

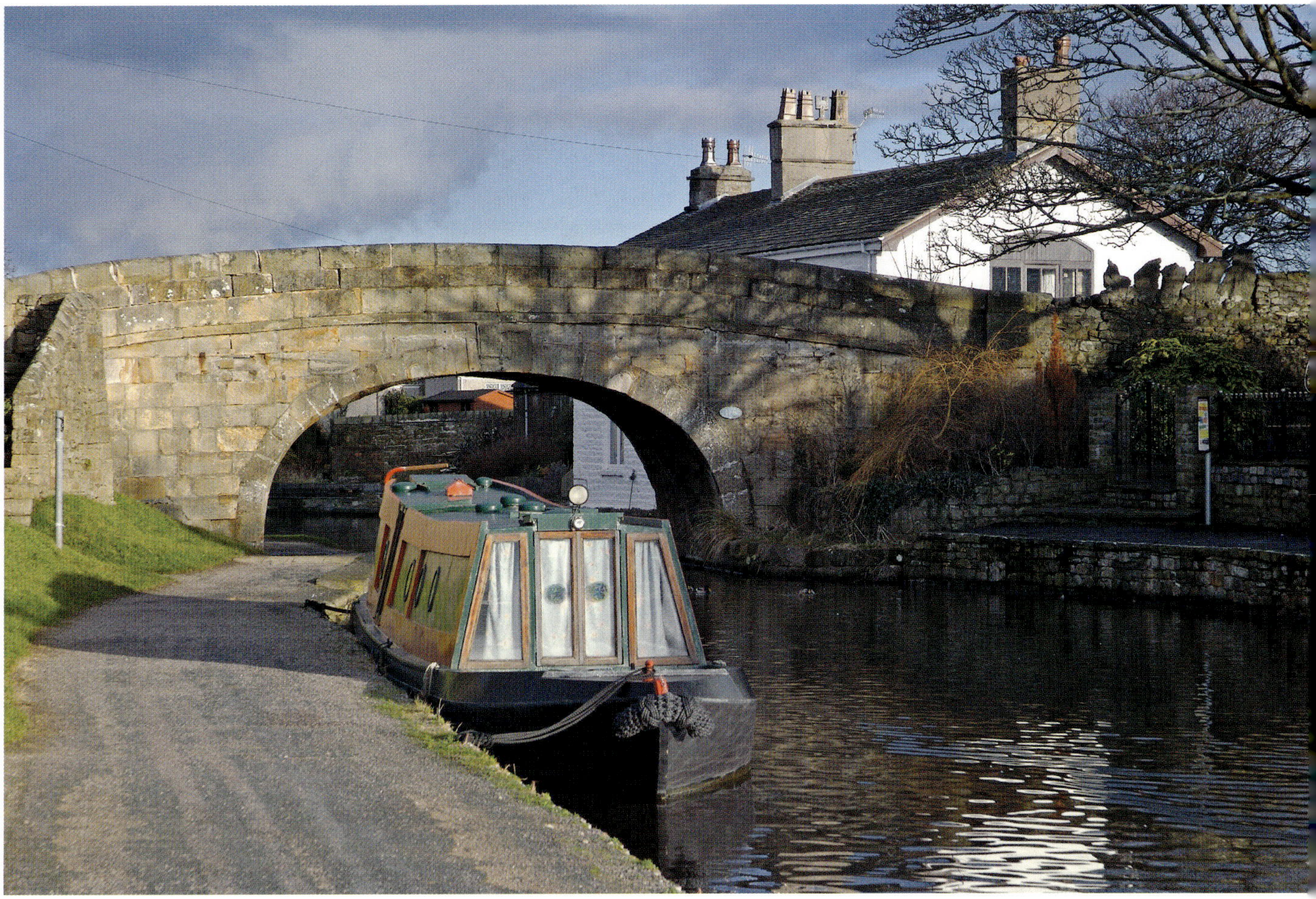

As they pass beneath this canal bridge at Hest Bank, narrowboats are just a stone's throw from the sea.

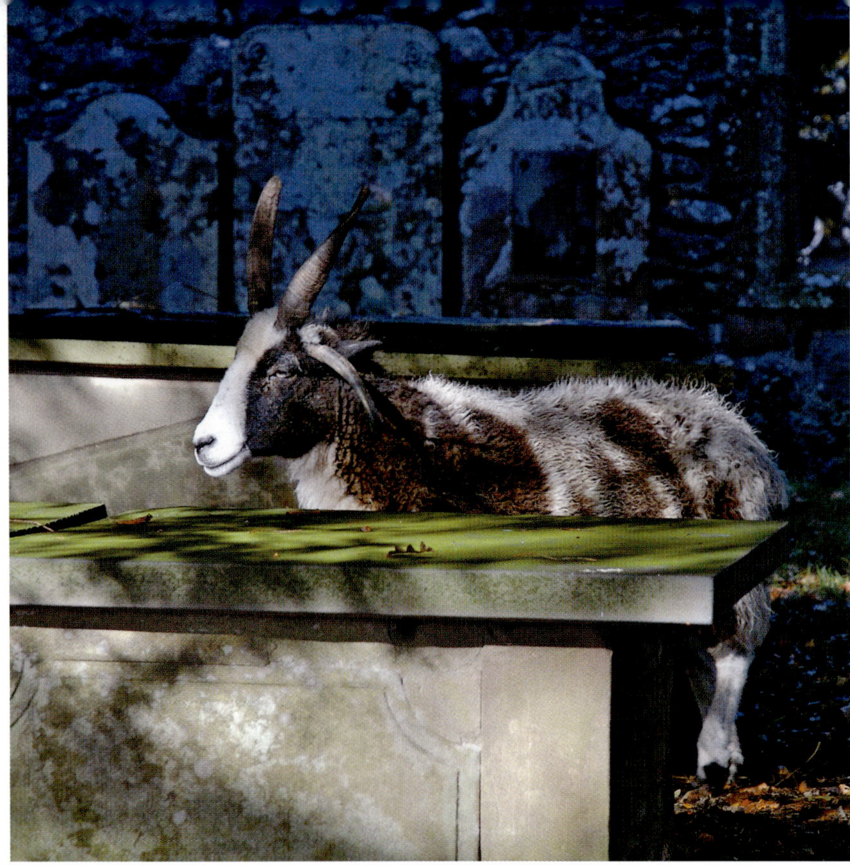

LEFT

Smirking sheep in the churchyard at Great Urswick.

BELOW

A few of the buildings, made from Coniston slate, to be found at the Lakeland Miniature Village in Flookburgh.

RIGHT, ABOVE

Blue skies reflected in the Walney channel, backed up by the ship-building hall: the biggest in Europe and now owned by BAE Systems.

RIGHT, BELOW

A typical scene in the Piel channel near Roa Island, with a line of offshore wind-turbines on the horizon.

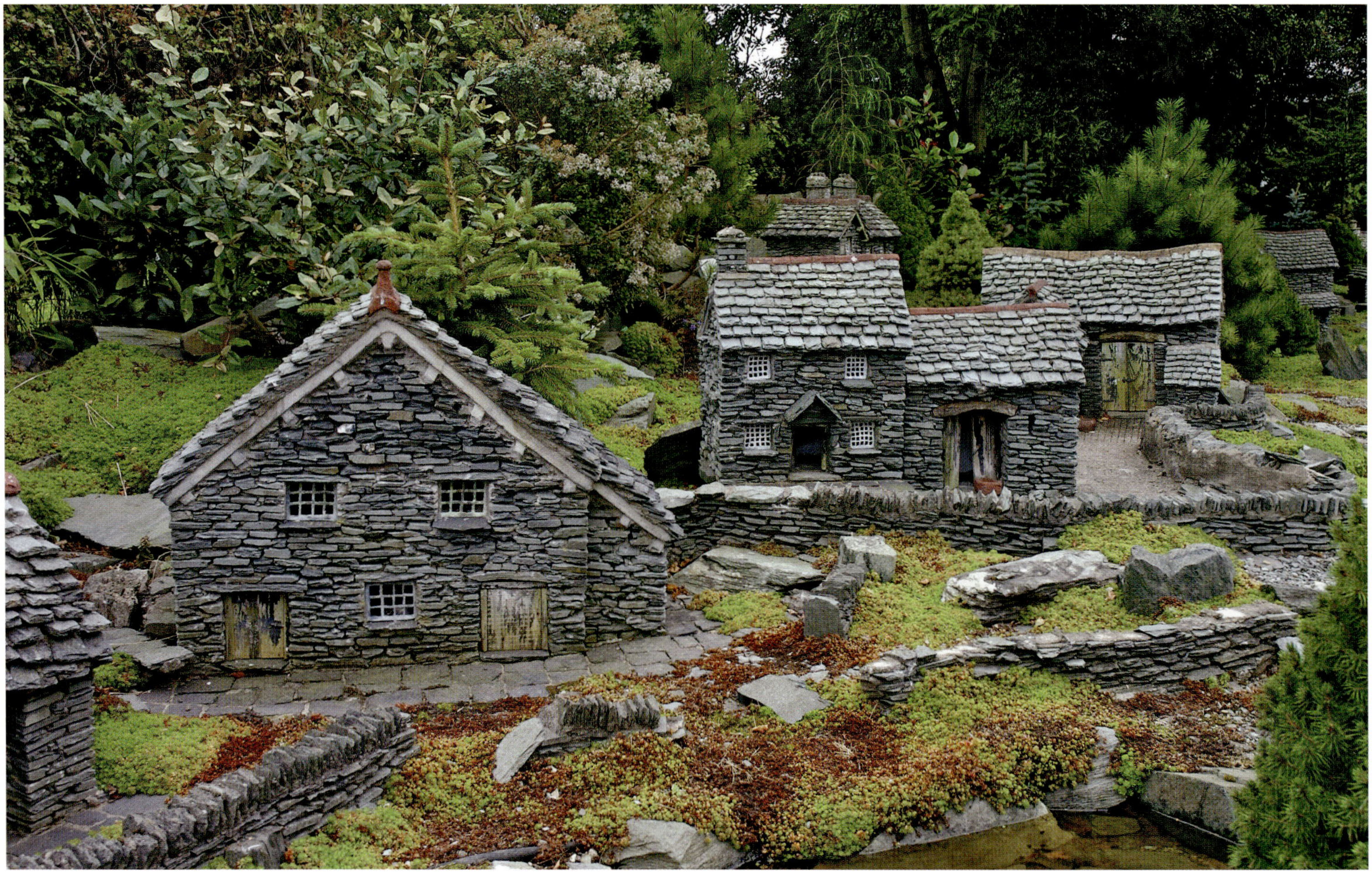

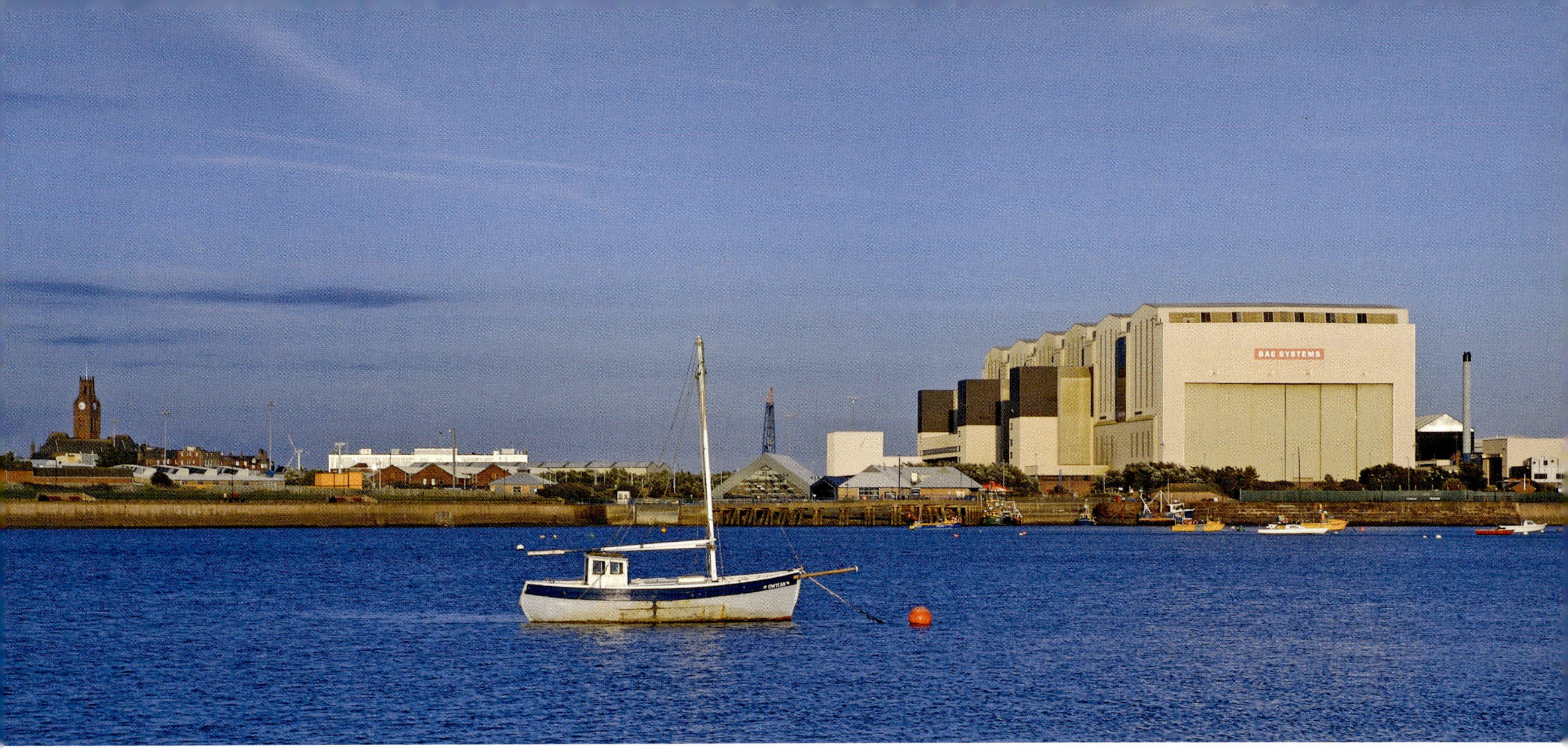

BAE SYSTEMS

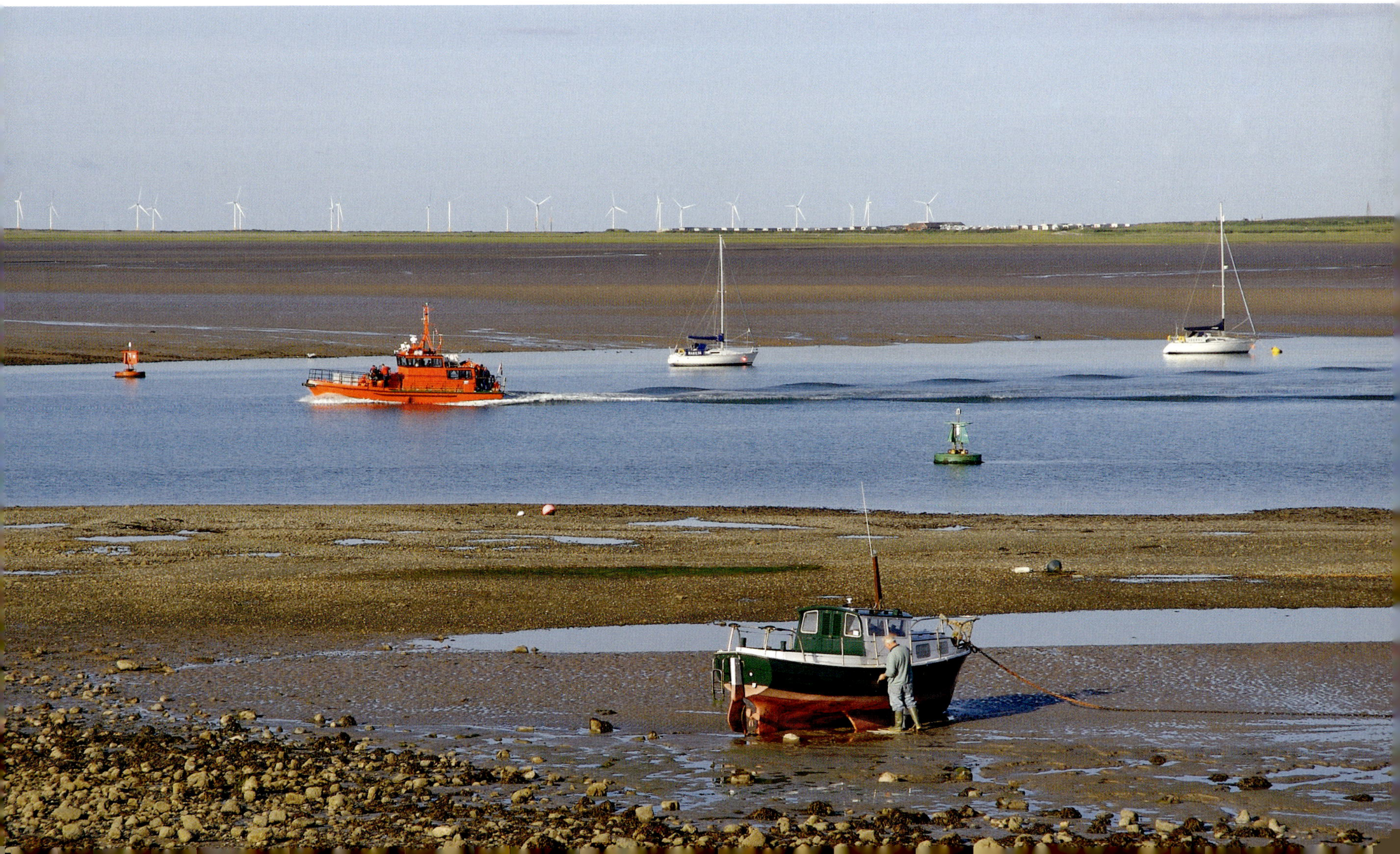

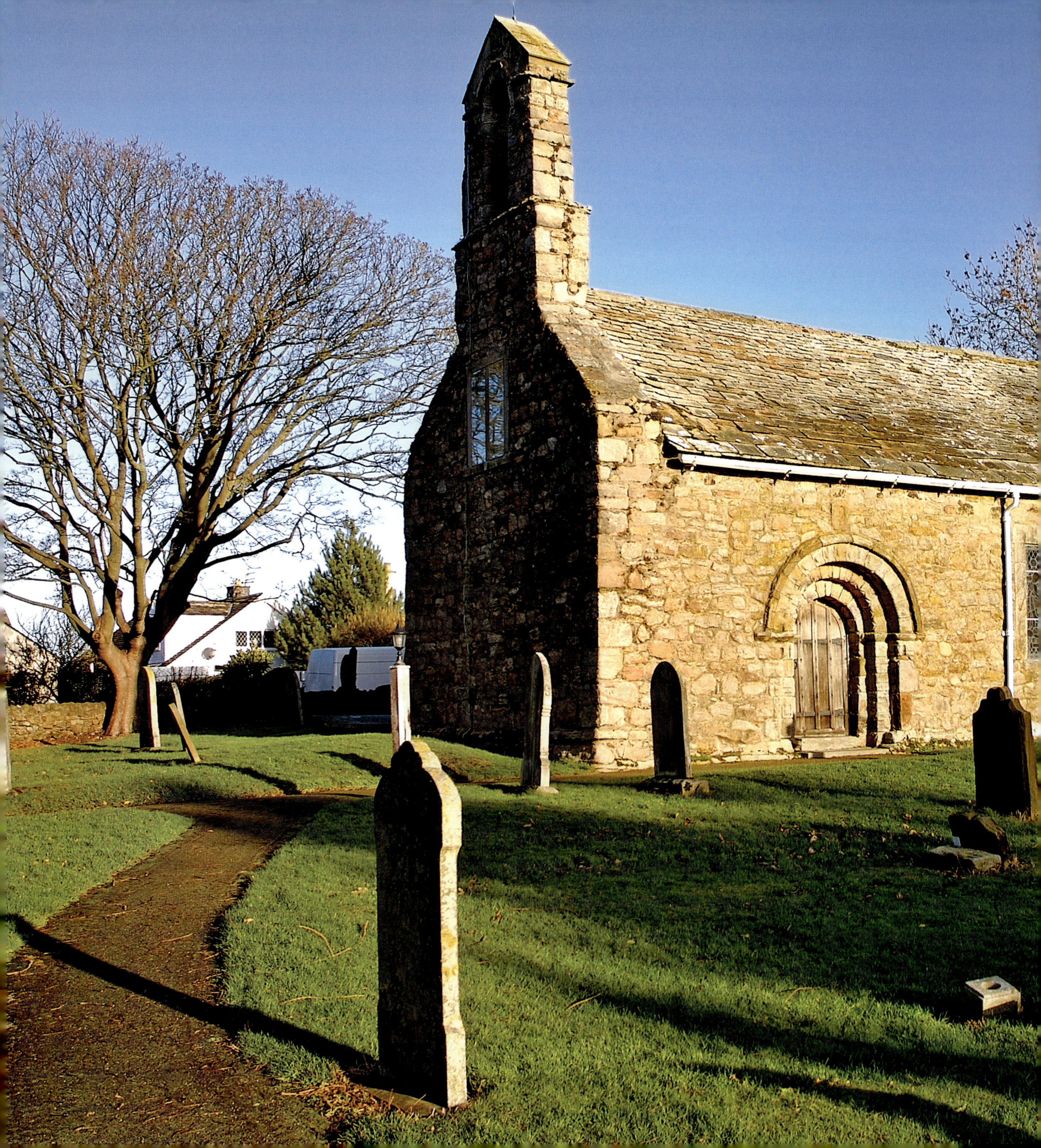

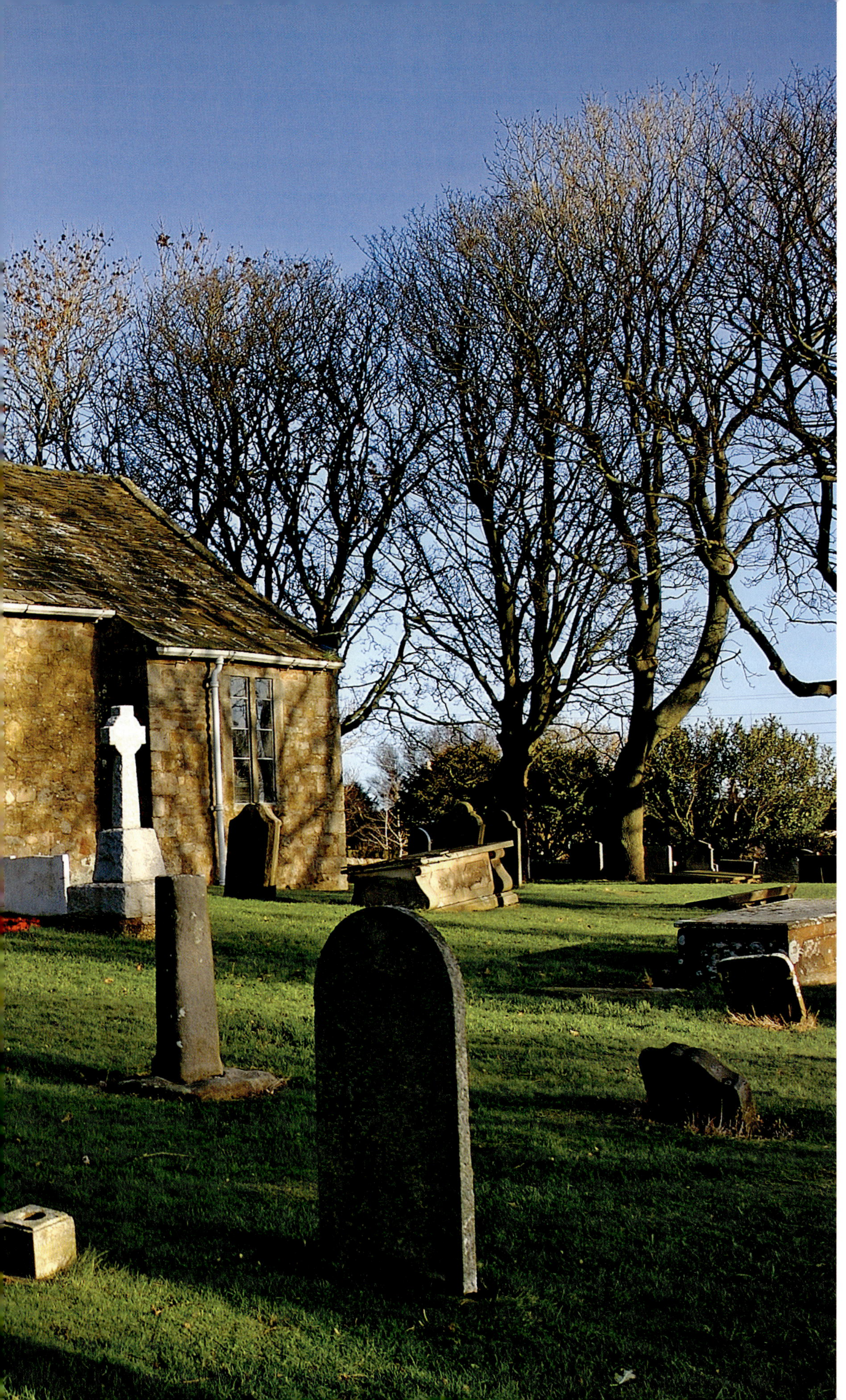

Overlooking the Lune estuary is the diminutive church at Overton, with its Norman doorway and simple bell-tower.

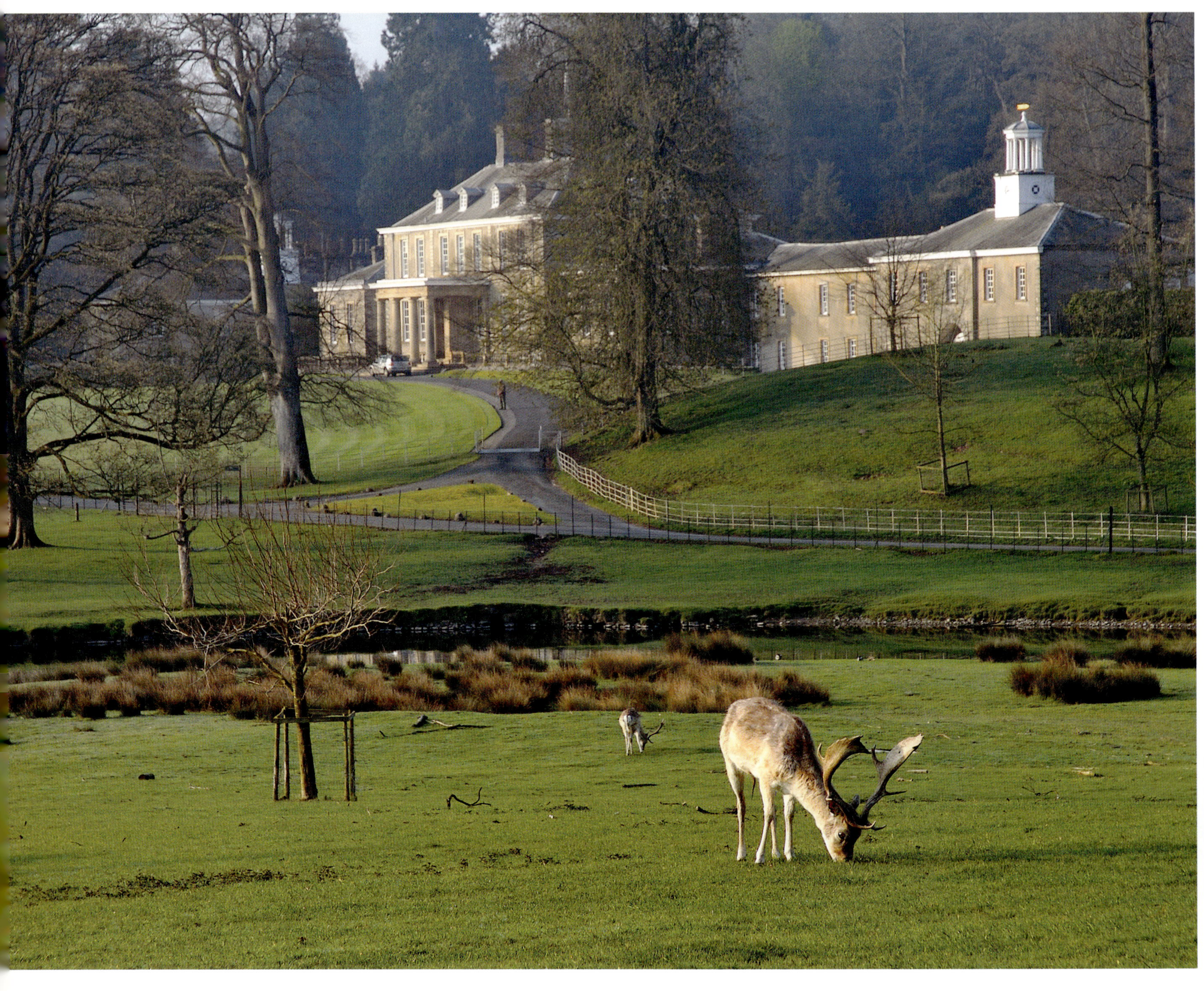

A fallow buck with a fine set of antlers grazing in the deer park of Dallam
Tower, near Milnthorpe.

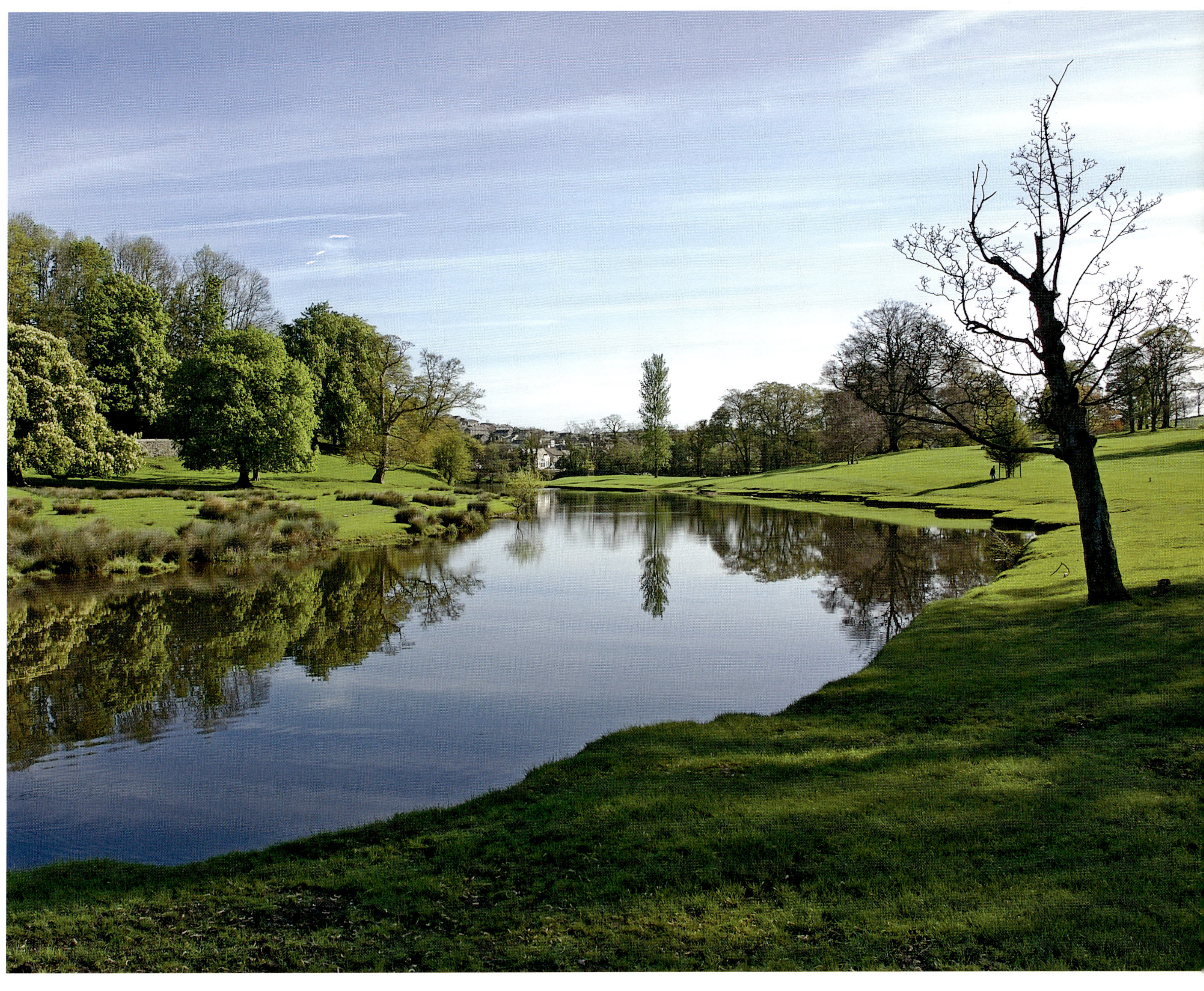

The tranquil River Bela runs through the deer park and into the Kent estuary.

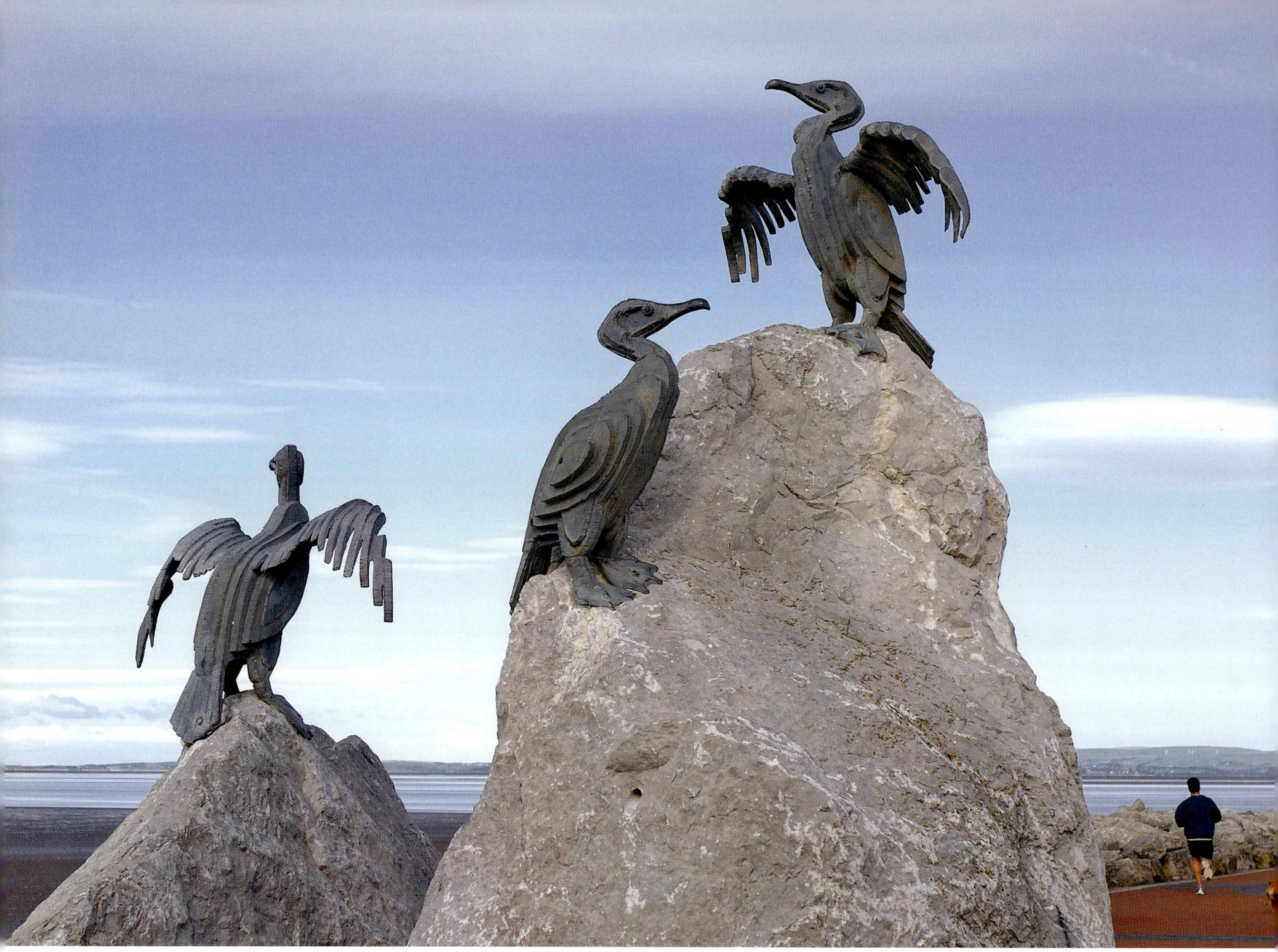

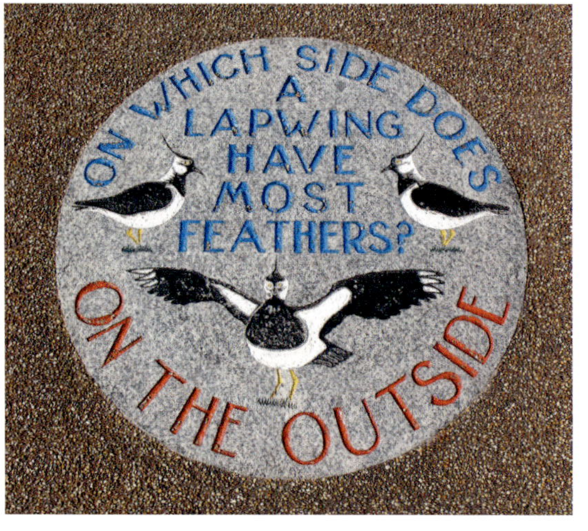


ABOVE

Cormorants – real and sculptured – can be seen from the promenade at Morecambe.

LEFT

An attempt at humour: one of the many artworks awaiting visitors to Morecambe.

RIGHT

The old lighthouse at Rampside – the only survivor of thirteen such 'range lights' built in the middle of the nineteenth century on the approach to Barrow.

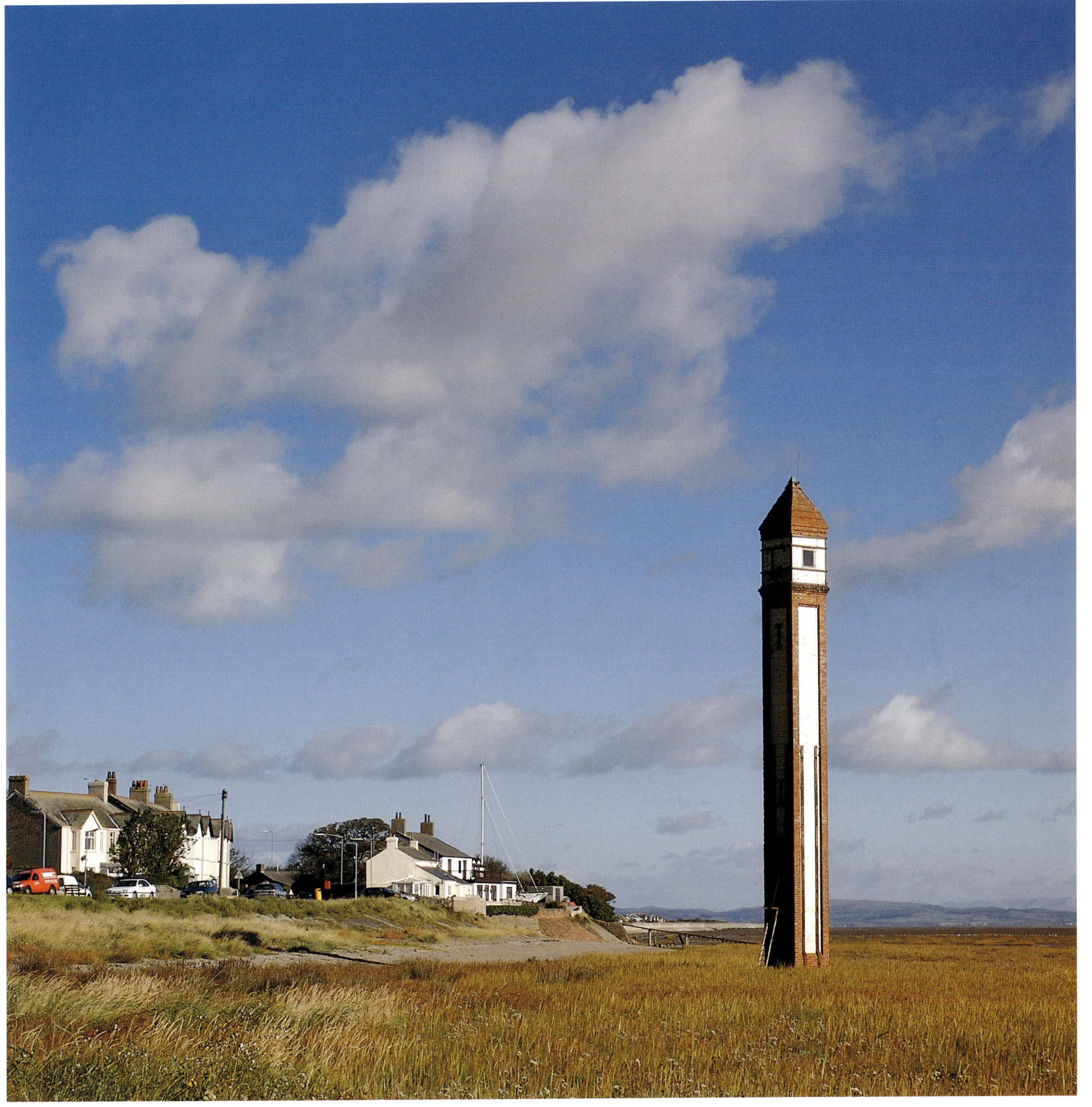

# THE EVER-CHANGING BAY

Change is the only constant around Morecambe Bay. Some changes occur with startling suddenness. When the River Leven changed course through its sandy estuary, for example, the resort of Grange-over-Sands found itself a mile from the sea. Other changes take longer, with the fortunes of local communities rising and falling like the tides. Some of them became over-reliant on a single, failing industry: fishing, for example, or ship-building. In the timescale of a single generation Barrow-in-Furness grew to become the biggest steel town in the country, while Sunderland, once a major port, declined into a quiet backwater.

The bay itself changes shape – over days, years, millennia. Ambitious attempts have been made to stem this natural ebb and flow, to impose a semblance of order on the volatile ecology of Morecambe Bay. Hopefully we've learned our lesson: it's better to work *with* these elemental forces, not *against* them. While we can protect a few sensitive places from the sea, the rest of the coastline will change and change again – leaving the last word to the tides and the waves, the wind and the weather.

A double rainbow above Foulshaw Moss and the Kent estuary, seen from the limestone landmark of Whitbarrow Scar.

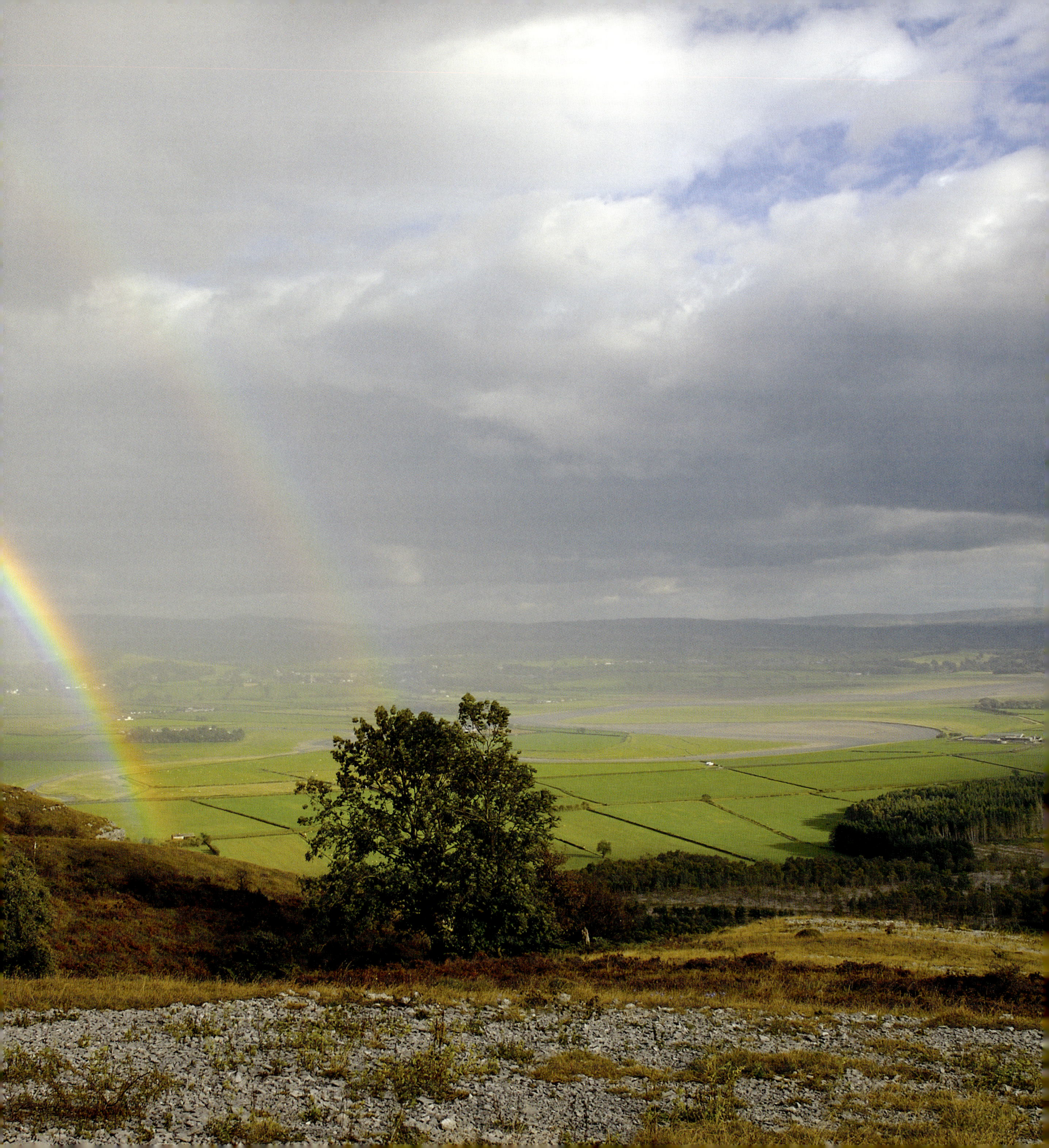

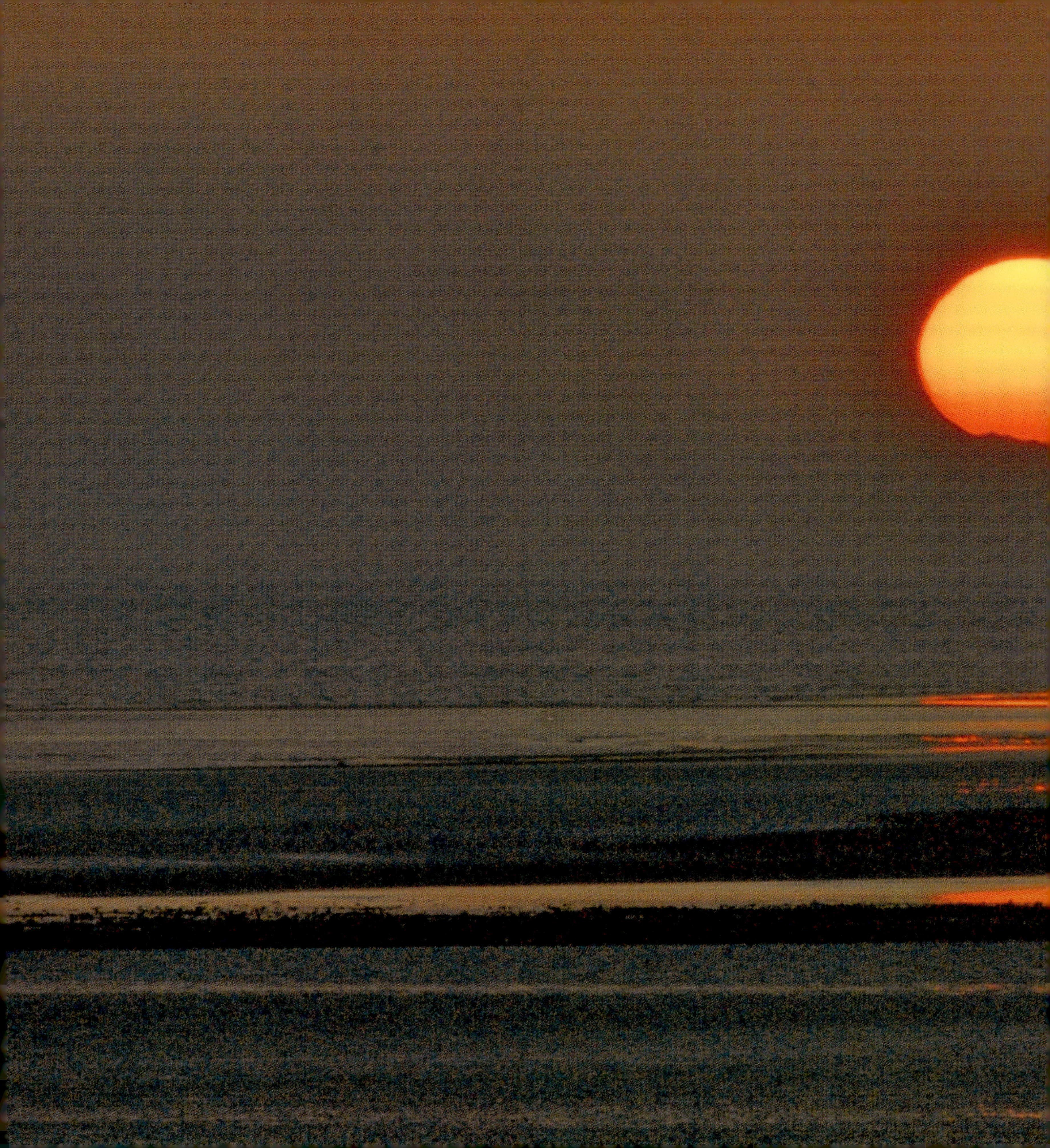

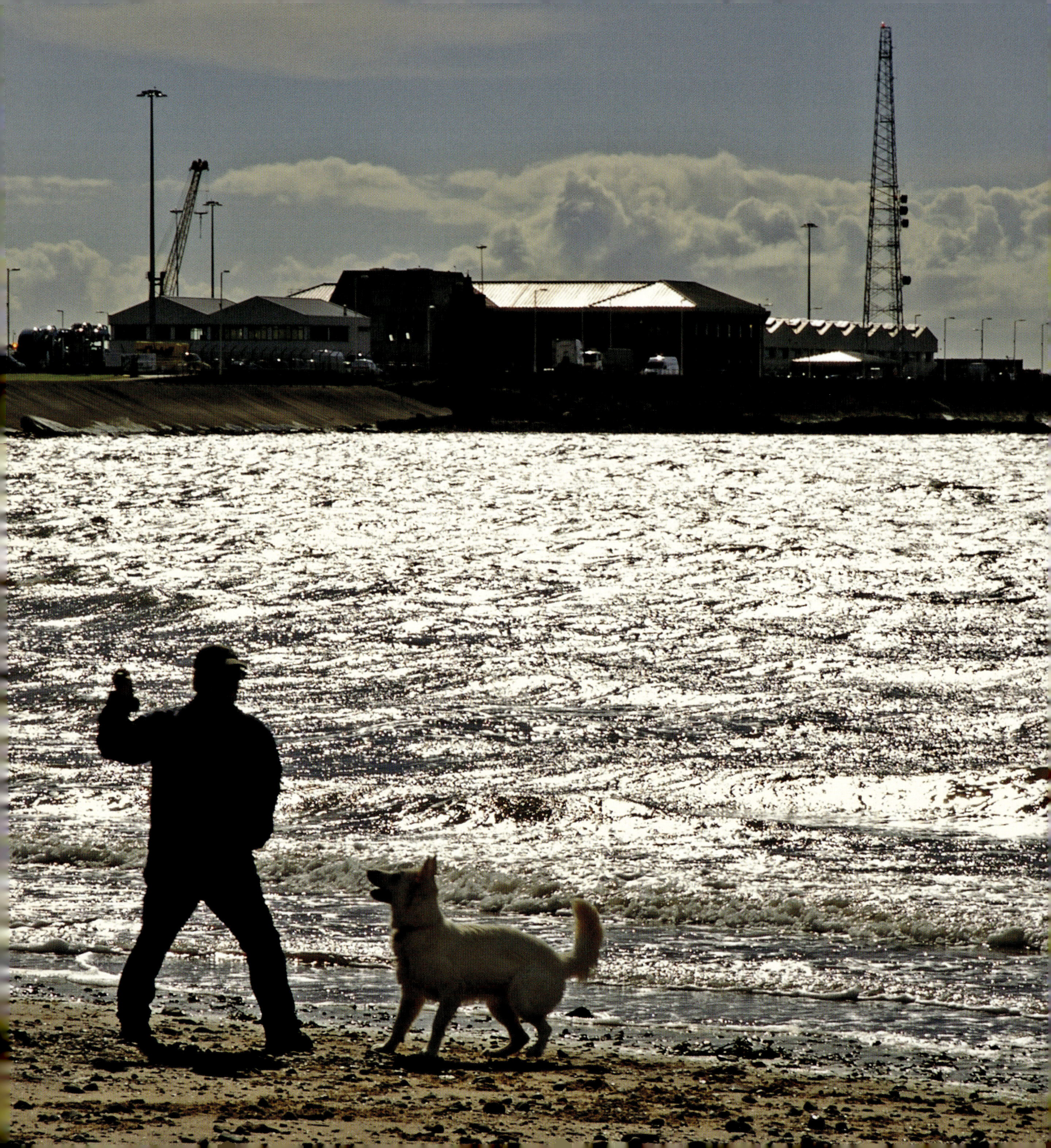

# INDEX



Half Moon Bay, near the harbour at Heysham –
where locals go to walk their dogs.

# DEDICATION

Dedicated to the twenty-three people who drowned in Morecambe Bay on 5 February 2004. 'Chinese cockle-pickers', or 'illegal immigrants', is how they're usually described, but they all had names and families. There were twenty men and three women; the youngest was eighteen, the oldest forty-five. Between them they had twenty-eight children.

| | | |
|---|---|---|
| Chen Al Qin | Lin You Xing | Wu Jia Zhen |
| Chen Mu Yu | Lin Zhi Fang | Xie Xiao Wen |
| Guo Bing Long | Dong Xin Wu | Zhang Ziu Hua |
| Guo Chang Mou | Liu Qin Ying | Xu Yu Hua |
| Guo Nian Zhu | Cao Chao Kun | Yang Tian Long |
| Lin Guo Guang | Wang Ming Lin | Yu Hui |
| Lin Guo Hua | Wang Xiu Yu | Zhou Xun Chao |
| Lin Li Shui | Wu Hong Kang | |

The tragedy led to the creation of the Gangmasters' Licensing Authority, to prevent the exploitation of workers in the agricultural industries.